INTRODUCING CATHOLIC THEOLOGY

The mystery of the Trinity

INTRODUCING CATHOLIC THEOLOGY
General editor: Michael Richards

This series, for theology students in colleges, universities and seminaries, offers comprehensive guides to the source material and to the research and reflection needed for a thorough understanding of Christian theology within the Catholic tradition. It provides reliable information and stimulates personal inquiry. The authors, who are drawn from a variety of countries and schools of thought within the English-speaking Catholic world, have constantly borne in mind the relationship of Christianity with other religions and the need to reconcile the faith of divided Christendom.

Father Michael Richards, formerly lecturer in church history, ecclesiology and pastoral theology at Heythrop College London and editor of *The Clergy Review* from 1967 to 1985, is now a parish priest in central London.

1 Revelation and its interpretation: *Aylward Shorter*
2 Interpreting Jesus: *Gerald O'Collins*
3 Being human: a biblical perspective: *Edmund Hill*
4 The mystery of the Trinity: *Edmund Hill*
5 Thinking about God: *Brian Davies*

In preparation:
Marriage
Eschatology
Sacraments of Initiation
The Church

INTRODUCING CATHOLIC THEOLOGY

The Mystery of the Trinity

Edmund Hill

GEOFFREY CHAPMAN
LONDON

A Geoffrey Chapman book published by
Cassell Ltd
1 Vincent Square, London SW1P 2PN

First published 1985

ISBN 0 225 66470 4

Nihil obstat: Anton Cowan, *Censor*
Imprimatur: Monsignor John Crowley, *V.G.*
Westminster, 3 July 1985

The *Nihil obstat* and *Imprimatur* are a declaration that a book or pamphlet is considered to be free
from doctrinal or moral error. It is not implied that those who have granted the *Nihil obstat* and
Imprimatur agree with the contents, opinions or statements expressed.

British Library Cataloguing in Publication Data

Hill, Edmund
  The Mystery of the Trinity.—
  (Introducing Catholic theology; 4)
  1. Catholic Church—Doctrines
  2. Trinity
  I. Title   II. Series
  231′ D44   BT111.2

Phototypesetting by Georgia Origination, Liverpool

Printed and bound in Great Britain by
Billing & Sons, London and Worcester

Contents

Editor's Foreword   xi
Abbreviations   xiii

I   Identifying the mystery   1

1   The starting-point of faith   3

      A.   The reference of faith in the Trinity to Christian
           experience   3
      B.   Statements of the faith: the Apostles' Creed and the
           Nicene Creed   3
      C.   The Athanasian Creed, or *Quicunque vult*   4
      D.   St Augustine's statement of trinitarian faith   6

      Notes   7

II   Being shown the mystery   9

2   The evidence for the mystery in the New Testament   11

      A.   Revelation and experience   11
      B.   The evidence of later New Testament texts:
           Matthew 28:19, John   12
      C.   The evidence of Paul's letters   15
      D.   A passage from Luke: 10:1–24   17

      Notes   19

3   The mystery prepared in the Old Testament   21

      A.   Father and Son   21
      B.   God and Lord   23
      C.   Word/*Logos* and Wisdom   24
      D.   Holy Spirit   25
      E.   Sending and proceeding   27

      Notes   28

4 The mystery revealed in the New Testament   **29**

   A. Jesus is the Christ   29
   B. Jesus more than just a man: Lord and Son of Man   31
   C. Jesus is truly divine   33
   D. Jesus, the Lord, as Son is really distinct from the
      Father   34
   E. The unity of the Father and the Son   35
   F. Recapitulation   36
   G. The Holy Spirit   38

   Notes   40

III Assimilating the mystery   **43**

5 The economic theologians   **45**

   A. Distinction between the economic and the
      transcendental approaches   45
   B. Justin   47
   C. Irenaeus   48
   D. The Monarchian reaction   50
   E. Tertullian and Novatian   50

   Notes   53

6 The transcendental approach   **54**

   A. Further assessment of the economic approach   54
   B. The Arians and the Council of Nicaea, 325   55
   C. *Homo-ousios* and *homoi-ousios*   57
   D. Person and hypostasis   58
   E. The problem underlying this battle of words, and
      attempted solutions   60

   Notes   62

**7 Augustine's combination of the two approaches:
missions, processions and relationships**   **65**

   A. Augustine's use of the economic approach   65
   B. Augustine's use of the transcendental method   68
   C. Missions, processions, and relationships   71

IV Communing with the mystery   **73**

8   Augustine's De Trinitate: purpose, method and structure   **75**

   A. Brief history of the *De Trinitate*   75
   B. Augustine's purpose in writing the *De Trinitate*   76
   C. Augustine's method in the *De Trinitate*   78
   D. Structure of the *De Trinitate*   80

   Notes   82

9   Missions: De Trinitate, books II–IV   **84**

   A. No obvious missions of the Son and Holy Spirit in the Old Testament: book II   84
   B. The mission of angels in the Old Testament: book III   86
   C. The mission of the one true mediator, Jesus Christ, in the new dispensation: book IV   87
   D. Summary: importance of the notion of mission   89

   Notes   90

10 Divine relationships: books V–VII   **92**

   A. Relationships considered before processions   92
   B. Subsistent relationships   93
   C. Relationships and substance   94
   D. Our relationships with the divine persons   95

   Notes   97

11 'Person' and 'hypostasis': appropriation of essential names to the persons: books V–VII   **100**

   A. The problem of 'person' and 'hypostasis'   100
   B. The scholastic solution of Aquinas   101
   C. Augustine's solution reconsidered   102
   D. The appropriation of names to the persons   103
   E. The appropriation of 'God' and 'Lord' in the New Testament   106

   Notes   106

12 The procession of the Holy Spirit **108**

   A. Introductory statement of the case 108
   B. Augustine's doctrine 108
   C. The *Filioque* in the subsequent Latin tradition 112
   D. The scholastic statement of the doctrine 113
   E. Orthodox objections to the *Filioque*: theological 115
   F. Orthodox objections to the *Filioque*: canonical 118

   Notes 120

13 The image of God: illustrating the divine processions: books VIII–X **122**

   A. Setting the context 122
   B. Constructing the image in the human mind 124
   C. What we learn from the image about the divine
       processions 129

   Notes 132

14 The trinitarian image of God: a programme for the Christian life: books XI–XIV **134**

   A. The image distorted by sin 134
   B. The re-integration of the image by the grace of Christ 137
   C. The invisible missions and the indwelling of the three
       divine persons 139

   Notes 142

V Losing sight of the mystery **145**

15 The drawbacks of scholastic method **147**

   A. Preliminary remarks 147
   B. The *Sentences* of Peter Lombard 148
   C. The *Summa Theologiae* of Thomas Aquinas, Ia, 27–43 149

   Notes 151

16 **Indigestible fruits of scholasticism: textbooks and**
    catechisms   **152**

    A.   Early twentieth-century textbooks   152
    B.   The doctrine in the catechisms   155
    C.   Comments on these catechisms   157

    Notes   159

VI **Recovering the mystery**   **161**

17 **After Vatican II**   **163**

    A.   Judgement on the texts cited in Chapter 16   163
    B.   Voices crying in the wilderness   164
    C.   The Council and after   166

    Notes   170

18 **Suggestions for a catechism of 'pro-trinitarian**
    boldness'   **171**

    Questions for discussion   **181**

    Bibliography   **185**

    Index of biblical references   187
    Index of references to Augustine's *De Trinitate*   190
    General Index   **191**

Foreword

Introducing Catholic Theology has been conceived and planned in the belief that the Second Vatican Council provided the Church with a fundamental revision of its way of life in the light of a thorough investigation of Scripture and of our history, and with fresh guidelines for studying and reflecting upon the Christian message itself. In common with every other form of human enquiry and practical activity, the Christian faith can be set out and explained in ways appropriate to human intelligence: it calls for scientific textbooks as well as for other forms of writing aimed at expressing and conveying its doctrines.

It is hoped that these volumes will be found useful by teachers and students in that they will supply both the information and the stimulus to reflection that should be taken for granted and counted upon by all concerned in any one course of study.

Conceived as expressions of the Catholic tradition, the books draw upon the contribution to the knowledge of God and the world made by other religions, and the standpoint of other patterns of Christian loyalty. They recognize the need for finding ways of reconciliation where differences of understanding lead to human divisions and even hostility. They also give an account of the insights of various philosophical and methodological approaches. It is hoped that the series will eventually cover the full range of theological themes.

The thought of St Augustine on the Church as the Body of Christ and on its constitution was particularly influential at the Second Vatican Council. In this volume a presentation of his teaching on the Trinity brings back to life in the twentieth century another of his highly important contributions to theology. St Augustine's understanding of the living reality of God, made known in Jesus Christ and shared by us through the power of his Spirit, will enlighten many for whom this mystery of faith has been made to appear as some sort of mathematical puzzle. This introduction to theological thinking at its most personal will help to eliminate the desiccated impression left in many minds by an instruction insufficiently nourished by the writings of the Fathers, the pastors and teachers by whom the Faith was first expounded and explained.

Michael Richards

Abbreviations

AH	Irenaeus, *Against Heresies*
AP	Tertullian, *Against Praxeas*
Dz	Denzinger-Schönmetzer, *Enchiridion Symbolorum*
ET	English translation
LXX	Septuagint Greek version of the Old Testament
parr.	and parallels in other gospels
PG	*Patrologia Graeca,* ed. J. P. Migne
PL	*Patrologia Latina,* ed. J. P. Migne
RSV	Revised Standard Version of the Bible
STh	Thomas Aquinas, *Summa Theologiae*

To the memory,
the blessed memory,
of Joan and Jimmy Stewart,
who died 11 and 16 July 1984:
'They were lovely and pleasant in their lives,
and in death they were not divided'.

I
Identifying the Mystery

1
The Starting-Point of Faith

A. THE REFERENCE OF FAITH IN THE TRINITY TO CHRISTIAN EXPERIENCE

Faith in the mystery of the Trinity is on the one hand something very immediate to ordinary Catholic Christians who have been even minimally instructed in the practice of their religion. They express it every time they make the sign of the cross 'in the name of the Father and of the Son and of the Holy Spirit' – perhaps their most familiar religious gesture and invocation. They were initiated into the trinitarian faith when they were baptized 'in the name of the Father and of the Son and of the Holy Spirit', and they are reminded of this every time they attend the baptisms of their children or their friends.

But on the other hand it is perhaps the article of Christian belief about which most ordinary Christians are most inarticulate, and which has the least meaning for their lives and their devotions. They mystery of the Trinity has somehow lost its moorings in common Christian experience – so much so that many people will doubt if it ever had such moorings in the first place, and will be tempted to assume that the doctrine is nothing but the product of the over-subtle speculations of theologians in academic ivory towers.

In this book I hope to demonstrate that the doctrine of the Trinity did indeed have such moorings in common and basic Christian experience; that furthermore it still does have them if only we would notice them; and that it always ought to have them. In this way I hope to make it easier for ordinary Christians (by which I mean Christians who are not professional theologians) to make sense of the mystery and so to perceive its profound bearing on their lives as Christians.

B. STATEMENTS OF THE FAITH: THE APOSTLES' CREED AND THE NICENE CREED

We begin the work in this chapter by just stating what Christian belief in the Trinity actually is. We are concerned to understand (as far as possible) what we believe; but first we must know accurately what it is we believe as Christians. We must articulate our faith in 'articles'.

We have already noted the simplest articulation of our trinitarian faith – 'in the name of the Father and of the Son and of the Holy Spirit'.[1] Those are its absolutely essential terms: what we believe in is the Father and the Son and the Holy Spirit. Forget, for the time being, all other terms such as 'trinity', 'person', 'procession', 'substance', 'three-in-one' and 'one-in-three'. They will all be introduced in due course, when they are needed. But introduce them too soon and they only serve to confuse and to give the whole doctrine an air of unreality and abracadabra. The basic statement is that we believe in, and sign ourselves in, and live in 'the name of the Father and of the Son and of the Holy Spirit'.

This basic statement is elaborated in the creeds – most simply in the Apostles' Creed, which came into existence as a baptismal creed, that is, as an expression of the assent of the baptized to faith in *the Father* (almighty, maker of heaven and earth), and in *the Son* (in Jesus Christ his only Son our Lord, who was conceived by the Holy Spirit . . . from thence he shall come to judge the living and the dead), and in *the Holy Spirit* (in the Holy Catholic Church . . . the resurrection of the body and life everlasting).[2]

The creed, to be sure, includes more than belief in the Father and the Son and the Holy Spirit – i.e. in the Trinity. But it fits all its articles, about Jesus Christ, for example, or about the Church and the resurrection, into a trinitarian framework.

A more elaborate creed, but one which was developed from a simpler baptismal formula like our Apostles' Creed, is the Nicene Creed, which we usually recite at mass on Sundays. It was drawn up at the Council of Nicaea (A.D. 325) and completed at that of Constantinople (A.D. 381) precisely to affirm unequivocally the full and equal divinity of the Son (begotten not made, born of the Father before all ages, God from God, light from light, true God from true God, consubstantial with the Father) and of the Holy Spirit (the Lord, the giver of life, who proceeds from the Father and the Son,[3] who together with the Father and the Son is adored and glorified). It is certainly a more stately affirmation of the faith, but perhaps generally felt to be 'more difficult'; it introduces that odd technical word 'consubstantial', which modern translations do not really succeed in making less technical by rendering it 'of one substance' or 'one in being'.

C.   THE ATHANASIAN CREED, OR *QUICUNQUE VULT*

The most complete formal statement of trinitarian doctrine, however, is to be found in the so-called Athanasian Creed.[4] This was quite unknown to St

Athanasius himself, the great hero of the Nicene doctrine, and in particular the defender of that word 'consubstantial', who died in 376 and who wrote in Greek. This statement was first composed in Latin, probably about 500, probably by St Caesarius of Arles in the south of France, who was a great admirer of St Augustine. He put together this statement of faith in what is practically a series of quotations from Augustine. It seems he composed it as a kind of test of orthodoxy for his clergy – or as a guide to orthodoxy for them – since they were in danger of being misled by Arian heretics.

To my ears the *Quicunque vult* has the charm of a splendid incantation. Other people, no doubt, find it simply bewildering. But I think it is worth setting out here the major part of it which deals with the Trinity, because even if it is bewildering now, it may begin to make sense once we have traced Augustine's thoughts on the mystery later on in the book. It runs:

Whosoever wishes to be saved must before all things hold the Catholic faith . . .
Now the Catholic faith is this: that we should venerate one God in Trinity and Trinity in unity,
Neither confounding persons nor separating substance.
For there is one person of the Father, another of the Son, another of the Holy Spirit;
But of Father, Son and Holy Spirit one is the divinity, equal the glory, co-eternal the majesty.
As the Father is, so is the Son, so the Holy Spirit:
Uncreated the Father, uncreated the Son, uncreated the Holy Spirit;
Infinite the Father, infinite the Son, infinite the Holy Spirit;
Eternal the Father, eternal the Son, eternal the Holy Spirit.
And yet there are not three eternals, but one eternal,
Just as there are not three uncreateds or three infinites, but one uncreated and one infinite.
Likewise almighty is the Father, almighty the Son, almighty the Holy Spirit;
And yet there are not three almighties, but one almighty.
So too the Father is God, the Son is God, the Holy Spirit is God;
And yet there are not three Gods but one God.
So too the Father is Lord, the Son is Lord, the Holy Spirit is Lord;
And yet there are not three Lords, but one Lord.
Because just as we are compelled by Christian truth to confess each person singly as God and Lord, so we are forbidden by the Catholic religion to say three Gods or Lords.
The Father is made by no one, nor created, nor begotten.
The Son is from the Father alone, neither made nor created, but begotten.
The Holy Spirit is from the Father and the Son, neither made nor created nor begotten, but proceeding.
Thus there is one Father, not three Fathers; one Son, not three Sons; one Holy Spirit, not three Holy Spirits.
And in this Trinity there is nothing before or after, nothing greater or less; but all three persons are co-eternal with each other and co-equal;
So that, as has already been said above, in every way unity is to be venerated in Trinity, and Trinity in unity.
Whoever therefore wishes to be saved, must so think about the Trinity.

The idea of being compelled to assent to such an esoteric rigmarole in order to be saved certainly offends most modern sensibilities. The point I would make here is that this text would not be an esoteric rigmarole for averagely well instructed Christians if their trinitarian faith were really rooted in their Christian experience – as was still the case for their spiritual ancestors 1,500 years ago for whom St Caesarius composed it.

But I agree that its highly schematic and abstract style, while having its own proper religious grandeur in some contexts, can in itself serve to divorce the mystery it presents from concrete Christian experience – and perhaps has contributed in part to this unfortunate divorce.

D. ST AUGUSTINE'S STATEMENT OF TRINITARIAN FAITH

So I conclude this chapter with what seems to me to be much the best statement (not explanation) of our trinitarian faith, which is made by St Augustine at the beginning of the first book of his great work on the Trinity. He writes:

The purpose of all the Catholic commentators I have been able to read on the divine books of both testaments, who have written before me on the Trinity which God is, has been to teach that according to the scriptures Father and Son and Holy Spirit in the inseparable equality of one substance present a divine unity; and therefore there are not three Gods but one God; although indeed the Father has begotten the Son, and therefore he who is the Father is not the Son; and the Son is begotten by the Father, and therefore he who is the Son is not the Father; and the Holy Spirit is neither the Father nor the Son, but only the Spirit of the Father and of the Son, himself co-equal to the Father and the Son, and belonging to the threefold unity.

It was not however this same Trinity [their teaching continues] that was born of the Virgin Mary, crucified and buried under Pontius Pilate, on the third day rose again and ascended into heaven, but the Son alone. Nor was it the same Trinity that came down upon Jesus in the form of a dove at his baptism, or came down on the day of Pentecost after the Lord's ascension, with a roaring sound from heaven as though a violent gust were rushing down, and in divided tongues as of fire, but the Holy Spirit alone. Nor was it this same Trinity that spoke from heaven *You are my Son*, either at his baptism by John or on the mountain when the three disciples were with him, or when the resounding voice was heard, *I have both glorified my name and will glorify it again*, but it was the Father's voice alone addressing the Son. Although just as Father and Son and Holy Spirit are inseparable, so do they work inseparably. This is also my faith, inasmuch as it is the Catholic faith (*De Trinitate* I, iv, 7).

This, he says, is his faith, as it is the Catholic faith. It is a description of what he frequently calls the *initium fidei*, the starting-point of faith (*ibid*. I, i, 1). This is the starting-point, faith, from which we proceed to understanding, and not the other way round. Refusal to believe until you understand is in Augustine's view an entirely wrong-headed attitude. It is in fact characteristic of intellectual pride, and it is invariably frustrated. One of his favourite quotations is in fact a misquotation of Isa 7:9, which in his version, following the LXX, read 'Unless you believe, you shall not understand'.

This then is the given faith (and notice how Augustine roots this given faith in the experience represented by events, visible realities in time and space, which the gospels record), which we believe as Christians, and which we should be eager to understand if our faith has any vitality at all. If we love God, presumably we desire to know him better. But this, our faith declares, is what God is – Father, Son and Holy Spirit. This then is what we desire to know better, to appreciate and savour, if we genuinely desire to know God better. This is certainly what moved Augustine to compose his work. He had embarked on an all-absorbing quest for God. Here we are undertaking to join him in that quest.

NOTES

1   More traditionally known in English, of course, as the Holy Ghost. But the English word 'ghost' has long since ceased to mean what it used to mean, the same as the German *Geist* ('spirit'), and has come simply to signify spooks. Whatever the Spirit of God may be, it/he/she is certainly not a spook, a phantom or a spectre. Except therefore in the occasional doxology of a hymn, where it serves the metre and rhyme, the term 'Holy Ghost' is nowadays always to be avoided, as misleading, if not disedifying.

2   The leading authority on the creeds is J. N. D. Kelly. See his *Early Christian Doctrines*, 2nd ed. (London, 1960) and *Early Christian Creeds*, 2nd ed. (London, 1960).

3   The original formula of Constantinople (381) does not include the words 'and the Son'. It simply quotes Jn 15:26, 'the Spirit of truth, who proceeds from the Father'. It was Western Churches, beginning with those of Spain, which later added the famous word *Filioque*, 'and from the Son'. This would become, and remain, a great bone of contention between the Latin and the Greek Churches: see below, Chapter 12.

4   Again see J. N. D. Kelly, *The Athanasian Creed* (London, 1964).

II
Being shown the Mystery

2

The Evidence for the Mystery in the New Testament

A. REVELATION AND EXPERIENCE

Having identified with some precision what it is we believe in – the Father and the Son and the Holy Spirit – we proceed to try and understand the mystery thus indicated or named. And the first step towards understanding what we believe is to see why we believe it.

The answer is that we believe it because it has been revealed by God. The first volume of this series, by Aylward Shorter, was devoted to the topic of revelation, which suggests that it is a subject of some complexity and depth. Here we are only concerned with the revelation of the mystery of the Trinity, and after asserting that it has been revealed by God we are immediately faced with the questions how? and when? The basic answer to both questions is 'In the person of Jesus Christ', and therefore at the time he lived, taught, died and rose again from the dead. A secondary answer is 'In the pages of the New Testament'.

The first answer represents what God has done to reveal the mystery: he has sent his Son Jesus Christ into the world. The second answer represents the reception, the acknowledgement, the realization of the revelation by the disciples and apostles of Jesus Christ – by the first generation of believers in him.

In Chapter 1 I gave it as my opinion that the doctrine of the Trinity has long been divorced from the religious experience of most Christians, and that if it is to mean anything for us and our lives it has to be re-connected with and rooted again in our experience. Now receiving revelation from God, I here go on to propose, is the fundamental Christian experience. Our word for it is faith. At least it is by faith and in faith that we acknowledge some experience as being a revelation from God.

Our experience, to be genuine and real and significant to us, does not have to be an immediate one. Indeed, for all Christians who come after that first generation of disciples and apostles it never is, in any obvious way. The experience of revelation is mediated to us through others, through the tradition of the Church going back to the apostles and to Jesus Christ himself, through the tradition of the good news of salvation contained in the writings of the New Testament. What is immediate to us, to any believer, is the response of faith to this mediated experience, a response prompted by God's grace, but somehow elicited in us by a sense that what we hear from others ('faith comes from what is heard': Rom 10:14–17) chimes in with some very personal awareness, longing, need, of our own. This immediate personal experience of faith continues to be engaged by our involvement in the Christian life of the Christian community we belong to, its sacraments, worship, prayer, study, good works, apostolate.

What I am saying is that it is in this complex of mediated and immediate religious experience that the mystery of the Trinity is revealed to us.

B.   THE EVIDENCE OF LATER NEW TESTAMENT TEXTS: MATTHEW 28:19, JOHN

What we find primarily in the words of the New Testament (as indeed of the Old as well) is not God revealing things to us, even when the texts purport to describe some divine action or to rehearse the very words of God; it is rather the expression of the faith of the writers, their response to the experience of God's revelation, which for them as for us was usually mediated by others. In the Old Testament it was mediated usually by prophets, in the New it was mediated by Christ, the one mediator between God and men (1 Tim 2:5).[1] But it is impossible to separate, in the texts, the revelation from its acceptance and interpretation in faith. What I shall attempt to do here is to trace the development of that interpretation of the mystery in the New Testament; but I shall work backwards[2] from the texts which give us the most complete interpretation to the original experience itself, in so far as that is possible.

Let us begin with Mt 28:19:

Go therefore and make disciples of all nations, baptizing them in the name of the Father and of the Son and of the Holy Spirit.

This simply shows that by the time this gospel was written (A.D. 80-90?) the basic formulation of the doctrine, the basic expression of trinitarian faith, was already fixed in a liturgical setting. It is precisely a formula, and it is the fruit of common reflection, over a generation or two, on the experience which Christian communities had had of Jesus Christ and the Spirit in the context of their inherited Jewish faith in the one God.[3] The Churches out of which and for which Matthew's gospel was compiled are generally agreed to have consisted mainly of Jewish rather than gentile Christians. On the strength of their Christian experience they have come, first, to refer to their ancestral God of Israel, almost exclusively, as 'the Father', and secondly, to associate with him, in the same name, the Son (Jesus Christ) and the Holy Spirit.

The gospel of John, according to the practically unanimous opinion of the scholars (in this case endorsed by the traditional view), was written – or at least edited into its final and present form – some time after that of Matthew, say about 100. Nonetheless, John spells out in his gospel the kind of reflection that must have gone into producing the simple Matthaean formula. In his gospel we can discern two lines of reflection that were presumably followed within the earliest Christian communities. One is concerned with the relationship of Jesus to God the Father, and the other with the relationship of Jesus (and the Father) with the Holy Spirit. (A third line of reflection is also evident in the pages of the New Testament, namely on the person of Jesus without explicit reference either to the Father or the Holy Spirit; e.g. 'Who do you say that I am? . . . You are the Christ', Mk 8:29.[4] But that is not our immediate concern here.)

John puts all these reflections in the mouth of Jesus as firm divine teaching or revelation. But they really represent the fruits of meditation, and no doubt discussion, in the Johannine school of theologians, or in the Johannine communities.[5] The relationship of Jesus, the Son, with the Father is most completely set out in the discourse of Jesus in Jn 5:19–47, the occasion for which was the cure of the cripple at the pool of Bethzatha, which led to an altercation with 'the Jews' of which the author remarks,

This was why the Jews sought all the more to kill him, because he not only broke the sabbath but also called God his own Father, making himself equal to God (5:18)

It was just this conviction that 'Jesus was equal with God' which forced the first generation of Christians to reflect on this mystery and 'evolve' the doctrine of the Trinity. They did it in terms of the concepts of 'Father' and 'Son'. And so in Jn 5:19–47 two points are set out at great length: the total dependence of the Son on the Father, by whom he has been sent; and at the same time his equality with the Father.

The Son can do nothing of his own accord, but only what he sees the Father doing (v.19).

I can do nothing on my own authority; as I hear, I judge; and my judgment is just, because I seek not my own will but the will of him who sent me (v.30).

And on the other hand,

For the Father loves the Son, and shows him all that he himself is doing; and greater works than these will he show him, that you may marvel. For as the Father raises the dead and gives them life, so also the Son gives life to whom he will. The Father judges no one, but has given all judgment to the Son, that all may honour the Son even as they honour the Father. He who does not honour the Son does not honour the Father who sent him (vv. 20–23).

In other texts the language is not so much of the Son being sent by the Father as of his coming forth from and going back to the Father (e.g. 16:28; cf. 13:1); or of his coming down from heaven and going up to heaven again (e.g. 3:13 and 6:38–42). Later theological reflection, as we shall see,[6] will find it convenient and even necessary to distinguish between the Son's coming forth or proceeding from the Father and his being sent by him. But for the evangelist the two phrases signify the same relationship. A text that strongly affirms their equality is 10:30, 'I and the Father are one'; and another that seems to negate it, but must be understood, as presumably it was by at least the final editor of the gospel, only to qualify it, is 14:28, 'For the Father is greater than I'. This too will call for much discussion and reflection later on.[7]

It is above all in Jn 14 – 16 that Jesus talks about his and the Father's relationship with the Holy Spirit, in terms that do oblige us, in the language that was to be developed in due course, to consider the Holy Spirit a distinct person from the Father and the Son. He is called 'another Counsellor [Advocate, Paraclete] . . . the Spirit of truth' (14:16–17); 'the Counsellor, the Holy Spirit which [RSV: whom] the Father will send in my name, he will teach you all things' (14:26). 'Counsellor' is a masculine noun in Greek, 'Spirit' a neuter; so the Holy Spirit is in these texts sometimes a 'which' and sometimes a 'who', sometimes an 'it' and sometimes a 'he'. Nor is this a merely grammatical point. In the Old Testament the Spirit is very much a divine force, an impersonal attribute of the personal God. Its (his) transformation in the New Testament into a masculine person is a significant revelational development.[8]

Later on Jesus talks of

the Counsellor . . . whom I shall send to you from the Father, even the Spirit of truth which [RSV: who] proceeds from the Father (15:26).

So the Spirit is sent by both Father and Son. Later still he says,

When he comes, the Spirit of truth, he will guide you into all the truth . . . He will glorify me, for he will take what is mine and declare it to you. All that the Father has is mine; therefore I said that he will take what is mine and declare it to you (16:13–15).

These texts are no doubt reflecting on some experience of the Spirit which the first Christians underwent, in addition to their experience of, or encounter with, Jesus. But the fact that the evangelist is so careful in these texts to relate the Holy Spirit firmly and inseparably to Jesus, as sent by Jesus or by the Father in his name, as receiving from what belongs to Jesus and proclaiming this and only this to the disciples, indicates very definitely that those first disciples experienced the Holy Spirit inseparably, though distinctly, from their encounter with Jesus. John explicitly connects the sending or giving of the Holy Spirit with what he calls the glorification of Jesus, i.e. his death and resurrection. 'As yet the Spirit had not been given, because Jesus was not yet glorified' (7:39). And after his resurrection Jesus 'breathed on them and said to them, Receive the Holy Spirit' (20:22).

C. THE EVIDENCE OF PAUL'S LETTERS

St Paul's letters are among the first of the New Testament writings to have been written; they are certainly earlier than the gospels. So in them we shall find evidence of an earlier reflection on the revelational experience we are interested in. I look at them, however, before examining a selected text from the synoptic gospels, because although these were composed in their present form after St Paul wrote his letters, they do record traditions that go right back to the revelational experience at its source, that is, to Jesus himself and his personal followers.

To start with the point where we left John, Paul is quite as determined to stress that experience of the Holy Spirit is inseparable from the experience of Jesus Christ. He had occasion especially to do so when dealing with the Corinthians, who were evidently a highly charismatic body of believers – so absorbed in the charisms or gifts of the Holy Spirit with which they had been favoured, that they were tending to overlook the context and the purpose of the favours received.

So Paul begins his discussion of spiritual gifts or charisms (1 Cor 12 – 14) with the very straightforward reminder that

no one speaking by the Spirit of God ever says 'Jesus be cursed', and no one can say 'Jesus is Lord' except by the Holy Spirit (12:3).

Belief in the Holy Spirit and in Jesus as Lord are inseparable, because the Holy Spirit is inseparable from Jesus. He drives the lesson home by going on to give us a characteristic Pauline trinitarian formula:

Now there are varieties of gifts, but the same Spirit; and there are varieties of service, but the same Lord; and there are varieties of working, but it is the same God who inspires them all in everyone (12:4–6).

We observe that St Paul does not use the terms 'Father, Son and Holy Spirit' – he never does so. The formula had not yet taken shape. We may also observe that there is for him no fixed order of the divine persons. In his time you could scarcely speak in Christian circles about 'the first, second and third persons of the Trinity' and expect to be understood. Here the Spirit is first and God (i.e. the Father) is third, while the Lord (i.e. the Son) remains in second place. When Paul talks of 'God' without qualification, he is nearly always referring to the Father; and when he talks about 'the Lord' without other qualification, he is nearly always referring to Jesus Christ, the Son.

There is a text earlier in the same letter which makes this usage clear. He is making a statement of traditional Jewish monotheism – saying it is something we Christians do not have to argue about; we all know it. The context is disagreement among the Corinthians about eating the meat of animals that had been sacrificed to idols.

As to the eating of [this], we know that an idol has no real existence, and that there is no God but one. For although there may be so-called gods in heaven or on earth [this a reference perhaps to the divine honours paid to Caesar] – as indeed there are many gods and many lords – yet for us there is one God, the Father from whom are all things and for whom we exist, and one Lord, Jesus Christ, through whom are all things and through whom we exist (8:4–6).

What Paul seems to be doing in the last verse here (from 'yet for us') is setting out, or quoting, a Christian variation on the theme of the famous Jewish *Shema'*, the affirmation in Dt 6:4, 'Hear, O Israel, the Lord is our God, the Lord is one'.[9]

We notice in both these instances (1 Cor 12 and 8) that Paul refers to the divine persons in connection with certain actual problems that arose in the life of the Christian community, and with a tacit reference to some kind of Christian experience. The relationships of the divine persons with each other are manifested to us only in terms of, and in the context of, our relationships with them.

This is even more evidently the case with St Paul's most important statement of the trinitarian mystery, Gal 4:4–7:

When the time had fully come,[10] God sent forth his Son, born of woman, born under the law, to redeem those who were under the law, so that we might receive adoption as sons.[11] And because you are sons, God has sent the Spirit of his Son into our hearts, crying 'Abba! Father!' So through God you are no longer a slave but a son, and if a son then an heir.

It is at the fullness of time, that is, at the moment of fulfilment of all the prophecies and expectations of ancient times, as the climax of God's revelation to man of his saving purposes, that God sends his Son and the Spirit of his Son – so revealing the triune mystery. And the Son is sent *to redeem* us, and to give us 'Son status'. We are sons[12] in the Son, and so we can pray the prayer of the Son, 'Abba, Father' (see Mk 14:36), because we receive the Spirit of the Son.

In this crucial text Paul tells us, as a fruit of his reflection on his experience of Christ and the Holy Spirit, just how the mystery was revealed: it was done by God's sending his Son as a man (born of woman), and a Jew (born under the law); and then by sending, not just his Spirit but the Spirit of his Son, into our hearts. And furthermore he tells us why the mystery was revealed, i.e. what the point of our knowing about it is. It was in order to change our status and our consequent relationship with God from a slave status to a Son status – to the one-Son status of God's onlybegotten Son. We may compare the saying of Jesus in Jn 15:15, 'No longer do I call you servants [slaves] . . . but I have called you friends'. In John God's saving grace makes us the equals of Jesus, his friends; in Paul it makes us his equals – his 'identicals' in fact – in his Sonship, a Sonship in which he is equal to the Father.

This text show us in a nutshell how the whole Christian experience, the Christian hope and aspiration, are contained in the mystery of the Trinity.

D.   A PASSAGE FROM LUKE: 10:1–24

Though Luke wrote his gospel perhaps a decade or two after Paul wrote his letters, he uses, like the other evangelists, both written and oral sources that go back eventually to Jesus and his disciples. But at the same time he is editing, moulding and interpreting this original material, and we must be aware of this as we consider this passage.

I do not intend to comment on the whole passage. My interest centres on vv. 21–24. But the story of the mission of the seventy/seventy-two[13] disciples and their return is the context which Luke gives to this saying (in Mt 11 it is given quite a different one). Notice first how Luke begins the episode by calling Jesus 'the Lord'. This is undoubtedly anachronistic. It is the title Paul gives Jesus, and Luke and the people he was writing for gave him. But we can gather from Mark that it is not what his disciples called him or how they referred to him during his earthly ministry, until perhaps the very end of it, after they had recognized him as the Messiah. They referred to him and addressed him as 'Master', 'Teacher', 'Rabbi'. The questions are, first how they came eventually to think of him as 'the Lord', and secondly what they meant by it. We shall return to the first question in Chapter 4.

As for the second one, we have seen what Paul meant by the title in 1 Cor 8:6; there it is clearly a divine title that places Jesus Christ on a par with God the Father. Thus it picks up the use of the title in the Old Testament as a name of God. I think it is fairly plain that Luke used it in much the same sense, here and elsewhere in his gospel, though perhaps not quite so explicitly. Thus in the very next verse he has Jesus telling his disciples to 'pray to the Lord of the harvest', where 'the Lord' clearly means God. So, 'the Lord said, Pray to the Lord'. If the second 'Lord' has a divine reference, why not the first? The argument is not, of course, conclusive. But Jesus goes on in this discourse to speak, if not in a divine, at least in a superhuman style. He addresses the towns of Galilee in the *persona* of the judge presiding at the last judgement (vv. 13–15). He identifies himself, or at least his authority, with 'him who sent me' in v. 16 – as he also, to be sure, identifies his disciples with himself. He saw Satan fall like lightning from heaven (v. 18). Finally, he congratulates his disciples on seeing (presumably in himself and his proclamation of the kingdom of God) the fulfilment of all the prophecies and expectation of the prophets and kings of the Old Testament – the fullness of time of which Paul writes in Gal 4:4, the final revelation of God.

This brings us to the crucial verses of this section, 21–22. First Jesus thanks his Father for a revelation, the revelation of the fullness of time, made to babes. This is perhaps an echo of Ps 8:2, 'by the mouth of babes and infants'. But what Luke intends us to understand by 'babes', as we can gather from the wider context of his gospel (e.g. the next episode, the parable of the good Samaritan), is tax collectors and sinners, Samaritans and gentiles. The revelation is thus something that surpasses as well as fulfilling the Old Testament revelation, which was a field in which the wise and understanding (scribes and Pharisees) were considered entirely competent.

In v. 22 he goes on to explain what the revelation consists in: it is the revelation of the Father, and who he is, by the Son. Now this language, of 'the Father' and 'the Son', is familiar to us from John. But it is entirely uncharacteristic of Luke, Matthew or Mark, occurring only once in each of these synoptic gospels (Mt 11:27, parallel to this passage in Luke, and Mk 13:32, a quite different saying). For Jesus to talk about 'my Father' (as here in v. 22a) is quite normal in the synoptics, as also to refer to himself as 'the Son of Man'. It is the absolute, unrelated terms 'the Father' and 'the Son' that are so unusual. John uses them to express his fully explicit trinitarian theology. Here in Luke and the other synoptics they can only be, either intrusions from the Johannine tradition (just possible in Luke, but hardly so in Matthew or Mark), or a reminiscence of authentic sayings of Jesus himself. The latter inference seems to me by far the more likely. It would provide the developed Johannine tradition with an actual source in the original Christian experience of the disciples, their personal encounter with Jesus.

One final observation on this passage. Jesus' words, like his discourse in Jn 5, refer only to the Father and the Son. Luke himself completes the trinitarian reference (unlike Mt 11:25) by beginning the passage with the words, 'In that same hour he rejoiced in the Holy Spirit and said, I thank thee, Father, Lord of heaven and earth . . . ' (10:21). Thus he shows his awareness of the trinitarian significance of Jesus' words.

There are, of course, many other passages in the New Testament which bear witness to the writers' faith in the mystery of the Trinity. Perhaps the most important are the prologue of John and the two trinitarian 'tableaux' of the baptism of Jesus in the Jordan (Mk 1:9–11 and parr.), and the transfiguration (Mk 9:2–8 and parr.). These may well represent one of the earliest, pre-

Pauline stages of the communities' reflections on the person and mystery of Jesus. The main point of both episodes is his designation by God himself as 'my Son' – i.e. the Son of God – and his consequent endowment with the Spirit of God, represented respectively by the dove and the bright cloud. What we learn from this is that you cannot reflect deeply on the mystery of Jesus Christ without, as it were, stumbling on the mystery of God himself, which is the mystery of the Trinity.

Having cursorily set out selections from the New Testament evidence that the mystery of the Trinity was revealed to the disciples of Jesus Christ, we will return in Chapter 4 to the question of how the revelation was achieved. On the evidence set out, we shall attempt to reconstruct the necessarily complex process by which such a radically new and strange concept of the deity was conveyed to and then transmitted by simple traditionally monotheistic Jews. How can that clarion call of Dt 6:4, 'Hear, O Israel, the Lord is our God, the Lord is one'[14] ever have been transposed into St Paul's equally convinced assertion, 'For us there is one God, the Father . . . and one Lord, Jesus Christ . . . ' (1 Cor 8:6)?

But first we must examine, in the next chapter, the Old Testament inheritance of language which made acceptance of the final revelation possible.

NOTES

1 In this text Christ Jesus is being called the mediator of salvation, not primarily of revelation. But in the last resort the two ideas are not all that far apart, since to receive God's revelation of himself is to be saved.

2 I am not maintaining strictly that the texts I begin with are the latest, and the ones I end with the earliest, chronologically. We should remind ourselves from time to time that there is a chronological difference between the time a text was written and the events it purports to record, not to mention the sources it incorporates.

3 In other words, the text is unlikely, in my opinion, to be a simple record of what was actually said and done on that occasion. It is not descriptive history, but theological history, in which the doctrine of the writer, or of the source he is using, is written into the story being told.

4 For the different kinds of early Christian confession, or credal formula, current in the New Testament Christian communities, see J. N. D. Kelly, *Early Christian Creeds*, 2nd ed. (London, 1960), pp. 14–23.

5 The discourses of Jesus in John should not be treated as his *ipsissima verba*. They have been written up by the evangelist, in his own style. See note 3 above. For a study of the background to the Johannine theology see Raymond E. Brown, *The Community of the Beloved Disciple* (New York/London, 1979).

6 In Chapter 7 below.

7 In Chapters 5 and 7.

8 But it is important to see that even in the New Testament the Holy Spirit retains something of his (its) impersonal character as a divine force. Nearly all the vivid images

for the Holy Spirit are impersonal forces: fire, wind, water, a dove.

9 The Hebrew runs 'YHWH our God, YHWH one'. YHWH is the proper name of the God of Israel, which out of respect was never pronounced *Adonai* ('the Lord') being substituted for it (see Chapter 3, B). So this declaration of faith can be rendered in various ways: as I have put it in the text; or the last phrase could be rendered 'the Lord alone'. The one way it cannot reasonably be rendered, I would have thought, given that 'the Lord' represents the proper name, is the way it is translated by RSV: 'the LORD our God is one LORD'; or the Jerusalem Bible's equivalent, 'Yahweh our God is the one Yahweh'. Of course he is – who ever suggested that he was two or more Yahwehs? These translations have the same (absurd) value as the sentence 'Elizabeth our Queen is one Elizabeth'.

10 I prefer the more literal and traditional translation, 'When the fullness of time had come'. Fullness, *plērōma*, is a very pregnant word with Paul. It suggests fulfilment, completion, perfection. The little adverb 'fully' can scarcely carry all that weight.

11 St Paul's word is *huiothesia*, which does indeed mean adoption as sons, but with a much stronger suggestion of a new status being conferred. We are given 'son status'.

12 Here I cannot say 'sons and daughters', not out of male chauvinism, but because the sons we all are, we are by identification with the Son. We share his filiation. The 'son status' mentioned in the previous note is really 'Son status', as I go on to argue in the next paragraph.

13 The MSS are about evenly divided between 'seventy' and 'seventy-two', and so are the arguments for preferring one number to the other.

14 See note 9 above.

3

The Mystery prepared in the Old Testament

Let us return to the text of Gal 4:4–7 and take it as the starting-point of our examination of the Old Testament background to the mystery. Paul is here, in effect, saying that the mystery of the Trinity has been revealed by God sending his Son and then sending the Spirit of his Son – both clearly New Testament 'events'. But these sendings occur and are observed in the context of first-century Judaism; as Paul puts it, 'under the law' (Gal 4:4). It is contemporary Judaism that necessarily provides the language, the terms in which faith in the revelation is expressed. That means that these terms are derived from the Old Testament. So study of their Old Testament history should make it easier for us to understand how they were developed and modified in the New Testament to express so radically new an understanding of the divine being and its inner relations.

The most important terms (a few do not occur in this passage) are: 'Father' and 'Son', which it is natural to take together; 'God' and 'Lord', also a natural pair; 'Holy Spirit'; 'Word'; and also the verbal concepts of 'sending' and 'proceeding' or 'coming forth'.

A. FATHER AND SON

In the Old Testament God is not originally thought of by Israelites as 'our father', but rather as being the God of the fathers (e.g. Gen 26:24, Exod 3:13). It is Abraham, Isaac and Jacob, rather than God, who are the first father figures in Israel's consciousness.

There are, however, in ancient, or deliberately archaic, texts[1] beings known as 'the sons of God'. They seem originally to have been lesser deities. Such they certainly are in the old Canaanite myths related in the Ugaritic texts.[2] But in the Hebrew scriptures they have been domesticated into what we can more decently call angels, or sometimes the stars – which were of course gods in the astral religion of Babylon. See for example Gen 6:2ff, Pss

29:1, 89:6, Job 1:6, 38:7, Wis 5:5. It is, no doubt, because of their awareness of these superhuman sons of God that the early Israelites were inhibited from thinking of themselves as God's sons, or of God as their father.

But at some point in Israel's history there is a remarkably original development of ideas: the nation itself is assimilated to these angelic or divine sons of God. It is possible that what stimulated the development was the name *Yahweh Sabaoth* for the God of Israel. He is the Lord of hosts, Yahweh of armies. Which armies? Well, both the armies of Israel and the hosts of heaven. The two military machines tend to coalesce, at least in the minds of the composers of war songs. And as the heavenly armies are sons of God, so too are the Israelite armies. Dt 32:8 is an interesting text here, when we compare the Hebrew with the Greek of the LXX.[3] In the Hebrew it runs, 'When the Most High gave to the nations their inheritance . . . he fixed the bounds of the peoples according to the number of the sons of Israel' (viz. seventy; cf. Exod 1:5 and the number of nations in Gen 10). But in the Greek, which presumably represents a variant Hebrew original, the text has 'according to the number of the sons of God'. Conceptual interchange was clearly possible.

In any case the development is explicit in the crucial text Exod 4:22: 'And you shall say to Pharaoh, Thus says the Lord: Israel is my first-born son, and I say to you, Let my son go that he may serve me'. There are two allusions to this text in the prophets: Hos 11:1, 'When Israel was a child, I loved him, and out of Egypt I called my son'; and Jer 31:9, 'I am a father to Israel, and Ephraim is my first-born'.

So the nation, personified in its ancestor Israel/Jacob or its biggest tribe Ephraim, is thought of as God's son, indeed as his first-born. But individual Israelites continue to think of themselves as 'sons of Israel', and of Abraham, Isaac and Jacob as their fathers. But inevitably, if God is thought of as the father of the nation, he eventually comes to be thought of as the father of its members. In one striking text, a post-exilic one certainly, he actually replaces the patriarchs in the role of father. In Isa 63:16 he is addressed like this: 'For thou art our father, though Abraham does not know us and Israel [the patriarch Jacob] does not acknowledge us; thou, O Lord, art our father, our redeemer from of old is thy name'. See also Isa 64:8 and Mal 2:10. It is to be noted that God's being our father is linked with his redeeming us – from Egypt. Having God as father is not associated in these texts with God's creating the human race, but with his creating Israel as his own peculiar possession. Having God for their father is what distinguishes Israel and Israelites from other nations.

In texts much older than these from Third Isaiah and Malachi there is an even more important development of the father/son relationship between God and the chosen people. He becomes in a very special sense the father of the people's divinely chosen representative, the anointed king; and the king becomes in a unique and privileged sense the son of God. The key texts are 2 Sam 7:14, Pss 2:7, 89:26–27, and also Isa 9:6.

The psalm texts and 2 Sam 7 apply this title to the king. Isa 9:6 is already applying it to the ideal king of the future, the Messiah, and the other royal texts come in due course, after the exile and return, to be read in a messianic sense. A final enrichment of the concept of the Messiah as the son of God is given by the picture of the just man, drawn in the book of Wisdom. His portrait is clearly influenced by that of the suffering servant in Isa 53, and in Wis 2:16, 18 and 5:5 he is called 'the son of God' and numbered among 'the sons of God' (the angels). It cannot be definitely asserted that the author was identifying his just man, pictured like the suffering servant, with the Messiah; it is perhaps unlikely. But he certainly prepares the way for that identification to be made in the New Testament.

Thus what the New Testament inherits from the Old is a way of speaking about God as father of all Israelites, and God as father in a very special sense of the most special of Israelites, the Messiah. In the synoptic gospels Jesus takes over this way of speaking when he talks about God to his disciples as both 'my father' (he is the Messiah) and 'your father' (they are Israelites). This is where we will start from in the next chapter.

B. GOD AND LORD

The word 'Lord' plays a very important part in the New Testament articulation of faith in Jesus Christ, as we shall see in the next chapter. To appreciate it, however, we need to see something of its history in the Old Testament, in connection with the word 'God'.

In English the word 'God' is nearly always used as a proper name; it is spelt with a capital G, and hardly ever used with the definite or indefinite article. We are so used to the notion of there being only one God that we do not need to give him any other name. But in fact and in origin the word 'god' is a common noun like any other, 'man' or 'cat' for example, and we know this because we are quite capable when necessary, which somehow is not very often, of so using it.

The same, on the whole, is true of the Hebrew word *Elohim* in the Old Testament. The main difference is that it is a plural form in Hebrew – a difference that is significant for the development of Israel's ideas about God. But construed with singular verbs as it most commonly is, it refers to God, and only rarely should it be translated 'gods'. However, the polytheistic past, in which there were indeed many gods around, was rather closer to the Hebrew Bible of the Israelites than it is to us with our Bibles in modern

European translations. At any rate, the time was still comparatively fresh in the nation's mind when their God (god) had to be distinguished from the gods of other peoples by a proper name of his own. That name was YHWH, usually spelt and pronounced nowadays as Yahweh.[4] Exod 3:14–15 gives us the story of how the sacred name was revealed to Moses at the burning bush. It is here interpreted as containing in itself the meaning of the strange sentence 'I am who I am'.[5] The story is told at this point, even though at least one of the ancient Hebrew writers had happily employed the name in his stories about the patriarchs in Genesis, and indeed in his story of paradise and the fall, Gen 2 – 3, where the deity is called, for some mysterious reason, *YHWH Elohim*, 'Yahweh God'. This, let us note, is a combination of a strictly proper name and a common noun.

The time eventually came when respect for the sacred name was such that people felt they ought not to pronounce it.[6] It continued to be written and transcribed in the biblical texts, but whenever readers came across it they were expected to read instead the word *Adonai*, meaning 'Lord'. When the Hebrew Bible was translated into Greek in the fourth and third centuries B.C. the divine name YHWH was consistently rendered by *Kurios*, 'Lord'.

So whereas we begin by having two principal names for the deity, one of which (*Elohim*/God) is really a common noun, and the other (YHWH) a proper name, we end up with these two principal names both being common nouns, *Elohim* and *Adonai*, 'God' and 'Lord'. But now, while the first one, 'God', which began by being a common noun, is in fact most commonly employed as a proper name, referring to one being only, the other, 'Lord', which is a substitute for a genuine proper name, remains in point of fact a common noun, applicable to all sorts of human and semi-human and divine individuals, such as great men (or even simple gentlemen) and kings and angels and pagan gods, as well as to the God of Israel. It is precisely this wide range of reference of the word 'Lord' which will make its application by the New Testament to Jesus so potent a 'developer' of Christian faith in Jesus.

C. WORD/*LOGOS* AND WISDOM

The concept of Jesus Christ as the Word of God (*Logos* in Greek) is not employed in our key text, Gal 4:4–7. Indeed it occurs extremely rarely in the New Testament – only in Jn 1:1–14 and casually, as it were, in Rev 19:13. But it acquires such extreme importance in the later theological tradition that we should examine its Old Testament antecedents before looking in the next chapter at what function it performs in the Johannine theology.

It is my opinion, which I will explain in the next chapter, that it is used in Jn 1:1–14 simply as a masculine substitute for the feminine noun *Sophia*,

'Wisdom'. Christ was early identified with the divine wisdom in Christian reflection (see 1 Cor 1:24; also Lk 11:49 compared with the parallel verse, Mt 23:34). Wisdom, in a number of striking Old Testament texts, is personified as a daughter or feminine companion of God the Most High. In Prov 8 in the course of a long speech Wisdom describes how she assisted at the creation of the world (vv. 22–31). In Sir 24, in another speech which she begins by stating that she 'came forth from the mouth of the Most High', she describes how she took up her abode in Israel and was established in Zion, and praises herself in very glowing terms. At the close of the speech the author (not Wisdom) remarks, 'All this is the book of the covenant of the Most High God, the law which Moses commanded us' (v. 23).

Thus the divine Wisdom is associated first with *creation* and then with the *law*. But creation is attributed in Gen 1 to the utterances of God – 'And God said, Let there be light, and there was light' (v. 3) etc. The process is summed up in Ps 148:5, 'he commanded and they were created'. The law in its turn is summed up in the ten *commandments*, known as the deca-*logue*, or the ten *logoi*, ten *words*.

Thus the substitution of the term *Logos*, Word for *Sophia*, Wisdom is quite natural, especially since Wisdom, as we noticed, describes herself as coming forth from the mouth of the Most High – as a kind of utterance or word, presumably (Sir 24:3). It is then this Old Testament figure of the divine Wisdom which lies behind the New Testament *Logos* concept, rather than the very common Old Testament expression 'the word of the Lord', which came so frequently to the prophets. The *Logos* is not merely a means of communication from God to man; it is, so to say, the content of God's mind.

D.   HOLY SPIRIT

As in English, so in Hebrew, the word 'spirit' (*ruach*, literally 'wind' or 'breath') has a wide range of meaning and reference. Here we are only interested in the word when it is referred to God.

Expressions like 'the spirit of the Lord', 'the spirit of God', 'my spirit', 'his spirit' (meaning God's) are extremely common in the Old Testament; the phrase 'holy spirit' is rather rare, but also rather significant in some late post-exilic texts which we shall be noting.

The spirit of the Lord is not of course a distinct entity, any more than the word of the Lord or the divine wisdom. It may be called, not inaccurately, a divine energy or force. In Judges and other books relating the earlier history of Israel it comes upon or falls upon people from time to time and transforms them, making them in some respect or other superhuman. It gives Samson, for example, superhuman strength, and other leaders like Gideon, Jephthah and Saul it fills with a more than ordinary energy and prowess and power of leadership in war. See Jgs 14:19, 15:14, 6:34, 11:29, 1 Sam 11:6.

The God of Israel, certainly, is a thoroughly personal God, who communicates constantly with his people by his word, and creates and governs the world by his wisdom, and whose chief attributes are justice, lovingkindness and faithfulness (see e.g. Exod 34:6, Ps 117). But, being God, he cannot be confined to the category of person, or adequately defined in its terms. He cannot, of course, be defined at all. He transcends this category as he transcends all categories, and so he also has to be depicted in non-personal terms and images. And it is here, I think, that the concept of the spirit of the Lord has its part to play. Ezekiel is the only one of the prophets who, so to say, encounters the spirit of the Lord extensively; and with him it is not usually the source of what we would call his prophetic inspiration – that is the word of the Lord, which comes to him as to the other prophets. What the spirit of the Lord is the source of is violent local movement. To put it rather crudely, it is Ezekiel's one and only means of rapid transport from Babylon to Jerusalem and back. It is also the principle of motion for the divine chariot – 'wherever the spirit would go, they went' (Ezek 1:20;[7] see also 8:3, 11:1, 24. The spirit of the Lord as the spirit of prophecy does fall on him in 11:5). The spirit of the Lord is very much the divine energy, or life force.

In a few later passages, some of which actually use the phrase 'holy spirit', the concept is, so to say, softened or refined somewhat, and almost identified with another important Old Testament term, the face – i.e. the presence – of God. In Isa 63:9–14 the prophet is recalling the exodus and he says,

In all their affliction he was afflicted, and the angel of his presence saved them; in his love and his pity he redeemed them . . . But they rebelled and grieved his holy spirit; therefore he turned to be their enemy, and himself fought against them . . . Where is he who put in the midst of them his holy spirit, who caused his glorious arm to go at the right hand of Moses, . . . who led them through the depths? . . . Like cattle that go down into the valley, the spirit of the Lord gave them rest. So thou didst lead thy people, to make for thyself a glorious name.

The expression 'angel of his presence' (v. 9) seems to be an invention of this writer. What I suppose he intends is to identify the angel of Exod 23:20 with 'my presence' of Exod 33:14. Then in the following verses this presence or face of God is further identified with his holy spirit. Thus the concept of God's spirit begins to take on a more personal quality, God as guide and protector.

This quality is again to be found in Ps 51:11, where it is probably a case of God's personal relationship with an individual worshipper rather than with the people as a whole; and even more significantly in Isa 11:2–3, where the Spirit of the Lord rests on the Messiah, the hoped-for king, as a spirit of wisdom, understanding, counsel and might, knowledge and the fear of the Lord. The divine spirit is coming close to merging with the divine wisdom. The same tendency is found in the latest of the Old Testament books, Wis 1:6-7, 7:22-23.

The same more personal quality appears in the spirit of the Lord in the eschatological context of Jl 2:28-29, the passage quoted by Peter at Pentecost. Here, in the last age, the spirit poured out on all flesh is the spirit of prophecy and vision, clearly closely akin to the spirit of wisdom and under-standing.

But for all these refinements and modifications, that impersonal, unpredictable, cosmic-force character of the spirit of the Lord which we have noted remains strong in the Israelite imagination, and will be manifest in the New Testament experiences of the first disciples of Jesus and their converts.

E. SENDING AND PROCEEDING

In our key text of Gal 4:4-7 Paul talks about God sending the Son and the Spirit of his Son, but not about their proceeding or coming forth. These expressions are found elsewhere (e.g. Jn 15:26, 16:28; see also Mk 1:38, and compare it with Lk 4:43). In the ordinary use of words one clearly implies the other: if you are sent (at least by God) you go, or proceed on your mission. See for example Isa 6:8.

A later necessary but highly artificial distinction between the procession and the mission of the divine persons will refer them, so to say, to two different 'moments', the one eternal (procession), the other temporal (mission).[8] But there is of course no hint of that in either Old or New Testament texts. As well as frequently sending various messengers, men, angels, prophets, God also sends things like plagues (Exod 9:14, Am 4:10), serpents (Num 21:6) – these are agents or manifestations of his power and anger – or like his fury and his terror (Exod 15:7, 23:27), that is to say, his own moods or attributes. This is a rather strong figure of speech. More benign attributes that are sent are his light and his truth (Ps 43:3), and his word, his spirit and his wisdom (e.g. Pss 147:18, 104:30, Isa 55:11, Wis 9:10, Sir 24:3).

Perhaps it could be maintained that the most proper object of divine sending is persons, human or angelic, and that when attributes of God are said to be sent they are at least to a slight extent being personified. And e converso, when a divine attribute like Wisdom is very explicitly personified, and starts speaking as a person, she is easily represented both as being sent by God and as going forth or proceeding from God.

NOTES

1 As a deliberately archaic text I think especially of Job, and as an ancient text of Gen 6:1–4. But in suggesting a development of ideas in this field, I am not to be taken as assuming that the texts I quote for the earlier stages of the development are necessarily the earlier texts. They may well not be.

2 Ugaritic is an early Phoenician language, closely related to Hebrew. It is named after the city of Ugarit, which was discovered during excavations at Ras Shamra, a site in northern Syria, where a whole library of cuneiform texts in this language were discovered, dating from about 1500 B.C.

3 LXX is the abbreviation for the Septuagint, the name for the oldest Greek translation of the Bible. The legend was that seventy scholars were put *incommunicado* in seventy cells by King Ptolemy III(?) of Egypt, and that when they had finished translating it was discovered that their seventy separate translations were in fact identical. The point of the legend is to assert the divine inspiration of this translation (the Bible of the Alexandrian Jewish community), and thus to put it on an equal footing of authority with the original Hebrew.

4 That this was its original form is a learned guess, backed up by ancient transcriptions of the name in Greek. The vowel points given to the four consonants in the Massoretic Hebrew Bible are those of the word *Adonai*, which is to be read instead. By combining these vowels with the four sacred consonants we get the form *Jehovah*, which may be described as a learned mistake. Or at least it was a learned mistake when first perpetrated by Hebrew scholars at the Renaissance; now it is simply an ignorant mistake, and it is rather regrettable that it has been perpetuated in Protestant translations of the Bible in the mission world – for instance into Sesotho.

5 *Ehyeh asher ehyeh* in Hebrew, from the verb *hayah* 'to be'. Some scholars do not accept the connection of the name with this verb. Those who do, differ about what the connection is. The name is perhaps most likely to be derived from the causative form of the verb, and so to mean something like 'He who brings into being'.

6 To show respect by never pronouncing the name of the person respected (a father-in-law, for instance, or mother-in-law) is a custom common to many African societies. Where names have common meanings, like *Thabo* for instance in Sesotho (meaning 'joy') or *Mpho* ('gift'), the avoidance of their use will often be rather inconvenient to the speakers and quite a tax on their ingenuity.

7 The Hebrew qualifies the spirit as being the spirit of the four living creatures supporting the divine chariot-throne. But the LXX and the Latin Vulgate call it the spirit of life – which might mean either the divine spirit or just 'a living spirit'.

8 See below, Chapter 7.

4

The Mystery Revealed in the New Testament

What we shall attempt to do in this chapter is to put ourselves in the shoes of Jesus' disciples, and also of the next generation of Christian believers, in order to achieve some understanding of how they came to a realization of the revelation being made to them in the person of Jesus Christ – and in the gift of the Holy Spirit – and of how they worked their way to an expression, or rather to several expressions, of their faith in the mystery revealed. I suggest their understanding went through the following stages, which we shall examine in turn: they came to realize, and to express the realization, (a) that Jesus was the Christ/Messiah;[1] (b) that he was something more than just a man; (c) that he was indeed divine in the full sense of the word; (d) that he was really a distinct entity from God the Father; (e) that nonetheless he is not a separate God from the Father, since *he and the Father are one*, and the monotheism inherited with Judaism remains inviolable; (f) that the Holy Spirit is also a distinct entity from the Father and the Son, while again not being a separate God, but one with the Father and the Son. Let us take each stage in turn.

A.   JESUS IS THE CHRIST

John tells us that Jesus' first disciples had been followers of John the Baptist (Jn 1:35ff.) Although John is the latest of the gospels, and represents the most developed theology of the person of Jesus to be found in the New Testament, and manifestly tailors its account of events to express that theology, it is nevertheless trustworthy in its details. In this detail it is supported by Acts 1:21–22, where Peter says they must choose a successor to Judas from among those who had been with Jesus 'all the time that the Lord Jesus went in and out among us, beginning from the baptism of John'.

Their first perception, then, of this man would have been of a prophet, as great as, if not greater than John. We need to make an effort of imagination to appreciate the religious ferment among the Jews at that time, caused above all by the appearance of John in the desert. The man was manifestly a prophet – and prophecy had ceased in Israel for three hundred years or so.[2] That a prophet should be sent by God again after so long an interval could only mean that the end of the ages was near (see 1 Cor 10:11).

And then comes Jesus; what could it all mean? Two prophets at once! Jesus himself said of John that he was more than a prophet (Mt 11:9, Lk 7:26).[3] What then could Jesus himself be? Mark is so constructed as to lead up to Peter's acknowledgement that Jesus was the Christ (Mk 8:29) as its first climax. All the deeds and sayings of Jesus up to that point are presented as so many hints and proofs that this is the case. At last, at Caesarea Philippi, with Peter, the light dawns. Jesus is the Messiah.

But what was the Messiah, and what was he expected to be? Undoubtedly an eschatological figure who would inaugurate the age to come. If Jesus was the Messiah and John the messenger before his face (Mt 11:10 etc.), then the end of the ages had undoubtedly come. Jesus himself had said 'The time is fulfilled and the kingdom of God is at hand' (Mk 1:15). The question was how he was going to inaugurate the kingdom. And to most Jews, including the disciples, the answer was clear: by a political and military victory over Israel's oppressors, achieved with supernatural assistance to be sure – twelve legions of angels, in fact (Mt 26:53) – he would redeem Israel (Lk 24:21) and restore the kingdom to Israel (Acts 1:6). The Romans knew of this answer too, and it is undoubtedly because Jesus was alleged to have claimed to be this kind of Messiah that he was crucified: 'This is the King of the Jews' (Lk 23:38).

Jesus himself, of course, had other ideas about how he would fulfil the role of the Christ, identifying it with the role of the Isaian servant of the Lord, and the poor man of the psalms, and the just man of Wisdom. He tried, without much success at first, to impart these ideas to his disciples. Hence his famous rebuke to Peter immediately after Peter had acknowledged him as the Christ (Mk 8:31–33).[4]

That the disciples thought of Jesus as the Messiah *and no more* right up to his death seems evident from the way the title 'Lord' is applied to him in the synoptic gospels. As we shall see in the next section, this title played a crucial part in carrying the disciples' notion of Jesus beyond the merely human level. Now in Mark the disciples never call him *Kurios*, Lord. In fact the only person in Mark to address him as *Kurie* – 'Sir' or even 'your lordship' – is the Syro-Phoenician woman; in her extreme anxiety she was, perhaps, employing extravagant politeness (Mk 7:28). His disciples, and everyone else, address him as Master, literally 'teacher' (*didaskalos*, a translation into Greek of *Rabbi*). Only once is he referred to as 'the *Kurios*' – the Lord – and that, oddly enough, is by himself, when he instructs the disciples to fetch him the foal for his triumphal entry into Jerusalem, and to say to its owners 'The Lord has need of it' (Mk 11:3).

In Matthew and Luke the disciples regularly address him as Lord, and Luke as the narrator several times refers to him as such, while his opponents and other non-disciples never do so. This would seem to be a historical anachronism on the part of the evangelists, reading back into the life of Jesus, and thus theologically justifying, the common usage of Christians when they were writing. Mark is more likely to represent the historical reality, and it is indeed what one would expect. How could good plain monotheistic Jews even begin to think that this man was anything other than a man – a man indeed with the most exalted divine mission, far greater than any of the prophets, the Messiah, the son of David – but still only a man?

It was their experience of Jesus risen from the dead that made them think again.

B. JESUS MORE THAN JUST A MAN: LORD AND SON OF MAN

In Acts 2:36 Peter ends his Pentecost sermon, in which he has related how God raised Jesus from the dead, with the words

Let all the house of Israel therefore know assuredly that God has made him both Lord and Christ, this Jesus whom you crucified.

'Both Lord and Christ.' God has made him this, Peter evidently means, by raising him from the dead. The term 'Christ', at any rate, signifies primarily a role or function. So even though Peter had acknowledged Jesus as the Christ before he was crucified, what he is asserting now is that it is the risen Jesus who is to fulfil the messianic role. And it is the risen Jesus, the Christ, who is to be accepted as Lord. Presumably the term 'Lord' is not a mere synonym for 'Christ'. The phrase 'both Lord and Christ' is even stronger in the Greek than in the English; two very distinct predicates are being employed.[5]

The term 'Lord' has a very extensive range of reference as we saw above (p. 24, Chapter 3, B); anything from a polite 'Sir' or possibly 'my lord', as with the Syro-Phoenician woman (Mk 7:28), right up to God himself. Here, and in all subsequent Christian use of the term (see e.g. 1 Cor 12:3), it is clearly at the upper end of the range. But not yet, I think, stating that Jesus is God. We must remind ourselves yet again what a well-nigh impossible thing it would have been for Jews to do that. Jews eventually did it, as we shall see – but it was hardly a conclusion they could jump to. They could only reach it step by little step.

So here, and in most places in the New Testament, the title is certainly raising Jesus above the merely human level. It is putting him on a level with the pagan gods and goddesses, who were called 'Lords' and 'Ladies' (*kurioi* and *kuriai*)[6] – and well above the *kurios*, Caesar, 'our sovereign Lord the King'. Hints had been given by Jesus himself, above all in his discussion of the Christ as the son of David and his employment of Ps 110:1:

David himself, inspired by the Holy Spirit, declared, 'The Lord said to my Lord, Sit at my right hand, till I put thy enemies under thy feet'. David himself calls him Lord; so how is he his son? (Mk 12:36–37).

More than just human, but not simply divine. This earliest Christology may be called innocently Arian.[7] It is also semi-mythical, and supported by the title 'the Son of man' which Jesus, and only Jesus according to the overwhelming evidence of all four gospels, had employed about himself. For this too was a very ambivalent expression. It had two meanings or references. First, it was simply a Semitic turn of phrase for 'a human being', 'a member of the human race', as in Ps 8:4.[8] So when Jesus refers to himself as the Son of man, he is using a title of modesty, as it were calling himself 'the guy'. He is one of us, a little, mortal human being. But secondly, in that period of Judaism the term 'Son of man' had come to have a more exalted reference, based on Dan 7:13, 'with the clouds of heaven there came one like a son of man'. So in the apocalyptic literature that followed Daniel, the Son of man becomes an eschatological and heavenly figure. He is the heavenly man who will come at the end of time. He is identified, it seems, in some circles with the Adam of Gen 1:26–28, who was created in the image of God, and whom these circles distinguished from the Adam of Gen 2:7 who was fashioned of dust from the soil. By people like Philo he is 'Platonized' into a Platonic idea, the ideal man laid up in heaven, distinguished from empirical man in all his earthly defectiveness, who begins his career in Gen 2.

So this Son of man is a curious mixture of mythical figure and Platonic idea. St Paul uses most of the language without apparently subscribing to the myth. In 1 Cor 15:45–49 he talks of the heavenly man and the earthly man (RSV: 'the man of heaven' and 'the man of dust'). But he emphatically reverses their order, thus implicitly rejecting the distinction between the Adam of Gen 1 and the Adam of Gen 2. He never uses the expression 'the Son of man', possibly because he doubted if it would make sense to his Greek readers. But when he calls Christ 'the last Adam' in 1 Cor 15:45 (and by implication in Rom 5:12–19) he has, in my view, the whole complex Son of man concept in mind. Finally the early Christian hymn he incorporates in Phil 2:5–11 is, according to Oscar Cullmann, a reflection on the Son of man theme, thoroughly Christianized – a contrast being made between Christ (the last Adam) and Adam (the Adam of Gen 2 who fell). The key to Cullmann's very convincing interpretation is to see that the word 'form' (*morphē*) in vv. 6 and 7 does not mean 'nature' (the traditional interpretation since at least the fourth century), but is a synonym for 'image'. Thus the hymn would be applying the Son of man myth fairly and squarely to Jesus Christ.[9]

C.   JESUS IS TRULY DIVINE

I have said Paul uses the language of this myth without subscribing to its content. I don't think there is much doubt that Paul's favourite title for Jesus is 'the Lord' or 'our Lord'. See for instance 1 Cor 12:3. And as we have observed, the title has a very wide range of reference. And Paul cannot have been satisfied with limiting its upward reference at this mythical Son of man figure. That he sees him as the divine Lord, as the Lord whose real but unspoken name is YHWH, seems clear from a passage like 1 Cor 8:6:

Yet for us there is one God, the Father, from whom are all things and for whom we exist, and one Lord, Jesus Christ, through whom are all things and through whom we exist;

which, as we remarked above (p. 16, Chapter 2, C), seems to be a Christian variation on the *Shema'* of Dt 6:4.

Though it seems clear from this text that Paul is putting Jesus Christ as Lord on an equality with the Father as God, attributing creation and redemption to each, nowhere does he either explicitly call Jesus God, or analyse his person into two component elements or natures, as the later definition of Chalcedon will put it,[10] a human and a divine. This is particularly evident from another early Christian hymn to Christ incorporated in Col 1:15–20. If Colossians is by Paul it is one of his later letters, and if it is not by him (as most critics aver) it certainly represents a development of his thought. The Son of man myth reappears here, God's beloved Son (v. 13) being called at the beginning 'the image of the invisible God'. Perhaps it is also this mythical concept that is being employed when he is called 'the first-born of all creation' – there could also be an allusion here to the Wisdom figure of Prov 8:22. But when creation is credited to him – 'in him all things were created' (v. 16) – we surely have a fully divine, theological not mythological, predication. See also Col 2:9.

Paul's, and the Pauline, statement of Christ's divinity remains, however, cabined, cribbed, confined in semi-mythical language and concepts. It is left to the Johannine tradition fully to demythologize, that is to say fully to theologize the doctrine of Christ. John does it by interpreting the title 'Lord' in those famous 'I am' sayings. The name YHWH is interpreted in Exod 3:14 as meaning I AM: 'Say this to the people of Israel, I AM has sent me to you'. So the best way of showing that Jesus is Lord in the sense of YHWH is to present him as I AM. Of course, it is possible for him to say 'I am' in an ordinary, less exalted sense, as when he says 'I am the bread of life' (Jn 6:35), or 'I am the true vine' (15:1). But when he says 'Truly, truly I say to you, before Abraham was, I am' (8:58), there can be, and there was, no possible doubt about what was meant. When they came to arrest him in the garden and told him they were looking for Jesus of Nazareth he answered 'I am', which is ordinary Greek for 'I am he' – as it is properly translated. But that John intends it to be taken as affirming I AM is clear from his comment: 'When he said to them "I am he" they drew back and fell to the ground' (18:5-6). John makes the final identification of the title Lord with the deity when he has Thomas acknowledge the risen Jesus as 'My Lord and my God' (20:28).

D.   JESUS, THE LORD, AS SON IS REALLY DISTINCT FROM THE FATHER

In themselves the developments we have traced so far could, and did, lead to heretical ideas about Jesus. The awareness of Jesus as more than just a man, expressed in the semi-mythical Son of man concepts held in isolation, easily lent itself to various Gnostic ideas of the Christ as some kind of *aeon* or lesser emanation from the ultimate One.

The awareness of Jesus as the Lord God, held in isolation and in a context of strict monotheism, produced the later heresy of Monarchianism or Sabellianism or Modalism, according to which Father and Son and Holy Spirit are just three names or modes of the one God.

But the Christian communities which produced the New Testament did not cherish these awarenesses in obsessive isolation. Paul and the Pauline tradition, and the bearers of the Johannine tradition never forgot that Jesus was a man, and that he was first recognized as the Christ or Messiah. See for example Jn 1:35-51, especially vv. 41 and 49, which is historically speaking a highly artificial passage (it certainly does not square with Mk 8:27-33), but theologically indispensable and harmonizing perfectly with the Marcan theology. And they also continued to give full value to the fact that the Messiah was also called the Son of God (see Jn 1:49 again – also Rom 1:4 and pp. 22-23 above, Chapter 3, A).

If Jesus, as well as being Lord/YHWH/I AM/God, is also the Messiah/Son of God, then he is really distinct from the God whose Son he is, and who is frequently referred to by Paul as the God and Father of our Lord Jesus Christ. Now we, with our analytical theological tradition behind us, could say, 'Yes, really distinct from God *as man*, and it is as man – the Messiah – that he is called the Son of God; but this does not entail his being really distinct from God *as God*'. But Paul does not seem to have thought like this. As we observed in the previous section (p. 33), he never analysed Jesus Christ, whom he knew as the risen Lord, knowing him no longer 'according to the flesh' (2 Cor 5:16; RSV: 'from a human point of view'), into, so to say, his component parts. It is the one Jesus Christ who is the divine Lord, through whom are all things, the first-born of all creation, and it is the one Jesus Christ who is the Son of God, of whom Paul also writes in our key trinitarian text, 'When the time had fully come, God sent forth his Son, born of woman . . . ' (Gal 4:4).

But 'Son of God', as we have just been saying, remains a messianic title, applied to that man who is the Messiah or Christ, as also to his prototypes the kings of Israel/Judah. To enable it, while continuing to express real distinction from God the Father of our Lord Jesus Christ, also to express divine equality with him, John abbreviates it to 'the Son', while symmetrically abbreviating God and the Father of our Lord Jesus Christ to 'the Father'. We discussed a sample of such Johannine language, 5:19–47, above on pp. 13–14 (Chapter 2, B) and need not repeat our comments here. I would just like to recall what was said above on p. 18 (Chapter 2, D), that the language of 'the Father' and 'the Son' occurs somewhat incongruously just once in each of the three synoptics (Mt 11:27, Lk 10:22, Mk 13:32). This suggests to me that it was a usage invented by Jesus himself, but only developed in the Johannine tradition – there is not a single instance of it in the Pauline corpus – until it becomes the common Christian style, as illustrated in the trinitarian formula of Mt 28:19.

E.   THE UNITY OF THE FATHER AND THE SON

The language of 'the Father' and 'the Son' certainly serves to distinguish really, and not just nominally, what we now call these two persons of the Trinity, because a son cannot be his own father nor a father his own son. In isolation, indeed, it serves only too well to distinguish them; its tendency is inevitably to present them as two distinct beings, and since we are here by common consent moving on the divine plane, this means as two distinct Gods. For the devout Christian Jews who preserved and developed the Johannine tradition such a thought was clearly anathema, and so we have the strong statement in Jn 10:30, 'I and the Father are one', and the scarcely less strong statement in 14:9, 'He who has seen me has seen the Father'.

But these Johannine theologians, like all Christians, were busy preaching the gospel to the gentiles, i.e. to people for whom believing in many gods was as easy as falling off a log. It was a log our authors clearly did not want them to fall off. But if they heard the message of a divine Father and a divine Son, what else were they to think but that these were two Gods like Zeus and his son Hermes? (See Acts 14:11–12 – not that that incident has anything to do with 'the Father' and 'the Son'.)

So to forestall any such temptation to ditheism John had to find another, less personal name for the Son, which would help us to see how, while being really distinct from the Father, he and the Father really are one – one God. The name he chose was *Logos* or Word. And he gave his gospel, which is really the gospel about the Father and the Son, its invaluable and indispensable prologue:

In the beginning was the Word, and the Word was with God, and the Word was God. He was in the beginning with God . . . And the Word became flesh and dwelt among us, full of grace and truth; we have beheld his glory, glory as of the only Son from the Father (Jn 1:1–2, 14).

Logos means 'thought' as much as, indeed, rather more than it means 'word'. As we saw above (Chapter 3, C, pp. 24–25), John's *Logos* is primarily a masculine form of the feminine *Sophia*, wisdom, a title already attributed to Christ in 1 Cor 1:24. Now whereas a son is not only distinguishable but really separate from his father, a person's thought or wisdom, while distinguishable from the person, cannot exist as a separate entity. So if the Son is the Wisdom of God (i.e. of his Father), and the *Logos*/thought that is with God (i.e. with his Father), it means that while he is indeed distinct from his Father, he cannot be a separate being from him but is indeed, with the Father, God – one and the same and only God. Monotheism is safeguarded.

F.   RECAPITULATION

Every stage of this deepening awareness of the mystery of Jesus Christ was, so to speak, supported by and read back into the memories and testimonies of his life and ministry, his death and resurrection. That is why, indeed, the gospels were written, as Luke says in his prologue to his own: 'that you may know the truth of the things of which you have been informed' (1:4).[11] What Theophilus had been informed of, presumably (the Greek word is, literally, 'catechized'), was doctrine about Jesus Christ – that Jesus is Lord, for example, and the Christ, and that the Christ had to suffer in fulfilment of the scriptures and so enter his glory, that salvation was to be preached in his name to all nations (see e.g. 1 Cor 12:3, Acts 2:36, Lk 24:26, 46–47, Acts 17:3).

So while before his death the disciples, according to our reconstruction, had got no further than recognizing him as the Messiah, after his resurrection they began to remember things he had said and done that pointed beyond this – and to record these memories in a way that would teach further lessons about him. For instance: 'Who then is this, that even wind and sea obey him?' (Mk 4:41). Now we can see that he is far more than just the Messiah, because the wind and the sea, as the Old Testament so consistently testifies (e.g. Pss 93:3–4, 104:3–4, Job 38:8–11), only obey their creator.

Or take the passage comparing Jesus with John the Baptist when John sent messengers asking 'Are you he who is to come, or shall we look for another?' (Lk 7:18–35, Mt 11:2–19). First of all, the message he sends back to John is an obvious allusion, among other passages, to Isa 35:3–6, where we read 'Behold your God will come with vengeance, with the recompense of God. He will come and save you'. 'You asked if I am the one who is to come', Jesus is in effect saying; 'well, that passage, which describes the things you have seen and heard, tells you who is coming'. Secondly, Mal 3:1 is applied to John: 'Behold, I send my messenger before thy face, who shall prepare thy way before thee' – so Luke (7:27) and Matthew (11:10). But when we turn to Malachi (as of course we are meant to do), we find: 'Behold I send my messenger to prepare the way before me, and the Lord whom you seek will suddenly come to his temple'. We surely conclude, as Christians of that first generation, to an identity between 'me' (God) in Malachi and 'thee' (Jesus) in the gospels.

The two most important of these 'readings back' or 'refurbished memories' are the stories of Jesus' baptism by John and his transfiguration. Both (like the story of his temptation in the desert) are theological legends rather than mere historical descriptions. Both are composed in the light of experience of the risen Christ. My guess is that the first represents an earlier stage of reflection on the mystery of Jesus than the second. The first relates him precisely as the Christ – and also as the Servant of the Lord – i.e. in his human roles, to both God the Father as his Son and to the Holy Spirit as the arch-recipient of this divine gift. Since the Spirit comes upon him in the form of a dove, which recalls the dove that brought back the olive branch to Noah in the ark, he is presented as being, in the Spirit, the reconciler of the whole human race to God; what Paul calls 'our peace, who has made both [Jew and gentile] one' (Eph 2:14). But for all that, we have what I like to call a very definite trinitarian tableau.

The transfiguration gives us another such tableau, one that takes us even deeper into the divine mystery. Jesus being transfigured appears at least as superhuman (the Son of man myth, the heavenly man), if not already as sharing the divine glory 'which thou hast given me . . . before the foundation of the world' (Jn 17:24). He is still the Christ, the Son of God, with a role to play (his death and resurrection). But Luke calls this role 'his exodus [RSV: departure] which he was to accomplish in Jerusalem' (9:31). Now it was God, and only God (YHWH) who accomplished the original exodus from Egypt. So the inference is that it will be Jesus as Lord (YHWH) who will accomplish the universal exodus of mankind from the dominion of sin and Satan.

In this second trinitarian tableau the Holy Spirit, not mentioned by name, appears as the 'bright cloud' (Mt 17:5) which overshadowed them, the cloud which in the Old Testament represents the divine protective and sanctifying presence, which accompanied the children of Israel out of Egypt (Exod 13:21–22), which filled Solomon's new temple after the ark had been placed in it (1 Kgs 8:10–11), which the Lord will create over Mount Zion and over her assemblies, presumably at the final vindication of Zion in the kingdom (Isa 4:5). In the baptism scene the Holy Spirit descended on Jesus alone; here it overshadows Jesus and his three disciples together.

G.   THE HOLY SPIRIT

The revelation of the mystery of the Trinity, whose progressive apprehension by the first Christian generations we are trying to recapture or reconstruct (hypothetically of course) in this chapter, was accomplished by the sending of the Son and the sending of the Holy Spirit, as suggested in Paul's key text, Gal 4:4–7. The sending of the Son in 'the form of a servant' (Phil 2:7), in the person of Jesus of Nazareth is the great objective assertion of the Christian religion. There he was, born of the virgin Mary at a particular time,[12] baptized by John the Baptist 'in the fifteenth year of the reign of Tiberius Caesar' (A.D. 28/29; Lk 3:1), crucified under Pontius Pilate, raised from the dead on the third day. And we have been tracing a possible, indeed, I modestly suggest, a likely way in which his disciples and subsequent believers, on the basis of their experience and memories of him, came to penetrate further and further into the mystery of his being.

But the Holy Spirit – when was he sent? Pentecost, you will say. But the New Testament also records his advent at the baptism of Jesus – not to mention the conception of Jesus. The first point I wish to make is that his mission or being sent does not terminate in an objective reality external to believers, something 'out there', as was the man Jesus, but in an internal, subjective experience *only*. Both stories or theological legends just mentioned, Pentecost and the baptism of Jesus, objectify this subjective experience into a dove and tongues of fire and a mighty rushing wind; but that is just part of the technique of theological story-telling. Press photographers, I am saying, could not have seized those moments with their candid cameras, as they could have photographed the crucifixion, and even the risen Jesus walking along the road to Emmaus, for example. St Paul in our key text will talk of God sending 'the Spirit of his Son into our hearts' (Gal 4:6), and that is of the essence of this sending; that is the only place – a subjective place – the Holy Spirit can be sent to.

I am not denying, far from it, that this purely subjective experience of receiving the Holy Spirit had objective consequences. It did, and it does, and it ought to have. I am only saying that it is of its essence a subjective experience, like being taught something, and that if that experience is lacking, then the sending cannot be said to have taken place. On the other hand, while the experience of perceiving the Son in Jesus Christ is certainly subjective – an experience of faith – like the experience of the Holy Spirit, Jesus the man is still an objective fact of history, out there, even for those who do not have the subjective experience of faith, and do not perceive the Son of God in him.

The second point I wish to make is that in spite of some apparent evidence to the contrary, the sending of the Holy Spirit is not subsequent *in time* to the sending of the Son. The evidence to the contrary is the fact, for example, that Pentecost comes after Easter and does not coincide with it; and especially the text of Jn 7:39, 'as yet the Spirit had not been given, because Jesus was not yet glorified'. But here, I think we can say that in John's view the Son himself was not yet fully sent until Jesus was glorified.

In fact the two missions, or from the human side the two experiences, the objective one of the Son in Jesus Christ and the subjective one of the Spirit, go together, each implied by or involved with the other. Both Matthew and Luke therefore rightly associate the virginal conception of Jesus with the Holy Spirit: Mary subjectively experienced the Holy Spirit in her heart when she objectively conceived the Son in her womb (Mt 1:20, Lk 1:35). At his baptism the man Jesus subjectively experienced the Holy Spirit (his anointing as the Messiah or Christ) at the same time as he perceived himself yet more clearly and objectively as 'my Son, my Beloved' (Mk 1:11, RSV alternative). In the ministry of Jesus there are enough references to the Holy Spirit to support this case. Besides the episode of the transfiguration which we have already noted, see the following texts: Lk 11:13, Mt 12:28, Mk 3:29 (a most difficult text indeed!), Mt 10:20.

The perception of who and what Jesus Christ really was, as is clear from the preceding sections, was a gradual, progressive process. Is the same true of believers' understanding of the Holy Spirit? There presumably must have been some process of development, governed by the experience which the first Christian generations had of the Holy Spirit. But what the process was, what the special nature of that experience, it seems impossible on the evidence (the New Testament texts) to say. We can only note where the process started and where it ended.

It started, presumably, where we left ideas about the Holy Spirit in the last chapter (pp. 25–27, Chapter 3, D). God's Spirit, like his Wisdom, is one of his attributes or qualities, rather more 'impersonal' than his Wisdom. It signifies his power, his vitality, and towards the end of the Old Testament development it comes to signify in a rather more refined notion something more personal – God's presence or 'face', a protective, guiding, indwelling presence. In many, perhaps most of the New Testament texts we have glanced at in this section there is no intrinsic reason for thinking that the term 'Holy Spirit' signifies anything more than this.

But at the end of the process the term undoubtedly signifies what we now call 'the third person of the Trinity' – a personal subsistent reality, (subsistently) distinct from the Father and the Son, while remaining inseparably one God with them. The formula of Mt 28:19 clearly bears this sense. So do Paul's various triadic formulae, including I think our key text of Gal 4:4–7. Here the sending by God of the Spirit of his Son is so clearly parallel to the sending of the Son, that it would be very odd to think of the Spirit as only a divine attribute, while the Son is manifestly a subsistent person. The same is true for 1 Cor 12:4–6.

The clearest statement of the Holy Spirit as a 'subsistent personality' is to be found in Jn 14 – 16, where Jesus calls the Holy Spirit 'another advocate' (14:16; RSV: Counsellor) – he himself being the first advocate – and talks about him teaching you 'all things' (14:26). See also 15:26, 16:7ff., 13.

But how the disciples of Jesus and those first Christian generations moved from one point to the other; what obliged them, so to say, to do so, is (to me at least) very obscure. Perhaps it was something in their experience of the Spirit, of the divine force or presence which possessed them so powerfully, as being *sent* to them as they knew the Son of God had been sent to them; a sense of that parallelism which we have just noted in Gal 4:4–7. And there is no reason to doubt that recollection of things Jesus had said about the Holy Spirit reinforced this quality in their experience. More than that I find it impossible to say.

NOTES

1 The Greek and Hebrew respectively for 'the anointed one'. There were a number of ideas circulating about who or what the Messiah would be, and what he would do. Common to all of them was his eschatological character. He was the figure who would usher in 'the age of the Messiah', which in most eschatological theories was identical with 'the age to come', but in one or two was just preparatory to that final age. For practically all Jews the Messiah would be a political liberator.

2 See 1 Macc 4:46, 9:27, 14:41. The sense one gets from these passages is that until a prophet arises again in Israel we are living in a kind of interim period when only provisional decisions about important matters can be made.

3 If any texts in the New Testament give us authentic sayings of Jesus, these must do so! Jesus' being baptized by John and his consistently expressed admiration for him must have been a real embarrassment to the first Christian theologians, suggesting that Jesus was a disciple of John.

4   See the other so-called predictions of the passion, Mk 9:31, 10:33–34 and parr.; also 10:45 and Lk 22:27. The most important Old Testament texts are Isa 53, Ps 22, Wis 2:10–20.

5   Literally, 'and Lord him and Christ made God, this Jesus . . . '.

6   See 1 Cor 8:5.

7   Arius taught his heresy at the beginning of the fourth century. We will meet it again in Chapter 6. His slogan, at least as quoted by his orthodox opponents, was 'there was a time when the Son was not'. In other words, the Son or Logos was a creature, not true God, not equal to the Father. He was the first and greatest of all creatures, and this was the being, a kind of demigod, who became man.

8   'What is man that thou art mindful of him, and the son of man that thou dost care for him?' Man in his littleness and weakness. But the psalmist goes on immediately to recall the great dignity bestowed on man by God who has 'crowned him with glory and honour' and 'given him dominion over the works of [God's] hands' (vv. 5–6). One might say that the psalmist goes on to hint at the 'high' meaning of the phrase 'son of man'. I think we can say he is harmonizing the contrasting views of man expressed by the P author of Gen 1 and the J author of Gen 2 – 4. (For J, the Yahwist, and P, the Priestly strand in the Pentateuch or first five books of the Bible, see my *Being Human* [London, 1984], pp. 16–17.)

9   *The Christology of the New Testament* (London, 1963). I am indebted to this book of O. Cullmann's for everything I say in this section about the Son of man.

10 The Council of Chalcedon, A.D. 451. After many decades of increasingly bitter dispute about Christ, the Council condemned both the Nestorian heresy that Christ is two persons, a human person united to the divine person of the Word, and the Monophysite heresy that the human and divine are united in Christ in one nature; and made its definition that one and the same Lord Jesus Christ is the one person of the Word or Son subsisting in two natures, the divine nature and the human.

11 The RSV translation is not entirely satisfactory. More precise would be 'that you may know the certainty of the things about which you have been instructed'.

12 The gospels do not tell us precisely when. The fifth-century monk, Dionysius Exiguus (Denis Little), who worked out the Christian era, took Luke's vague statement of Jesus' age in 3:23 – 'about thirty years of age' – as a precise statement, and so placed his birth fifteen years before the accession of Tiberius, in A.D. 1. But both Matthew and Luke say that Jesus was born in the reign of Herod the Great, who died in 4 B.C. So if that point of the infancy narratives has any historical validity, and nobody has found any reason to doubt it, then Jesus must have been born before then. The most favoured date seems to be 6 B.C.

III
Assimilating the Mystery

5

The Economic
Theologians

A. DISTINCTION BETWEEN THE ECONOMIC AND THE TRANSCENDENTAL APPROACHES

Karl Rahner, in his 'Remarks on the Dogmatic Treatise "De Trinitate" ' (*Theological Investigations* 4), states his basic thesis as follows: 'The Trinity of the economy of salvation *is* the immanent Trinity and *vice versa*'. To anyone not used to Rahner's style this is indeed a baffling statement. Whoever suggested that there were two Trinities in any case? Perhaps someone has done; if so, I myself remain baffled. But the way I interpret Rahner's thesis is to treat it as theological shorthand. 'The Trinity of the economy of salvation' means the mystery of the Trinity as revealed in, and as studied through, the economy of salvation. 'The economy of salvation', or 'the economy' for short, is an old theological expression going right back to St Paul and the Pauline circle. Thus Eph 1:9, 10: 'For he has made known to us . . . the mystery of his will, according to his purpose which he set forth in Christ as *a plan* for the fullness of time'; and Col 1:25: ' . . . the church, of which I became a minister according to *the divine office* which was given to me for you'. In the first text 'plan' translates *oikonomia* or 'economy', and in the second 'the divine office' renders 'the *oikonomia* of God'.

The Greek word *oikonomia* means literally 'housekeeping' or 'household administration'. So what Paul means in these texts is God's administration of his household, his creation, with particular reference to the salvation of mankind. Hence the theological expression 'the economy' (sc. of salvation) means God's plan of salvation, or rather his execution or administration of that plan in such a central mystery, for example, as the incarnation. Thus this mystery, and the doctrines of creation, the Church, the sacraments, grace, eschatology, will all be called mysteries or doctrines of the economy.

'The Trinity of the economy of salvation', in Rahner's phrase, therefore means (or at least I am taking it to mean) the Trinity as revealed in and then approached through such saving events and realities as the incarnation, Pentecost, the Church. It is in fact how we have been approaching the mystery so far. We have been pursuing the economic approach.

By 'the immanent Trinity' Rahner means the mystery of the Trinity considered in itself, without reference to creatures. The difference lies, surely not in the Trinity (as I remarked, there can hardly be two Trinities), but in the way we consider the Trinity. The word 'immanent', I think, can be misleading, since it usually means, in theological or philosophical discourse, one thing 'residing' in another. So God as immanent – hence the Trinity as immanent – would normally signify God as being present in his creatures, in the world, in us. But that is precisely *not* how we are thinking of the Trinity in this case (that would be identical with the Trinity considered economically). So I have substituted the word 'transcendent' – the Trinity (God) as being in itself (himself) above and beyond all creatures.

So then, we have two ways of considering or approaching the mystery. The economic way reflects on the mystery as revealed in Jesus Christ, Pentecost, etc. – and also as manifested, if you think this is the case, in creation and in the divine *gesta* of the Old Testament. The transcendental way reflects on the mystery in itself, on the mutual relations of the divine persons to each other, on their unity and distinctness without reference to creatures or to our salvation.

Now the fact is that the earliest Christian theologians all followed the economic way, which is after all the way of experience. And by the beginning of the fourth century it had become clear that this approach had led to a dead end and given rise to insoluble problems. So (roughly speaking) from the crisis of Arianism[1] onwards – the crisis that in fact stated the inadequacy of the economic approach – and from the Council of Nicaea in 325, it was the transcendental (Rahner: immanent) approach that came to be more and more favoured, until eventually it monopolized the field. This too ended up by producing unfortunate effects, which were briefly recorded in Chapter 1 and which Rahner is surveying in his 'Remarks'.

Meanwhile we must now follow three of the earliest 'economic' theologians in their exploration of the mystery. I think they are the most important ante-Nicene writers on the subject. They are Justin (d. 165), Irenaeus (d. *c.*195) and Tertullian (d. *c.*225). If I were writing a history of the doctrine I would certainly have to include Origen (d. 253), the greatest of all the ante-Nicene Fathers in learning and intellectual genius. But my aim in this book is to present the mystery intelligibly and 'experientially' to the reader; and while in order to do this I am indeed following a historical procedure, my historical survey does not need to be exhaustive. In my view the high point of the history of the doctrine is Augustine's reflection on it in his great work, the *De Trinitate*. So here I am content to follow the earlier historical line that leads up to him; and I do not think that that line went through Origen. But it did go, from the New Testament, through Justin,

Irenaeus and Tertullian, with an extension from him to Novatian. They then are stages on our journey.

B. JUSTIN

Justin was born in Palestine in what is the modern town of Nablus, ancient Sichem or possibly Samaria. But he seems to have been a pagan, not a Samaritan. He devoted his life to the quest for the true philosophy, which he did not find among the Platonists or the Stoics or the Aristotelians or the Epicureans – but did find among the Christians, probably at Ephesus. Then he set up his own school of philosophy (i.e. in fact Christianity) in Rome about 145. To the world at large he appeared as a professional philosopher, to the Church he was probably a *didaskalos* or teacher, in charge of, or at least on the staff of the Roman catechetical school.

He was one of the so-called Apologists, whose writings were intended to defend Christianity against the criticisms of the pagans, and also if possible to avert persecution. He addressed two *Apologies* (the Greek word for 'Defence' – cf. J. H. Newman's *Apologia pro Vita Sua*) to the emperor Antoninus Pius, and he also wrote a defence of Christianity against Jewish criticism in dialogue form, the *Dialogue with Trypho*. These are his writings which survive. They all contain autobiographical information. He was put to death in Rome about 165 for refusing to sacrifice to the gods.

It is his *Dialogue with Trypho* that interests us here, since in it he sets out to prove from the scriptures, which of course Christians have in common with Jews, first that Jesus was the Christ/Messiah, and secondly that the Christ is divine and 'pre-existed', i.e. existed as the *Logos* (Word) before the incarnation.[2] He undertakes to show 'that there is, and is stated to be [in the Old Testament scriptures] another God and Lord under the maker of all things'[3] and also 'to provide evidence from the scriptures that in the beginning before all creatures God begot a certain "logical" power out of himself,[4] which is also called the glory of the Lord, and sometimes Son, sometimes Wisdom, sometimes Angel, sometimes God, sometimes Lord and Logos'.[5]

The evidence Justin provides to prove his point all comes, of course, from the Old Testament, and the texts he chooses remain standard proof texts for centuries. The most important element in his method is to assume that all the manifestations of God recorded in scripture, whether visible or audible (e.g. to Adam in the garden, Gen 3; to Abraham at Mamre, Gen 18; to Moses at the burning bush, Exod 3), were appearances of the Son or Logos. So they prove the 'pre-existence' of Christ. Here he develops a tradition of interpretation which begins perhaps in the New Testament (for example, Jn

12:41). It became standard practice until it was subjected to devastating criticism by Augustine.[6] It illustrates the economic approach very well, because all these theophanies recorded in scripture are stages in the divine economy or plan of salvation.

C.   IRENAEUS

The same method is employed by Irenaeus in his four-volume work *Against Heresies*, although he is fighting, so to say, on the opposite front from Justin; not against Jewish critics with whom Christians share the common ground of scripture (Old Testament), but against the various Gnostic heretics with whom we share very little common ground at all.

Irenaeus was born in Asia Minor, probably at Smyrna, and as a boy he knew the venerable bishop Polycarp who had himself as a youth been a disciple of the apostle John. He migrated to Lyons in Gaul (France), and became bishop of the Christian community there in 177 or shortly afterwards.

One of the opinions of the Gnostics which he had to refute is that the God of the Old Testament was different from the God and Father of Jesus Christ – was in fact rather a nasty God, whom they called the cosmocrat. So it suits Irenaeus' purpose to use the same texts and method as Justin in order to prove that both testaments speak of one and the same God – and what is more, of one and the same Son of God. Thereby he shows that 'the Son of God is scattered (*inseminatus*) everywhere in the scriptures; sometimes talking to Abraham, sometimes to Noah, giving him the measurements [of the ark], sometimes looking for Adam, sometimes bringing judgement on the men of Sodom; and again when he appeared and guided Jacob on his way, and talked to Moses from the bush'.[7]

Irenaeus improves on Justin by suggesting a theological reason for its being the Word or Son who figured in the Old Testament theophanies. It is that the Word is the means of communication between God the Father (who is God at his most ultimate, absolute and godly, so to say) and his creation. Irenaeus, though obviously no Gnostic, inhabited the same thought-world as his Gnostic opponents – which is why he could meet and refute them in their own terms. It was a world of ideas which almost axiomatically needed intermediaries or links between the absolute Being beyond being which is what nearly everyone with any education meant by God, and the relative, corruptible sub-being of this visible world. The Gnostics postulated whole chains of emanating *aeons* (one of which would be called *Logos*, another *Christos*, another *Sophia*, for example); the Christians as represented by

Irenaeus found the necessary intermediary much more simply and economically in the Logos incarnate in Jesus Christ.

But the linking or communicating function of the Logos did not begin only with the incarnation. It began at creation and continued until the incarnation, when it reached its full perfection. Commenting on Exod 3:7, 8, 'Seeing I have seen the affliction of my people who are in Egypt . . . and I have come down to deliver them', Irenaeus writes: 'The Word of God was accustomed from the beginning to go up and come down, for the salvation of those who were in evil straits'.[8]

His key trinitarian statement is perhaps that 'by the Word made visible and palpable [he is not referring to the incarnation but to Old Testament phenomena, especially those of the divine revelation at Sinai] the Father was being shown, even though all did not equally believe him. But all saw the Father in the Son; for the Father is the invisibility of the Son, and the Son is the visibility of the Father'.[9] He will, however, go on to make a very necessary qualification of this bold statement by remarking, 'It is not, as some people say, that the Father of all things being invisible, there is another who could be seen by the prophets'.[10]

A superficial sceptic might consider that this statement contradicts, not qualifies, the previous one. But it would indeed be a superficial criticism. Irenaeus is struggling, with an inadequate set of terms, to express profound insights into God's revelation of himself, which is really identical with his saving of man. He (God) intends us to see the unseeable – that is what our salvation consists in. So, 'Man of himself does not see God; but he is willingly seen by what men he will, when he will, as he will. For God is powerful in all things. He was seen then [in the Old Testament] through the Spirit of prophecy; he was seen [in the New Testament] through the Son adoptively (*adoptive*); he will be seen in the kingdom of heaven paternally (*paternaliter*). It is the Spirit who prepares man in the Son, it is the Son who leads to the Father, it is the Father who bestows incorruption unto eternal life, which comes to anyone from his seeing God'.[11] Elsewhere he calls the Word 'the interpreter of the Father'.[12]

To sum up the contribution of Justin and Irenaeus, the pre-existence of the Son or Word is clearly affirmed, and so is his real distinctness from the Father. This is seen to lie in his function, with reference to the created world and to man in particular, of being the operative principle in the divine order, that is of being the creator, saviour, revealer, above all being the revealer of the Father. This is really the essence of the economic theology of the Trinity; the three persons are seen as distinguished from each other by their differing functions or roles in the economy of salvation.

D.   THE MONARCHIAN REACTION

These developments and this kind of language – especially that of Justin saying 'there is another God and Lord under the maker of all things' – must have struck many Christians as a betrayal of the traditional faith in one God: what we in our abstract, 'transcendental' way call monotheism, but what they in their more concrete 'economic' way of thinking called the 'monarchy' of God. The God of Israel alone, the true God, the Father of our Lord Jesus Christ alone is the creator and only ruler, the mon-arch, of all things. In their reaction against what seemed to them to be a multiplication of gods and a disintegration of the divine monarchy, some went so far as to deny that there is any real distinction between Father, Son and Holy Spirit. They said that these three names are just that: three different names for God, given him by the scriptures according to the various ways or 'modes' in which he has revealed himself to men. Hence the name of *Modalism* for this heresy. It is also called *Sabellianism* from Sabellius its chief propagator, and sometimes *Patripassianism* from the inference drawn from it that it was the Father, identical with the Son, who suffered on the cross. It was a primitive Unitarianism.

E.   TERTULLIAN AND NOVATIAN

It was against this heresy of Modalism that Tertullian wrote his *Against Praxeas* at the beginning of the third century, carrying on the work of Justin and Irenaeus, to whom he is greatly indebted.

Tertullian was a native of Carthage in the Roman province of Africa, the son of a soldier, born into a pagan family about 155. He studied and practised law in Rome. When he became a Christian he returned to Carthage, and wrote a vast number of books, nearly all of them very fierce, in defence of Christianity. He is the first Christian writer of note to have written in Latin. Towards the end of his life he joined the fierce, puritanical sect of the Montanists, and died about 225.

Tertullian, of course, does not deny the principle of 'monarchy', but to balance it he brings in quite explicitly the principle of 'economy'. He seems to go further than Justin and Irenaeus, who had indeed stated the distinction of the divine persons in economic terms, i.e. in terms of their functions or activities in the created world. Tertullian says (as I understand him) that these different economic functions actually produce the distinctions between the persons. In this he carries the economic approach to its logical conclusion.

All that monarchy means, he says, is unity of empire or rule and its concentration in a single individual. But it does not disallow the monarch having a son, or administering (an economy word) his empire by whatever agents he likes, or sharing his monarchy with his son. 'So if the divine monarchy or empire is administered by so many legions and armies of angels, and does not cease to be a monarchy for all that . . . , how is it that God should be thought to suffer division or dispersion in the Son and in the Holy Spirit, who share so intimately in the Father's substance, though he suffers none in all those angels, who are so alien to him in substance?'[13]

Elsewhere he calls the Trinity 'a mystery of the economy (*sacramentum oeconomiae*) which arranges the oneness into threeness, setting forth three, Father, Son and Holy Spirit'.[14] And he goes on to say that his opponents 'assume that the number and arrangement of a threesome [trinity] means the division of unity; whereas the unity, deriving the threesome out of itself, is not destroyed by it but administered'.[15]

Tertullian is certainly not easy to understand. But I think it is clear from the context of these quotations that the divine unity, like the monarchy which manifests it, is preserved and embodied in the person of the Father, who remains impregnably monarch, and one, while the mystery of the economy administers his unity into trinity by deriving the Son and the Spirit from his substance. G. L. Prestige considers that the idea of 'economy' as used here by Tertullian does not mean quite the same thing as when the incarnation, for example, is called a divine economy, but that it has a secondary meaning of 'arrangement of parts'. He is trying to save Tertullian from putting the derivation of the Word and the Spirit from the Father into the same category of act, that is to say an act in the order of creation, as the incarnation or any other saving act of God.[16]

I do not think he really succeeds, as Tertullian's subsequent unfolding of his case makes clear. For example, with reference to the original act of creation itself he writes, 'It is then that the Word receives its shape and form, its sound and voice, when God says Let there be light. This is the complete nativity of the Word, when it proceeds from God'[17] – presumably it was only conceived but not yet born while it was still only thought by God without being uttered.

Later still, developing and hardening Irenaeus' idea about the Son being what is visible of the Father, he says 'and consequently we must understand the Father as invisible in the fullness of his majesty, but we must acknowledge the Son as visible in the measure of his derivation'.[18] Finally, he treats the generation of the Son by the Father as being on a par with his being sent by the Father, and regards both as meaning a derivation of substance from the Father, which makes the Son less than the Father.[19]

Let us now try to assess how Tertullian's contribution has reset the trinitarian problem. He has followed Justin and Irenaeus in asserting the real distinction of the Son and the Holy Spirit from the Father (and from each other), and proved it by the same means, above all by the frequent manifestations of the Word in the Old Testament theophanies before the incarnation. He has on the other hand asserted the monarchy of God in the person of the Father.

But his use of the idea of the economy to explain the relationship of Son and Holy Spirit to the Father, and his association of this idea with the execution of God's providence as attested by scripture, and the whole drift of his argument – all this implies that the Son and the Holy Spirit have the role of lieutenants of the sole monarch, the Father. It also implies that God *has become* a trinity, that the divine unity has been distributed into a trio in the course of putting into effect the economies of creation and redemption.

Tertullian is nowhere concerned to defend the equality of the divine persons. The last text quoted shows him quite happy with the idea of the Father being greater than the Son. It is true he vehemently maintains that the Son and the Holy Spirit share in the Father's substance (an expression which was going to give rise to the term *consubstantialis*, though Tertullian himself does not use this word); and this makes them quite different from creatures. But his idea of the divine substance was such that it admitted of extension and gradation within it, differences of degree though not of kind.[20]

So the effect of his use of economy, associated with the idea of the essential visibility of the Son and his frequent appearance in the Old Testament, is to subordinate the Son to the Father, i.e. to jeopardize his absolute equality with the Father. This was the tendency of most third-century theology. Novatian, a Roman presbyter in the middle of the century who started a rigorist schism not unlike the Montanist sect which Tertullian had joined, wrote a book *De Trinitate* in which he does little more than put a hard cutting edge on the tendencies that were beginning to show in Tertullian. For Novatian, to argue the divinity of Christ, which he does with great vigour, actually involves arguing his inequality to the Father. The assumption is that Christ can only be both divine and other than the Father if he is divine in a different and lesser degree. Novatian interprets the famous text of Phil 2:6, 'who, though he was in the form of God, did not count equality with God a thing to be grasped', as meaning that though Christ was divine, in the form of God, he never dreamt of claiming equality with God.[21]

Again, he states the visibility of the Son, as against the invisibility of the Father, even more unequivocally than Tertullian, and connects it with the Son's title of being the Image of the Father, the image according to which man was created.[22] Like Tertullian, he interprets Jn 10:30, 'I and the Father are one', as meaning that they are one by concord and love and unanimity.[23] Finally, he explicitly states, as I think Tertullian had not done, that the generation of the Son by the Father is an act of the Father's will, something he chose to do but need not have done.[24]

Thus the economic approach to the mystery, if followed consistently (as by

Tertullian and Novatian) leads to a very questionable, indeed heretical conclusion – though its heretical nature was only formally declared after the time of these writers. One last defect, and perhaps its greatest, is that consistently pursued it subjects God in his own nature and being to a temporal process; that is to say, it makes the being of God dependent on his relations with his creation and variable in accordance with those relations – and that is an inherently contradictory state of affairs.

NOTES

1 See Chapter 6 below.
2 *Tryph.* 48 (*PG* 6,580A).
3 *Ibid.* 56 (*ibid.* 597B).
4 i.e. the *Logos* or Word. As we saw above in Chapter 4, E (p. 36), *Logos* means thought or reason before it means the spoken word; the capacity for 'logic'.
5 *Tryph.* 61 (*PG* 6, 613C).
6 See Chapter 7 below.
7 *AH* IV, 10, 1 (*PG* 7, 1000A). Irenaeus, like Justin and all the earliest Christian writers, wrote in Greek. But this work of his only survives in its entirety in an early Latin translation.
8 *Ibid.* IV, 12, 4 (*ibid.* 1006A).
9 *Invisible enim Filii Pater, visibile autem Patris Filius: ibid.* IV, 6, 6 (*ibid.* 989C).
10 *Ibid.* IV, 20, 5 (*ibid.* 1034C).
11 *Ibid.* IV, 20, 5 (*ibid.* 1035A–B).
12 *Ibid.* IV, 20, 11 (*ibid.* 1040A).
13 *AP* 3 (*PL* 2, 158C).
14 *Ibid.* 2 (*ibid.* 157B).
15 *Ibid.* 3 (*ibid.* 158A).
16 *God in Patristic Thought*, pp. 99–106. See also A. Grillmeier, *Christ in Christian Tradition* (London, 1965), pp. 132ff.
17 *AP* 7 (*PL* 2, 161B).
18 *Ibid.* 14 (*ibid.* 171A).
19 *Ibid.* 9 (*ibid.* 164B).
20 Tertullian seems, curiously enough, to have been a materialist in his philosophy of being. For him 'substance' meant 'body'. If there is no body, there is no reality, only an abstraction. So for him to deny that God was or had a body would have been to deny that God was real, and to reduce the divinity to an abstraction. See *AP* 7 (*PL* 2, 162C) where he writes, 'Who can deny that God is a body, even though God is spirit? For spirit is body of its own kind'. It is odd that so highly educated a man should have been untouched by the highly spiritual (or idealist) philosophies that dominated the thought of the Hellenistic and Roman worlds, chief of which was Platonism in various forms. But then one remembers Augustine saying in his *Confessions* that it was his inability to conceive of substance that was immaterial or spiritual which first made him susceptible to the teaching of the Manichaeans and then held him back for a long time from being able to see the truth of Christianity.
21 *Trin.* 22 (*PL* 3, 958A).
22 *Ibid.* 18 (*ibid.* 946C–D); 28 (970–971); 31 (979B); cf. 17 (945B–C).
23 *Ibid.* 27 (*ibid.* 966C).
24 *Ibid.* 31 (*ibid.* 978A).

6
The Transcendental Approach

A. FURTHER ASSESSMENT OF THE ECONOMIC APPROACH

From what was said at the end of the last chapter it might be concluded that the economic approach to the Trinity proved ultimately sterile – at the very least a dead end, at the worst erroneous and misleading. But this would be too hasty a judgement. It had, and still can have, great virtues. It took the scriptural evidence for the mystery seriously; which means it took the historical dimension of the revelation seriously; which means it kept the mystery of the Trinity relevant to the historical human situation, and thus accessible to the experience of faith. The mystery of the Trinity *is* manifestly connected with the mystery of the incarnation; it is equally manifestly connected with the Pentecostal coming of the Holy Spirit; and so it has everything to do with our redemption and sanctification.

It was not, in fact, the economic approach of these theologians in itself which led to the unfortunate consequences we mentioned in the last chapter, but their pursuit of it without an adequate doctrine or metaphysics of God – a fault we have already noted in Tertullian (and Novatian) and surmised in Justin, with his language (clumsy to say the least) of 'another Lord and another God under the maker of all things'.[1] I think Irenaeus does not deserve such strictures.

The defect was to be remedied by the transcendental theologians who began to dominate the ecclesiastical scene from the end of the third and the beginning of the fourth century, both before, and above all after the Council of Nicaea in 325. It is in fairness to be remarked that the transcendental approach also had its disadvantages. Not only did it eventually lead, when followed without any economic reference, to that severing of the trinitarian mystery from any strong anchor-hold in the experience and religious consciousness of ordinary (Western?) Christians which we remarked on in Chapter 1; it also led directly to a much graver heresy and crisis of faith than any we have so far observed – that of Arius the presbyter of the Alexandrian Church, to whose movement we now turn.

B. THE ARIANS AND THE COUNCIL OF NICAEA, 325

As far as I know, none of the writings of Arius or his disciples, explicitly setting forth their teaching, has survived. Since they were in the end the losers of what was to be a very long ecclesiastical war, this is not surprising. No orthodox monk, no professional scrivener keen on keeping in business, was going to copy works of such heretical depravity. So we are left to reconstruct their teaching from the polemical writings of orthodox theologians against them.

Now from the sustained arguments of Augustine against them in books V–VII of his *De Trinitate* it is clear that they had a very mature doctrine of God, what we would nowadays call, perhaps, a natural theology. This was no doubt due to the influence of Plotinus, the mid-third-century Neoplatonist philosopher, on the religious thought of succeeding generations. At any rate the Arians taught very clearly the crucial doctrine of the absolute simplicity of the divine being. Perhaps they were the first Christian theologians to stress this cardinal point of doctrine. It has certainly remained at the very centre of the orthodox doctrine of God ever since.

What it amounts to is this: the infinite, uncreated being beyond all being (beyond all being as we know it) cannot in any sense whatever be composite or made up of parts. Certainly not of material parts, because such being is necessarily immaterial or spiritual. But it cannot even have what may be called spiritual or immaterial parts. That is to say, it cannot *have* qualities or attributes that adhere to it but are distinct from it. Such a being, of course, is the God we worship and whom we call 'he' rather than 'it' – though we ought to do so with full awareness of the total inadequacy of so doing. Thus while we attribute all sorts of qualities to him, such as goodness, justice, wisdom, power – qualities we also attribute to some of his creatures – we find that we cannot correctly say that he has these qualities in the way that some people have them, by acquiring them; and he certainly is not liable to lose them as we are if and when we have them. Of God we have to say that he *is* these attributes. They are quite simply identical with the divine substance or being.

Now this profound theo-logy, this mature metaphysics of divine being, knocks the bottom out of the implication of the trinitarian doctrine of Novatian and Tertullian that there are degrees of more and less, of higher and lower within the divine being. There cannot be any more and less, any before and after or higher and lower in the absolute simplicity of God.

This would seem logically to land the Arians in the Modalist position. There can be no real distinction between Father, Son and Holy Spirit since they cannot be 'parts' of the deity, so they must only be different names for the one simple divine being. But that was not the line Arius took. The real distinction of the Son/Logos from the Father was for him a datum of faith, something established by scripture and tradition. The Son is not the Father. Therefore, concluded Arius, the Son is not God in the full, true sense. He is of another substance or being from the simple divine being which the Father is. The dictum is attributed to Arius, concerning the Son, 'There was a time when he was not'. The Son is not God; he is therefore a creature.[2]

Arius is talking, we must remember, of the Logos/Son, not of the man Christ Jesus. So he does not deny the doctrine of the incarnation. But he maintains that the Logos which became flesh in Jesus Christ is not God but the first of creatures: 'perfect creature of God, but not as one of the creatures'.[3] The Arian Logos/Son is not unlike that mythical Son of man figure with whom Jesus was possibly identified in the early stages of the New Testament development of Christological understanding.[4]

But of course by this time ordinary Christians had been accustomed for more than two hundred years to worshipping 'Christ as a god',[5] and the outcry against the teaching of Arius was loud and widespread in the East. The bitter wrangling in the Church disturbed the emperor Constantine, who had only recently issued his edict of toleration of Christianity at Milan in 313, and who clearly intended the Christian Church to bestow the seal of divine approval, previously expected from the pagan gods, upon the imperial government. So he invited all the bishops to meet him in 325 at Nicaea – or at least the Greek-speaking bishops of the eastern provinces of the Empire – and there 318 of them assembled, in what came to be known and venerated – not to say canonized – as the first ecumenical council.

The dogmatic definition of the Council is contained in the creed which it issued. This is in fact shorter than what we now recite at mass as the Nicene Creed, which includes additions made by the Council of Constantinople in 381. This creed is worth recording here, together with the anathemas attached, to show how it is designed to repudiate the Arian teachings. Its basis, according to J. N. D. Kelly,[6] is some local creed from Syria.

We believe in one God, the Father almighty, maker of all things visible and invisible;
And in one Lord Jesus Christ, the Son of God, begotten from the Father, only-begotten, that is from the substance of the Father, God from God, light from light, true God from true God, begotten not made, consubstantial with the Father, through whom all things came into being, things in heaven and things on earth; who because of us men and because of our salvation came down and became incarnate, becoming man, suffered and rose again on the third day, ascended to the heavens, and will come to judge the living and the dead;
And in the Holy Spirit.
But as for those who say, There was when he was not, and, Before being born he was not, and that he came into existence out of nothing, or who assert that the Son of God is of a different hypostasis or substance, or is created, or is subject to alteration or change – these the Catholic Church anathematizes.[7]

The specifically anti-Arian clauses are evident: 'that is from the substance of the Father', against the Arian contention that the Son came into being from nothing; 'true God from true God', asserting that the Son is God in the full sense, the same sense as the Father is, against the Arian interpretation that he could be called God, so to say, only by courtesy; 'consubstantial with the Father' – this is the key Nicene statement of doctrine; the phrase before it, 'begotten not made', as against the Arian view that being begotten is a way of being made or created. Thus the true and full divinity of the Son is unambiguously asserted. His real distinction from the Father is not made so clear, and this is what worried many bishops who were by no means Arians, but who cannot have been at all happy with the anathema against those 'who assert that the Son of God is of a different hypostasis', and with the underlying assumption that 'hypostasis' and 'substance' (*ousia* in Greek) are mere synonyms. These difficulties, hesitations and ambiguities will be examined in the next two sections.

C. *HOMO-OUSIOS* AND *HOMOI-OUSIOS*

This definition of faith by the Council of Nicaea did not solve the problem of the Trinity for the orthodox. It is always important to realize that ecclesiastical definitions of faith never do solve problems. What they do, and what the Nicene creed did, is to force the orthodox to realize that there is a problem to solve – in this case by rejecting the Arian solution as unacceptable and heretical. This, like all such definitions, simply reset the problem.[8]

By declaring that the Son is in no sense a creature and that therefore the generation of the Son by the Father is quite different from an act of creation; and that the Son is as fully and equally God as the Father, consubstantial or *homoousios* with the Father – the Council's definition left the orthodox with two questions to answer. The second we shall come to in the next section.

The first is about the precise meaning of that word *homo-ousios* or *consubstantial* in this instance. Its primary meaning is 'of the same substance or essence (*ousia*)'.[9] Thus human beings are consubstantial with each other, since they all have the same human nature, or substance or essence. The Council of Chalcedon in 451 will say that Jesus Christ, truly God and truly man, is 'consubstantial with the Father as regards deity and consubstantial with us as regards humanity'.[10]

Now is the Son consubstantial with the Father in the same way as he is consubstantial with us? Are we merely asserting that he is the same sort of thing as the Father is, as one human being is the same sort of thing as another? One school of thought, rather unfairly dubbed semi-Arian by the Church history books, said 'Yes'. They went so far as to suggest that a better word than *homo-ousios* would be *homoi-ousios*, 'of like substance' instead of 'of the same substance' – there is no neat Latin equivalent to *homoiousios*. They were afraid that at least the Greek *homoousios* was more likely to be taken in the secondary sense of 'consubstantial', namely 'of one and the same numerically identical concrete substance', in the way that my ego is consubstantial with my self. But this, they objected, would be to fall into the error of the Sabellian modalists, fusing Father and Son into one numerically identical thing, and so denying any real distinction between them.[11]

However, it was certainly in this latter sense that Athanasius,[12] the great champion of Nicene orthodoxy, understood *homoousios*. For the objection to *homoiousios* (and even to *homoousios* interpreted in the primary sense) is that it makes Father and Son two separate divine beings, two Gods. So Athanasius will insist that it means they are numerically one and the same God. He too, with the Arians, had learned the lesson of the absolute divine simplicity.

D.   PERSON AND HYPOSTASIS

This immediately faces us with the second question. If Father, Son and Spirit are one numerically identical substance (the absolutely simple, infinite divine being), in what sense are they really and distinctly three? Three what? In the third century, from Tertullian onwards, the habit had grown of calling them three *personae* (persons) in Latin, three *prosōpa* in Greek. But Basil of Ancyra, the leading homoiousian theologian in the mid-fourth century, was chary of this word, because he thought the Sabellians had used it in its original sense of a theatrical mask (representing the character or 'person' of the drama – the Latin *persona* had the same primary sense), to mean that the three were only three modes or facets or faces of the one indistinguishable deity – thus making the God of the Christians a kind of three-faced Janus. What no doubt justified Basil in his fears was the theology of his predecessor in the see, Marcellus, who had been a staunch supporter of Athanasius, but was accused and convicted of Modalism (see Chapter 5, D above, p. 50), and was deposed from his see in 336. So he answered the question 'Three what?' by replying 'Three hypostases'. God is one *ousia*, three *hupostaseis*.

This terminology was adopted by Basil's namesake and disciple, St Basil of Caesarea, the eldest of the three great Cappadocian Fathers,[13] who were in sympathy with the homoiousians, and laboured to reconcile them with Athanasius and the homoousians. This they eventually succeeded in doing. Once the homoousians accepted the terminology of three hypostases, the homoiousians ceased to fear that the word *homo-ousios* implied Modalism. Both parties in the great Church could now unite in directing their attack on the real successors of Arius in the mid-fourth century, the Anomoeans (who said quite bluntly that the Son is *anomoios*, unlike the Father), and their chief spokesman Eunomius.

Unfortunately a problem arose when these Greek words were translated into Latin. 'One *ousia*, three *hupostaseis*' sounds very nice. But the Latin for both of these words was *substantia*, so what the Latins heard was 'one substance, three substances'.[14] If this is not to be a contradiction in terms, it can only be made sense of if the first 'substance' is taken to mean 'nature' or 'essence' (the primary meaning of the Greek *ousia*), and the second to mean 'concrete reality'. This may make sense, but the sense it makes is like saying 'One divine nature, three divine individual beings', and what does this amount to if not tritheism, saying in fact 'three Gods'? Back to what the Monarchians had rebelled against (rightly; see again Chapter 5, D above, p. 50), and also back to a metaphysically untenable concept of the divine being, or of the nature of deity and divinity.

Soon enough tacit agreement was reached that the Latins would accept the Greeks saying 'one *ousia*, three *hupostaseis*', and the Greeks would accept the Latins saying 'one *substantia*, three *personae*'. The mutual acceptance, though, was sometimes grudging, and in times of tension Greek Christians would too easily suspect and accuse Latins of Modalism, and Latins respond with the counter-charge against the Greeks of tritheism.

St Augustine's eventual comment on these particular words, 'substance', 'person', *hupostasis*, *ousia*, is in my view the right one. When applied to the divine mystery they lose (or should be deprived of) practically all their own proper content or signification, and should be treated as simply the least inconvenient of labels. There is one God – that is the great truth. But one in what way? Well – you have to give some answer – you can say one in being, nature, substance, *ousia*, essence. But you are making a very great mistake if you think these words in their ordinary signification (i.e. as when applied to realities of this world) tell us anything about God and what his (its, her, their) being one really means. You might just as well say he is one A, B or C – and you would not be any the less wise. Why, even the word 'one' applied to God is not to be construed as meaning what it means in any other context, e.g. in the slogan *ein Volk, ein Reich, ein Führer*.[15]

And again we believe in the Father and the Son and the Holy Spirit; that also is the great truth. These are three names, certainly; but we are not Modalists. The three names represent three distinct . . . three distinct . . . er . . . three distinct *what*? Well, the Latins say 'persons' for preference, but they would allow you to say 'subsistences' if you like (not 'substances', though; that word has been pre-empted for the divine unity). And the Greeks say 'hypostases' for preference, though they will allow *prosōpa*[16] at a pinch. But taken rigorously, *all* these words are hopelessly misleading. Don't take them rigorously, then; treat them as equivalent to three

Xs, Ys or Zs. God is one A, three Xs – or one P, three Qs; why not? Our technical terms do not *tell* us anything about his (their) threeness – nothing at all. They do not even make clear that it is not an arithmetical threeness of $1 + 1 + 1 = 3$, any more than his oneness or unity is an arithmetical oneness of $1 = 1$. There is no divine arithmetic, no possible procedures of addition or substraction, division or multiplication.[17] When we are talking about God, above all when we are talking about the Trinity (we could equally well call it the X-ity or the Q-ity), we are always using words that are not merely inadequate but *improper*.

E. THE PROBLEM UNDERLYING THIS BATTLE OF WORDS, AND ATTEMPTED SOLUTIONS

Whether you call them persons or hypostases or Xs or Qs, the problem remains: what is it that makes Father, Son and Holy Spirit to be really distinct from each other, while being at the same time one and the same God? What are their distinguishing marks or properties?

Two of the Latin Fathers of the mid-fourth century, Hilary of Poitiers and Victorinus Afer, propose a variety of divine attributes as distinguishing properties of the three persons. Thus Hilary in his *De Trinitate* assigns them special properties as follows: 'Eternity in the Father, form in the Image [i.e. in the Son], use in the Gift [i.e. in the Holy Spirit]'.[18] Augustine quotes this passage, naming its author in his own *De Trin.* VI, x, 11 (*PL* 42, 931), combining some mild criticism with his attempt at elucidation.[19]

Victorinus wrote a work *Against Arius*. He was evidently much better grounded than Hilary in Greek philosophy, and also, it would seem, better acquainted with contemporary works of Christian theology in Greek. In some ways he was a scholastic before his time, freely coining technical Latin terms to deal with the mystery of the Trinity – such as *filietas, existentialitas, intelligentialis, essentitas, substantialitas*.[20] In the matter of 'person' and 'hypostasis' he coined the Latin *subsistentia* to stand for the latter, and so he talked of one *substantia*, three *subsistentiae*[21] in God. He declared, with Basil of Ancyra, 'one ought not to say, nor is it lawful to say, there is one substance, there are three persons'.[22] In taking this line he was a loner among the Latins. In the text just referred to (see below, note 21) he offers this way of distinguishing the three persons: 'The being (*esse*) which the Father is, the life which the Son is, the knowledge which the Holy Spirit is, are all one thing, one substance and three subsistences'. Elsewhere he says that the Father, in his absolute transcendence, is *inoperans operatio*, the Son *operans operatio*; the Father as *actio inactuosa* is greater than the Son.[23] The paradoxical terms 'inactive action' and 'inoperative operation' suggest an interesting insight into the ineffableness of the mystery of God; but Victorinus' thought, or at least his expression of it, is almost impenetrably obscure.

But in any case none of these ways of distinguishing the three persons will really work, by themselves, though they may be acceptable enough as what one may call decorative meditations on the mystery. The trouble is, once again – the absolute simplicity of God. God does not have distinct and distinguishable attributes; he *is* all his attributes, and his attributes *are* the divine substance or being. Thus in God these attributes are not really distinct from one another; they are only distinct in our minds, in our manner of thinking and talking about God. Thus we have not, so far, managed to improve on the economic method of distinguishing between the persons in terms of their functions or actions. Nor can we introduce that into our present transcendental consideration of God. For in this perspective all God's actions, e.g. his acts of creation and redemption, are also identical with his substance, just as his attributes are. God *is* his actions, *is* his attributes. But the Father is not the Son, the Son is not the Father, and neither is the Holy Spirit. Why not, and how not? Clearly not by being identified with different actions and attributes, which in fact in God are not different.

Two of the more philosophically experienced of the mid-fourth-century Greek Fathers, Gregory Nazianzen (the life-long friend of Basil of Caesarea) and Didymus the Blind, did propose what was to become the definitive solution, as developed in detail by Augustine. What makes the divine persons really, not just nominally, distinct from each other can only be their mutual and mutually exclusive *relationships*, which are expressed by their proper names, and which are relationships of origin. The name 'father' expresses a relationship whose correlative is the name 'son', such that they cannot be two different names for the same relationship. It is impossible for the father of X to be X or the son of Y to be Y, because the relationships stated in these words imply that one (son) originates from the other (father). So Gregory writes: 'For "Father", O wisest of men [the Arians], is not a name of substance (*ousia*) or activity, but of relationship (*schesis*) and of how the Father is related to the Son, or the Son to the Father'.[24] Didymus says the divine hypostases are 'manifested in mutual relationship (*kat'allēlōn prosēgoria*)'.[25]

On the question of how we are to distinguish the relationship of the Son to the Father (arising out of his being begotten by or born of the Father) from that of the Holy Spirit to the Father (let alone that of the Holy Spirit to the Son) Didymus maintains a holy, and to be quite honest a rather irritating agnosticism.[26] For what he thereby devoutly declines to examine is not the holy mystery itself, but the question of how we should talk about it and express it; and to be agnostic on principle about language and its proper use is really to be obscurantist.

It is on this point that Augustine will make one of his most original, and in this case fateful, contributions to trinitarian theology. For he will propose that the Holy Spirit can only be really (not just nominally) distinguished from the Son, only have a real relationship of opposition[27] to the Son, if we say that he proceeds from the Son as well as from the Father. In this too he had precursors, Ambrose[28] and Epiphanius of Salamis,[29] but it was he who watered the idea and made it grow until it became the universal Western, Latin orthodoxy – which was not accepted by Eastern, Greek orthodoxy. But more of this in the next chapter, and especially in Chapter 12.

NOTES

1 See above, Chapter 5, p. 47 and p. 53, note 3.

2 Dz 126/54, the anathema of the Council of Nicaea. See also *A New Eusebius*, early Church documents edited by J. Stevenson (London, 1965), nos 290–296, especially 294, quoting a letter of Arius, and 296, quoting from a work of Arius called *Thalia* (which means 'blooms' or 'flowers').

3 *A New Eusebius*, no. 294.

4 See above, Chapter 4, B, pp. 31–33.

5 The way Pliny the younger described Christian worship, as he had been told about it, in a letter to the emperor Trajan *c.*112 (*A New Eusebius*, no. 14, 7).

6 *Early Christian Creeds* (London, 1963), pp. 220, 227–230.

7 The translation is Kelly's, *op. cit.* pp. 215–216, except that I have changed 'of one substance' to 'consubstantial'. The original Greek, with Latin translation, can be found in Dz 125, 126/54.

8 This is why the Council of Nicaea did not in fact settle the Arian controversy, but rather inaugurated fifty years and more of bitter theological strife. The same sort of thing was to happen with the disputes about the person of Christ; the classic definition of faith was made by the Council of Chalcedon in 451 – and they were still arguing furiously over its finer implications two hundred years later and more. This is because dogmatic definitions are not solutions to problems, but statements of faith. They exclude certain solutions, to right and to left, as it were, but offer no solutions themselves, simply leaving the way ahead open, and challenging the Christian mind to go forward along it.

9 The distinction was first formulated by Aristotle in his list of categories that can be predicated of anything: you can say *what* it is, and that is the category of *ousia* or *substance*; and you can say a number of other things about it, such as when and where and how it is, and these are the nine categories of *sumbebēkos* or *accident*. Now substance can be predicated either in the abstract – What is that? That is *human*, it is an instance of *humanity* – and Aristotle called this subdivision of the category *ousia prōtē*, in Latin *substantia prima*; or it can be predicated in the concrete and particular – What is that? That is a man/woman/child/human being – and this he called *ousia deutera*, *substantia secunda* in Latin.

10 Dz 301/148.

11 This was the accusation levelled against Marcellus of Ancyra, one of the staunchest supporters of Athanasius, who was deposed from his see in 336 and never restored in spite of appeals to the Pope. See above, section D.

12 At the Council of Nicaea Athanasius, who had been born in 295, was a deacon and

assistant to his bishop Alexander. He succeeded him as bishop of Alexandria in Egypt, the second see of Christendom, in 328, and remained at the centre of the theological battles over Arianism until his death in 376. Many of these forty-eight years of his episcopate were spent in exile, because the emperor Constantine in his last years, and his successors for the next forty years tended to favour the Arians. Or rather, to be fair to them, what they sought was a satisfactory compromise, and this Athanasius would never concede. For an outline of his career and writings see any *Patrology*, e.g. that of Berthold Altaner (ET; 2nd ed., New York, 1961), p. 312.

13 See Altaner, *op. cit.* pp. 335–356. The Cappadocian Fathers is a term usually applied to Basil (surnamed the Great), his friend Gregory Nazianzen (so called because he was the son of the bishop of Nazianzus), and his younger brother, Gregory of Nyssa, so called because he was made bishop of Nyssa in 371. Cappadocia was the central province of Asia Minor. Basil was a great bishop, the metropolitan of Caesarea in Cappadocia. Neither his friend nor his brother was very good at being a bishop (Gregory Nazianzen was for a short while after Basil's death bishop of Constantinople), and they much preferred the contemplative and intellectual life.

14 The Greek word *ousia* is formed from the participle of the verb 'to be'. But when the Romans, led by Cicero, were beginning to create their own philosophical vocabulary, they felt that Latin did not lend itself to forming words with quite the same ease as Greek, and Cicero at least shrank from coining the word *essentia* to stand for *ousia*. In fact he could not bring himself even to form the word *substantia*, and it was left to Quintilian, the leading grammarian of the first century A.D., to coin both words. It was generally felt by Latin speakers that *substantia* was a more suitable equivalent for the Greek *ousia* than *essentia* was. But it comes from the verb *sub-sto*, which means literally 'stand under'. And so it is also the verbal equivalent of the Greek *hupo-stasis* which comes from a verb with the same literal meaning. Thus both 'substance' and 'hypostasis', to Anglicize both these words, literally mean that which stands under, or underlies, the observable appearances or accidents.

15 'One people, one state, one leader'; the slogan of the Nazis in Germany, 1923–45. Augustine discusses 'substance', *hupostasis* etc. in *De Trin.* VII, iv, 7 – v, 11 (*PL* 42, 939–945).

16 The Greek equivalent for the Latin *personae*. See above, p. 58; for subsistence (*subsistentia*) as an equivalent for *hupostasis*, coined by Victorinus, see above, section E, p. 60.

17 Raimundo Panikkar in his excellent book *The Trinity and the Religious Experience of Man* (London/New York, 1973), to which I will be referring again, writes: 'One day at Rome during the Vatican Council some African Bishops confided to me their embarrassment at not being able to find in their own languages suitable words to convey the meaning of *nature* and *person*: the very concepts were unknown to those tongues. In reply I could only express my admiration for such languages . . . and my hope that one day they would contribute notably towards the rejuvenation of the central body of dogma of christianity' (p. 41).

18 II, ii (*PL* 10, 51A). The Latin text, as quoted by Augustine (see next note), runs: *Aeternitas in Patre, species in imagine, usus in munere.* An alternative reading of the first phrase, perhaps more likely to be original, is: *Infinitas in aeterno.*

19 Quoting other authors by name, unless you were actually attacking them, was extremely unusual in ancient literature, especially where contemporaries or near contemporaries were concerned. It is in fact hard to see why Augustine bothers to quote Hilary here. His criticism runs, 'I am afraid I do not follow him in his employment of the word "eternity", unless he only means that the Father does not have a father from

whom he is, while the Son has it from the Father both to be and to be co-eternal with him'. He interprets 'form' (*species*) as signifying 'the beauty involved . . . in that primordial equality and primordial likeness . . . with that of which it is the image'; of 'use' [*usus* – 'familiarity' would perhaps have been a slightly less inadequate translation] he writes: 'Then that inexpressible embrace, so to say, of the Father and the Image is not without enjoyment, without charity, without happiness. So this love, delight, felicity or blessedness . . . he calls very briefly "use", and it is the Holy Spirit in the triad, not begotten, but the sweetness of begetter and begotten pervading all creatures . . . with its vast generosity and fruitfulness'. An unashamedly erotic analogy.

20   *Adv. Arium* (*PL* 8, 1060D, 1065A, 1078B, 1103C). Victorinus was a very eminent African rhetor and philosopher who worked in Rome and became a Christian there late in life. Augustine had read his translation into Latin of the *Enneads* of Plotinus, which had at last freed him from his youthful materialism; and the story of Victorinus' conversion, told him by the Milanese priest Simplicianus, seems to have been the last impulse but one in bringing about Augustine's own conversion (*Confessions* VIII, ii, 3–6: *PL* 32, 749–751).

21   *Adv. Arium* III, 9 (*PL* 8, 1105B).

22   *Ibid*. I, 41 (*ibid*. 1072A).

23   *Ibid*. I, 13 (*ibid*. 1047C).

24   *Orationes* 29, 16 (*PG* 36, 96).

25   *De Trin*. I, 11 (*PG* 39, 293–294). Didymus was the head of the catechetical school in Alexandria for the last half of the fourth century (he died in 398) – thus a successor of the great Origen in a position of enormous theological influence. Like many *didaskaloi* in the early Church (Justin, for example) he was not a priest or indeed a cleric of any sort. There was no foolishness in those days about theology being the proper preserve of the clergy. He went blind at the age of four (which may, of course, be the reason why he was never ordained). See Altaner, *Patrology*, p. 324.

26   *De Trin*. I, 9 (*PG* 39, 281–282); II, 1, 4 (447–448, 481–482).

27   A relationship of opposition is one like that between parent and child, master and servant, teacher and pupil, where the mutual relationships are not interchangeable. Compare the relationship of friendship, or of brotherhood; two friends, two brothers, two sisters, two siblings, two cousins stand in the same relationship to each other. The same relationship of friendship etc. applies to each party so related.

28   *De Spiritu Sancto* I, xi, 119 (*PL* 16, 731). Ambrose was the great bishop of Milan 374–397. He was elected bishop while he was still a catechumen, but happened to be the chief magistrate of the city. He baptized Augustine in 387, and is famous for withstanding the emperor Theodosius to his face, over a massacre for which Theodosius had been responsible, in 390. See Altaner, *Patrology*, pp. 443–450.

29   *Ancoratus* 6; *Panarion* 76, 6 (*PG* 43, 25; 42, 525). What he says of the Holy Spirit in both texts is: 'proceeding from the Father, and receiving from the Son'. Epiphanius was born in Judaea, but became bishop of Salamis in Cyprus in 367. Really rather an unpleasant man, whom it would be only slightly unjust to label a narrow-minded bigot. But he is very dear to patrologists because his own rather dreary writings are a mine of information about many early Christian sources now lost. See Altaner, *Patrology*, pp. 365–368.

7

Augustine's Combination of the Two Approaches: Missions, Processions and Relationships

The next part of this book, Chapters 8 to 10, will be devoted to a fairly detailed presentation of Augustine's *De Trinitate*. This chapter is only intended to show how his great work makes use of, criticizes and harmonizes the somewhat confused tradition he inherited. Here I am therefore just rounding off the present section and leading into the next. I hope to do it fairly briefly, and shall not trouble the reader with detailed references. These will be amply furnished in the next part. Augustine, born in 354 at Tagaste in Numidia (eastern Algeria), was converted and baptized by Ambrose at the age of thirty-three in 387 at Milan, and shortly afterwards returned to Africa, where he became bishop of Hippo Regius (Bône, now Annaba, in the same province) in 396. There he died in 431. He began writing his *De Trinitate* about 400, but did not finish it until twenty or twenty-five years later. Thus he comes at the end of the fourth century's reflection on the mystery in the wake of the Council of Nicaea.

A. AUGUSTINE'S USE OF THE ECONOMIC APPROACH

We should start with Augustine's statement of faith, quoted in full in Chapter 1, D (p. 6 above). The first paragraph states the faith of Nicaea-Constantinople very clearly: the equality and unity of the divine persons, together with their real distinctness or non-identity with each other. It is a perfect summary of the transcendental view of the mystery.

The second paragraph, by contrast, is a succinct statement of the divine economy of the manifestation or revelation of the divine persons. The Son alone was incarnate in Jesus Christ, the Holy Spirit alone was manifested in the dove at Christ's baptism and in the Pentecostal wind and tongues of fire, the voices from heaven spoke in the person of the Father alone.

This is the faith Augustine wishes to establish and understand. He devotes the first book to establishing from scripture (in fact almost exclusively from the New Testament) the total equality of the divine persons, in particular of the Son to the Father. There is an easy rule for dealing with passages that suggest the Son is less than the Father: they apply to him in his humanity, 'in the form of a servant' as Augustine likes to put it in the words of Phil 2:7.

But it is not very long before we come up against a scriptural stumbling-block which had in fact led at least Tertullian and Novatian among the economic theologians to regard the Son in his divine nature – and also the Holy Spirit – as less than or subordinate to the Father. In his statement of faith Augustine has already referred to the Son being incarnate and the Holy Spirit being manifested at Pentecost. And it is the consistent testimony of the New Testament that the Son and the Holy Spirit were so manifested because they had been *sent* by the Father. Hence the technical term of 'the missions of the divine persons', i.e. the sending of the Son and the sending of the Spirit.

Now when one person is sent by another, the normal inference is that the one sent is subordinate or inferior to the sender. Heads of state send ambassadors, not *vice versa*. And in this case of the missions of the Son and Holy Spirit we cannot apply the rule just mentioned which allows that the Son in his humanity is inferior to the Father. For (a) he is not sent in his humanity, as a man, but he is sent as God the Son, as the Word, to become man; his humanity is the term of the mission, not the subject of it. And (b) the Holy Spirit is also sent, and he has no human nature to be inferior to the Father in. So if being sent implies inferiority, then the Son and the Holy Spirit are inferior to the Father in their divinity: the subordinationist position of Tertullian and Novatian.

Augustine's response is twofold. First, he simply denies that being sent *necessarily* means being inferior to the sender. That is indeed the normal inference. But as we have observed several times, words or concepts applied to the divine sphere cannot be expected to behave (i.e. to signify) in quite the same way as when applied to the world we know. So in this case all that being sent implies is that the one sent is from the sender. All implications of inferiority must simply be set aside. The only reason why the Father sends and is not sent is that he is not from the Son or the Holy Spirit, while they are both from him. Augustine simply asserts, if you like, that in this case we have to say being sent does not imply inferiority, nor does sending imply superiority.

Secondly, he does something which is really rather odd when you think of it, but extremely ingenious when you think of it further: he separates and reverses 'being sent' and 'proceeding'. Both these terms, of course, are applied to the Son and the Holy Spirit in the New Testament. They are said both to be sent by the Father and to proceed or come forth from the Father.

Now in ordinary contexts proceeding follows immediately on being sent. If you are sent on a mission, you then proceed on your mission. People sent come or go forth from the place they are sent from. And this is how the economic theologians saw the matter in the case of the missions and processions of the Son and the Holy Spirit. Because they have been sent, they have proceeded. Mission and procession, being sent and proceeding, are practically identical. Another expression for the Son's proceeding from the Father is his being born of or begotten by the Father. We have seen that the economic theologians did not confine the mission of the Son (or of the Holy Spirit, but they do not discuss this case so much) to the New Testament. The Son has been sent by the Father, and thus has come forth from or been born of the Father, from the beginning of the world. Hence from the beginning he has been inferior and subordinate to the Father. Hence also – this was evident at least with Tertullian – God the Father unfolded himself into a trinity in the process of his economy of creation.

Augustine simply cut, if not the Gordian knot, then the Tertullian tangle. As we have just seen, he stated that in this divine case being sent indicates no more than being from the sender. So being from comes before being sent. First the Son proceeds from, i.e. is born of or begotten by the Father, then he is sent by the Father. The same is true of the Holy Spirit. The procession is an eternal activity/passivity, co-eternal with the divine being. The mission is a temporal happening or happenings, it takes place in time and in the world, it is part of the economy.

In fact, Augustine finally concludes (to put it rather drily), the divine missions in time of the Son and the Holy Spirit reveal their eternal (transcendent) processions. The way he puts it towards the end of book IV (we shall examine the text more carefully in Chapter 9) is to say that 'as being born means for the Son his being from the Father, so his being sent means his being known [by us] to be from the Father. And as being the Gift of God means for the Holy Spirit his proceeding from the Father, so being sent means for the Holy Spirit his being known to proceed from the Father' (IV, xx, 29).

Augustine's interest in the missions of the divine persons shows his concern with the economic aspect of the trinitarian mystery – because that is precisely what the missions are: the mystery's economic aspect. The text I have just quoted comes indeed at the end of three books which are all devoted to the question of the missions; devoted in fact to a long and detailed criticism

of the axiom of the economic theologians that all the appearances of God
recorded in the Old Testament had been appearances, i.e. missions, of the Son
(see Chapter 5, B, pp. 47–48 above). He painstakingly examines all the Old
Testament instances quoted by Justin, Irenaeus, Tertullian and no doubt
many others in support of this axiom, and shows that in none of them is there
sufficient reason for supposing that it was the Son rather than the Father or
the Holy Spirit who was manifested to the eyes or ears or awareness of men.
And whichever person it was – or just God without distinction – Augustine
is insistent that what was seen or heard or apprehended was some created
effect which represented, but was not, the divine being. In other words, he
ruthlessly demolishes the economic assumption that the Son is the visible
member of the divine triad. All the persons are equally invisible (and
inaudible etc. – i.e. immaterial), because all are equally the totally simple and
unchangeable divine being.

So Augustine only acknowledges the divine missions, and hence the
revelation of the mystery, in the New Testament – precisely with the incarnation of the Son and the several manifestations of the Holy Spirit that
accompanied it. There can now be no more confusion at all between
processions and missions. Processions are eternal, in God, transcendent.
Missions are temporal, datable in fact to a few hundred years ago, in the
world, economic. They reveal the eternal transcendent mystery.

B. AUGUSTINE'S USE OF THE TRANSCENDENTAL METHOD

Having employed scripture to establish and defend the equality of the Son and
the Holy Spirit with the Father against the subordinationist tendencies of the
economic theologians, Augustine next proceeds to a more metaphysical or
transcendental battle in the same cause against the Arians, as represented
above all by Eunomius. The problem, let us remind ourselves, is to reconcile
the absolute simplicity of the divine being or substance, of God, with the firm
assertion of faith that the Father is not the Son and the Son is not the Father,
that they are really distinct identities, persons, hypostases, Xs, Qs.

Eunomius did this by saying that the Son is of a different substance from
the Father; i.e. he is not true God, but a created substance. He said: all God's
attributes – what would be called 'accidents' if we were talking about
worldly objects – are his substance (an accident in this logical/philosophical
sense is something which *accidit* or happens to a substance by modifying or
changing it). They are predicated of him not as accidents but as substance,
and thus are identical with each other. Therefore the attribute of being
unbegotten, predicated of the Father, is identical with the divine substance. If
the Son were also of the divine substance, then the attribute of being

begotten which is predicated of him would also be identical with the divine substance – which would thus manifest the impossible contradiction of being both begotten and unbegotten in its absolute simplicity.

Augustine countered by saying that while there are indeed no accidents in God, because he is totally unchangeable (he uses the concept of immutability for preference rather than that of simplicity to indicate the fullness of divine being), and that while in consequence what would be predicated as accident of other beings is predicated as substance of God; there can, all the same, be predications of God that are not predicated as substance. These are predications of relationship. About creatures we can say or predicate things either *substantively* or *accidentally*; about God we can predicate things either *substantively* or *relatively*. He can be called Father and he can be called Son. These are certainly not accidental predications, because in God they do not imply change or 'happening'. God is eternally and unchangeably both Father and Son. But these words are not substantive predications either, since they do not say something about God *in himself* (*in se* or *ad se*) but only in relationship or relatively to each other (*ad alterum*). They are relative predications.

The relatedness is usually shown in English by the preposition 'of'. The Father is the Father *of* the Son, the Son is the Son *of* the Father. Therefore as Father the Father is not the Son; as Son the Son is not the Father. They are really distinct, non-identical. But as God, as Lord, as good, wise, eternal, creator, redeemer, each is one and the same God, and hence in these respects not distinct from each other. Only as mutually exclusive, opposite relationships are they really distinct from each other.

To return briefly to Eunomius' pair of opposites, 'unbegotten' and 'begotten'. Augustine merely remarks, fairly enough, that 'begotten' is just a way of saying 'Son', and 'unbegotten' is the negative of that and just means 'not Son', since we do not have a word 'unson'. In other words they are what one could call latent relationship terms, one positive, asserting the same relationship as 'Son', the other negative, denying this relationship. The Father is not related as Son to any other person: there is no divine Grandfather. We should perhaps not forget that in the Greek pantheon there *was* a divine grandfather, even a great-grandfather if we take Zeus to be the father of gods and men. His father, the grandfather god, was Kronos, and Kronos was the son of Uranus. So to call God the Father the unbegotten one was not, in those days, entirely superfluous.

But the term 'begotten' as an equivalent to 'Son' reminds us that these mutually opposite relationships are founded in, or arise from a procession of the Son from the Father. They arise from his being from the Father, being eternally begotten by the Father, eternally born of the Father.

This brings us to the problem of the Holy Spirit. He too can only be really distinct from the other two persons in terms of his relationships with them.

Augustine grants that the name 'Holy Spirit' does not in itself signify a relationship. Its two parts can properly be predicated substantively of God; God is holy, God is spirit (Jn 4:24). As holy, as spirit, the three persons are not distinct. We could say, on the model of the Athanasian creed, 'The Father is holy, the Son is holy, the Holy Spirit is holy, and yet not three holies but one holy. Likewise the Father is spirit, the Son is spirit, the Holy Spirit is spirit, and yet not three spirits but one spirit'.

But by a theological convention we treat the name 'Holy Spirit' as a term of relationship and say he (it/she – the Hebrew word *ruach* is feminine) is the Spirit *of* the Father and the Spirit *of* the Son. In his search for a more specific relationship name Augustine eventually picks on the word 'Gift' for the Holy Spirit, for which he has ample New Testament warrant, e.g. Jn 4:10, Rom 5:5. The name 'gift' implies a relationship with the giver. (It also implies relationship with the recipient, but that need not concern us for the moment, provided we do not make the mistake of assuming that Augustine thought of the Holy Spirit as the Gift given by the Father to the Son, or of thinking like that ourselves. Not at all; he is the Gift both of the Father and of the Son to us – still the Gift, potentially, even before we are there to be given this divine Gift.)

This relationship too, if it is to be a mutually exclusive or opposite, and thus a distinguishing, relationship, must be based on a procession, on an originating and a being originated. It must be a relationship of origin. The procession founding the Holy Spirit's relationship with the Father is evident enough from the New Testament: he 'proceeds from the Father' (Jn 15:26).

So, however, does the Son. What then is the difference between the Son's relationship to the Father and the Holy Spirit's relationship to the Father? This amounts to asking what is the difference between the Son and the Holy Spirit, because if their relationships to the Father are the same, it follows that they themselves are the same – just two names for one person in fact. We know by faith that that is not the case. But why not, and how not?

The Son's procession from the Father is called in scripture a *generation*, i.e. a begetting and a birth. This is not said of the Holy Spirit. But again, why not? We have to establish (always on the scriptural evidence, of course) a mutual relationship between the Son and the Holy Spirit, as well as between each of them and the Father. The only way Augustine can think of doing this is by saying that the Holy Spirit proceeds from the Son as well as from the Father. It is true, the New Testament nowhere says this. But it does talk about the Son sending the Holy Spirit (Jn 15:26, the same verse which mentions the Holy Spirit proceeding from the Father; cf. also Jn 20:22), and about the Holy Spirit being the Spirit of the Son (Gal 4:6). For Augustine, as we have seen, mission reveals procession. If the Spirit is sent by the Son, this reveals that he proceeds from the Son. To be of the Son also amounts in this case to being from the Son. Not that the preposition 'of' always designates being 'from'; quite the opposite in the case of 'the Father of the Son'. But in this context it has to signify one being from the other, and no one has ever suggested that the Son is from the Spirit. It remains that the Spirit is in some way from the Son.

It might also be added that the New Testament was probably not using the words 'send' and 'proceed' in the highly technical, artificial way Augustine and the theological tradition use them, but in the looser way in which they were taken by the economic theologians. In this way being sent involves proceeding, proceeding involves being sent. So again the inference holds from the Son sending the Spirit to the Spirit proceeding from the Son.

This clarification of Augustine's became a characteristic feature of all subsequent Western and Latin theology, indeed of its dogma, and this proved later to be unacceptable to the Eastern and Greek tradition. It remains a bone of contention to this day. We shall enter more fully into the debate in the next Part, Chapter 12 below.

C. MISSIONS, PROCESSIONS, AND RELATIONSHIPS

To summarize then what Augustine has done with the tradition he received: He begins, like the economic theologians, with the missions, with the sendings/being sent of the Son and the Holy Spirit. He rightly assesses the importance of the missions for our understanding of the mystery, because it is precisely through these missions that the mystery has been revealed to us. To quote the text of Gal 4:4–6 once more,

When the time had fully come, God *sent* forth his Son, born of woman, born under the law, to redeem those who were under the law, so that we might receive adoption as sons. And because you are sons, God *has sent* the Spirit of his Son into our hearts, crying *Abba, Father*.

Following St Paul, Augustine very firmly limits the missions to the New Testament economy or dispensation.

These missions, he tells us, taking place in time as the climax of the history of salvation/revelation, reveal to us the eternal divine processions: the eternal procession of the Son from the Father by way of being eternally born or begotten of the Father, and the eternal procession of the Holy Spirit from both the Father and the Son. These processions are eternal, not only because everything about God is eternal (timeless), but also in so far as they do not terminate in a created event in created time as do the missions. They are wholly within God, belonging to the transcendent, or in Rahner's language the immanent divine reality. They are not part of the economy of salvation. They are what God is, they are part of what it means to be God, quite apart from their effect on God's creation.

These processions give rise to mutual relationships. Discussion of these is almost wholly a discussion of words and names and how most suitably to employ them. Divine names expressing relationships can be applied exclusively to one or other of the persons, and always imply at least a tacit corresponding relationship name in another person. Divine names not expressing relationships are common to all three persons and declare their identity with and in the absolutely simple, immutable divine being or substance.

The most obvious relationship names are 'Father' and 'Son'. But there are others. The Son is also the Word/*Logos* of the Father. There is no corresponding name for the Father in traditional use, but we could give him the name of 'Utterer' of the Word. The Father is also Origin or Source (*Principium, Fons totius deitatis*, source of all godhead). The Son is also called Image of the Father.

'Holy Spirit', as we have seen, is only by theological convention a name of relationship. Thomas Aquinas, giving full force to the derivation of the word 'spirit' from *spirare*, 'to breathe', will suggest that we can think of the Holy Spirit as the Breath of God, analogously to the Son's being the Word of God. Strange that Augustine never seems to have thought of this, seeing that a hint to this effect is given in Jn 20:22, where the risen Lord 'breathed on them and said to them, Receive the Holy Spirit'. So the Holy Spirit is the Breath of God, the Father and the Son together being the breathers. He is also the Gift of God, Father and Son together being the giver.

There are, to be sure, complexities about the appropriate naming of the divine persons in terms of their mutual relationships which we shall be examining in detail in Chapter 10 below.

IV
Communing with the Mystery

8

Augustine's *De Trinitate:* Purpose, Method and Structure

In this part of the book we shall be concentrating on the teaching of St Augustine's *De Trinitate*. In my opinion this is the greatest and most profound work on the mystery that has ever been written. I do not think it has been improved upon in the subsequent centuries. If I can here help the reader to appropriate Augustine's faith in and understanding of the mystery of the Trinity, then I shall have achieved my goal and completed my task. In our present situation, it seems to me, it is not a question of surpassing Augustine's teaching, but of retrieving it. We must begin, then, by introducing the great work itself.

A. BRIEF HISTORY OF THE *DE TRINITATE*[1]

When Augustine eventually finished his great work, he sent it with a covering letter[2] to Aurelius, bishop of Carthage, the primate of all the African Churches. It is, I think, worth quoting extensively. After the opening salutation he proceeds:

I was a young man when I began these books on the Trinity which the one true God is, and I am now an old man as I publish them. I stopped working on the project when I discovered that they had been lifted from my possession, and prematurely at that, since I had not completed them nor revised and polished them as I had planned to do. It had been my intention to publish them all together and not one by one, because the enquiry proceeds in a closely knit development from the first of them to the last. So when these people managed to get at some of them before I was ready, and thus made it impossible for me to carry out my plans, I did not resume the work of dictation that other preoccupations had interrupted . . .

However, at the urgent request of many of the brethren and above all at your command, I have felt obliged to attend with the Lord's assistance to the completion of this laborious task. I have corrected the books as best I could, though hardly as I would, or they might have varied too widely from the pirated copies that were already in people's hands. I now send them to your reverence by our dear son and fellow deacon, and give permission for anyone to listen to them, read them or have them copied . . . Some people have the first four books, or rather five, without their prologues, and the twelfth without its considerable concluding section; but if they manage to learn about this edition, they will be able to correct their copies . . . May I ask you to give instructions for this letter to be placed at the head of these books, though of course separately? Pray for me.[3]

So it took a long time to write – begun when he was a young man, published when he was an old one. What does that mean in terms of dates? We have a little more information from his *Retractations* II, 15,[4] an invaluable piece of self-criticism which he composed at the end of his life, going over all the works he had written and correcting what he thought wrong in them. Here again he briefly describes the history of the work, but rather more calmly and without the note of irritation that can be detected in the letter to Aurelius. It is listed among the works he began as a bishop, after the *Confessions* but before his major works against the Donatists,[5] who were his prime pastoral preoccupation during the first fourteen years of his episcopate. He became bishop of Hippo in 396, at the age of forty-two. The conventional age in ancient Roman society at which you ceased to be a young man, *juvenis*, and became an old man, *senex*, was forty-five. So if Augustine is speaking strictly here, it means he began the work within three years of becoming a bishop, i.e. before 399. In any case it cannot have been long after that.

In the same place he specifies that it was before he had finished the twelfth book that over-impetuous admirers filched a copy of the incomplete work and published a pirate edition – to his intense annoyance, as we can gather from the letter to Aurelius. This explains why, as he says in the letter, some people have the twelfth book without its considerable concluding section. From references in various other letters we can gather that his friends were getting impatient in 412;[6] and that he still had not finished or published it by the end of 415.[7] So the pirate edition may be dated to about 416. I think we can allow him a four-year sulk over this unforgivable behaviour. So he would have relented about 420, when he was sixty-six, and finally completed and published the work any time between then and 425 when he was seventy-one.

B. AUGUSTINE'S PURPOSE IN WRITING THE *DE TRINITATE*

This curious history gives us some clue about Augustine's intentions in writing the work. Why was he so slow that his friends and admirers finally lost patience? It can only have been – for so professional and prolific a writer – that he cannot have considered it pastorally urgent. Work on it kept on being elbowed aside by more immediately important matters, controversies with Donatists, pagan critics, Pelagius and his followers – and all the time his letters and sermons.[8]

But if there was in his mind no urgency about the work, this does not mean that he was only marginally interested in the topic. Quite the contrary. Of all his mature works the *De Trinitate*, I would say, is the most personal – yes, even more so than the *Confessions*. Notice why he was angry when his impatient admirers filched the first eleven-and-a-half books from his cupboard (*armorium*) and published them. It was because he wanted to publish the work as a whole, since he conceived it as a whole, as a very tightly argued and structured unity, not at all suitable for serial publication. The work has a plot and a very elaborate one, the germ of which must have been in his mind when he began writing it about 398, and which went on maturing and deepening over the years of slow composition and careful reflection.

'Plot' is not an inappropriate word, strange though it may seem, because there is a lot of action in the *De Trinitate*, as well as argument. It is argument about action. First it is about God's action in sending the Son and the Holy Spirit, and whether he sent them before the New Testament dispensation or not. Then after an interlude of pure argument with the Arians about the divine relationships there is a kind of action in book VIII, the centre-piece of the work in which Augustine as it were launches himself at God in order to try and grasp the divine mystery in itself. He fails, of course, and in the last seven books sets out to discover it in its image – man. And here we both follow the dramatic story of the break-up of that image by sin and of its restoration by Christ, and we also begin to penetrate the mystery of the eternal divine activity of the processions.

But above all – and this is where we finally perceive Augustine's intention – the work has the plot or structure of a *quest*. In the *De Trinitate* Augustine is searching for God. He knows what he is looking for – it is stated in his declaration of faith. But he does not yet know as he is known. And so three times he quotes Ps 105:3, 4: 'Let the hearts of those who seek the Lord rejoice! Seek the Lord and his strength, seek his presence continually!'; at the beginning of the quest, I, iii, 5; at the crucial turn it takes when he begins to look for God in his image, IX, i, 1; and at the end when he is about to sum up and declare the quest to be a magnificent and indeed a most successful failure, XV, ii, 2.[9] It is bound to be a failure for the time being, because it will only be achieved when Christ has handed over the kingdom to his Father, by leading us to the 'then' when we shall see face to face instead of in a glass darkly (the image), and shall know as we are known instead of knowing in part (1 Cor 13:12).

One last word about his purpose. His quest is not his alone but that of any keen Christian – particularly those impatient admirers who so ruffled his feathers before he had finished. And it is a quest which really *is* the Christian life. In his investigation of the divine image in man Augustine does not merely set up a model through which to contemplate the divine mystery; in doing this he also sets us, as images of God – images which we have to realize, to make come true – a programme for the full Christian life.

C. AUGUSTINE'S METHOD IN THE *DE TRINITATE*

Augustine's theological method is always governed by a principle perfectly expressed in his favourite misquotation of Isa 7:9, 'Unless you believe, you shall not understand' (RSV: 'If you will not believe, surely you shall not be established'). It is a misquotation because he is quoting the old Latin translation of the Greek translation of the Hebrew known as the Septuagint or LXX (see Chapter 3, note 3).

The point is: understanding presupposes faith, not *vice versa*. First you must believe; then you have a base from which to seek understanding. Few people in the history of Christian thought have been less anti-intellectual, less obscurantist than Augustine. But his own experience convinced him, not merely that human intellect has its limits and needs to be enlightened by God's grace before it can perceive the things of God, but above all that its pride, its cardinal sin, needs to be humbled before it can begin to understand God's truth. It is humbled by submitting in faith to what it does not yet understand. When one believes, of course, one understands the terms in which the faith is expressed; one confesses one's faith in one's own language, not as a piece of gibberish. But one does not yet understand *how* the statements of faith can be true; one simply believes. Then and only then, because such uncomprehending faith is deeply uncongenial to the nature of the human mind, which will insist on asking 'Why?', can faith set out on its journey of seeking understanding.[10]

So Augustine begins by stating his faith – we have seen how he did it in Chapter 1 (section D, p. 6). Then he proceeds, in his own words, 'to establish this starting-point of faith', this *initium fidei*, by showing how it is required by an honest and thorough reading of scripture. Faith in the authority of scripture as God's revealing word is simply presupposed – and in the *Confessions* Augustine tells us what intellectual humiliation that had been for him: having to accept these (by classical standards) barbarous writings as ultimately authoritative.[11] This task occupies him for the first four books.

Next, after so establishing the faith as set out in that brief statement, he moves on, in his own expression, to *reddere rationem*, to give a rational and reasoned account of this faith. This means in fact two things: (1) defending it against the logico-metaphysical attacks of Eunomius and the Arians; (2) clarifying the proper use of terms in discussing the mystery. The basic principle, as we saw in the last chapter (7, B, pp. 69–71), is that only terms signifying relationships can properly be used to distinguish the divine persons from each other. But there are a great many other words, like 'wisdom' for example, or 'love', which are applied by scripture and the subsequent tradition to one person rather than another, even though they do not primarily signify relationships. Later scholastic terminology will call this the *appropriation* of certain terms and concepts to particular divine persons. The terms are appropriated, be it noted, to a particular person (e.g. wisdom to the Son) because they are not in fact 'proper' to that person. Wisdom, properly speaking, is said absolutely of God; it is identical with the divine substance, and therefore common to all three persons. But it is 'appropriated' for various reasons to the Son. So a meticulous examination of such uses of language, including the uses of words like 'person', 'hypostasis', 'substance', forms the major part of this task of *reddere rationem*, and it occupies Augustine in books V–VII.

The rest of the work does not illustrate this method quite so clearly. Perhaps, indeed, Augustine abandons it. At any rate, he is quite clear that by the end of book VII he has not yet succeeded in his quest – he has not discovered what he is looking for, which is God. So in the prologue to book VIII he says he is going to go over what he has already discussed – the divine missions, relationships, processions – to go over it all again *interiori modo*, in a more inward manner. The implication seems to be that what he has said up till now has been merely superficial! And so in a sense it has been; it has been almost entirely about words. About the words of scripture to begin with, then about the right use of words in our theological tradition with which to talk about God. A very necessary superficiality too. But not, in the last resort, satisfying.

So he sets about his quest now 'in a more inward manner'; a typically Augustinian phrase. First of all, in book VIII, he apparently attempts to penetrate directly into the inner being of God. God is truth – surely then we can see God when we see the truth of anything that is true. God is goodness itself, or 'the good', *ipsum bonum*; surely then we can see God when we see the good that we love in anything that is good. But no – in fact we cannot see truth itself and the good in itself, any more than bats can gaze at the light of the sun.

He makes one last attempt at direct intellectual or mental contact with God, so to speak: God is love. So when we love and see our love and ourselves loving with it, surely we see God, But again, no. We may indeed here have a direct contact with God, but it is not the contact of direct vision.

However, in this last case Augustine begins to discern a trinity or threesome: that of love, lover and beloved. And this reminds him that if we cannot penetrate directly and immediately into the inmost being of God, we can perhaps get more thoroughly acquainted with the divine mystery by looking at it indirectly, through its reflection or image in ourselves.

This occupies him for books IX–XIV, leaving book XV for summary and survey of results. His method is complex, but in outline it is apparently the reverse of the one we have just sketched as governing the first seven books. He now begins with reason, that is to say with a kind of psychological intro-spection, and constructs a triad of mental acts – the acts of the mind remembering, understanding and willing itself, with special emphasis on the relations of these acts to each other in order to cast light on the eternal divine processions of the Son/Word and of the Holy Spirit from the Father, which constitute the inner mystery of God.

But then he moves on more and more to cast the light of faith, i.e. the light of the whole scriptural revelation, on this image. And this shows up two things: first, that the image of God in man is not to be thought of as something just given, static, like a statue or a photograph, but as mobile and active, like a reflection in a mirror; that it does in fact have a history, like God's revelation or economy, a history of first being spoiled, defaced or distorted by sin and then of being restored by God's grace in Christ; and that therefore it involves us in a project or programme of realizing what we are (God's image), and through faith in Christ and his grace becoming more and more like God. Secondly, it shows that the ultimate realization of the trinitarian image in us, the final achievement of the wisdom of God offers us, is not our remembering, understanding and willing ourselves, but our remembering, understanding and willing or loving God. Thus finally, by proceeding 'in a more inward manner', *interiori modo*, we reach God who is 'deeper within me than my inmost self', *intimior intimo meo*.[12]

I say this seems to be a reversal of his earlier method of beginning with faith and going on to employ reason in order to understand it. But it is not a reversal of the primary insight or value of that method, such that we must envisage Augustine now withholding faith until he can prove its assertions by reason. Not at all. The whole project of constructing a trinitarian image by psychological reflection is undertaken under the aegis of the faith already stated, established and explored in the first seven books. The apparent reversal of method is simply a grand completion of the circle, a return to the original starting-point.

D. STRUCTURE OF THE *DE TRINITATE*

Having spoken at length on Augustine's method, we can be briefer over the structure of his work. It is really controlled by what has just been said at the end of the preceding section – that in the whole work he goes full circle and returns to the point he started from.

This was a favourite literary form or pattern with the ancient classical writers, so much so that it may be said to have dominated even the way they thought. It is named, not altogether aptly, 'chiastic' from the shape of the Greek letter *chi*, χ. The point is that the lower half of this letter is a replica in reverse, a reflection, of the top half. The pattern or structure can also be illustrated by the graph of the parabola, which ends up symmetrically at the same level as it started from. In rhyming poetry it can take the form of a rhyme scheme, a b c d c′ b′ a′.

So that is how, as I read him, Augustine constructed his *De Trinitate*. We remember how he said in his letter to Aurelius that he did not want it to be published serially, book by book, because 'the later books are closely tied to the ones that precede them by the progress of the enquiry' – to give a more literal translation of his text. From the beginning, then, he must at least subconsciously have had the chiastic structure in mind. This is how I reconstruct it, using the a b c d c′ b′ a′ model (the numbers represent the number of books in each section):

a	1	Book I:	the absolute equality of the divine persons, proved from scripture;
b	3	II–IV:	the missions of the divine persons, examined in scripture;
c	3	V–VII:	rational defence of faith so far established, language of relationships etc.;
d	1	VIII:	centre book; attempt to 'storm' God, break surface, emerge from mirror world;
c′	3	IX–XI:	construction of mental image of God by rational introspection;
b′	3	XII–XIV:	history of this image in Everyman, and from Adam to Christ, explored in the light of scripture;
a′	1	XV:	the absolute inadequacy or inequality of the trinitarian image to the divine exemplar Trinity.

We can first notice the elementary pattern of numbers: 1 – 3 – 3 – 1 – 3 – 3 – 1. That it is deliberate is proved to my mind by the extreme artificiality of the second trio, books V–VII, in particular. There is really no reason at all where subject-matter is concerned why book VI, which is unusually short, should be separated from book VII. But the author wanted three books to perfect his pattern.

As regards subject-matter and treatment, XV does correspond both in length and by contrast to book I, contrasting the infinite inequality of the image to its exemplar with the perfect equality of the divine persons. The b, b′ sections, books II–IV and XII–XIV, correspond in that they both have a certain dramatic and quasi-historical character, the first investigating what we could call the history of God in the world, which culminates in the mission of the divine persons in order to redeem fallen man; the other observing the history of God's image in the world, i.e. of man's fall and redemption. Both sections are extended reflections on the scriptural record and data.

The two c, c' sections, books V–VII and IX–XI, only refer to scripture incidentally, though both presuppose the whole scriptural revelation. And it is interesting to see how the trinitarian image of three mental activities, remembering, understanding and willing of self, is constructed in books IX–XI with constant and explicit reference to the language of relationship and procession which had been painstakingly elaborated in books V–VIII. That is in fact why I think it is more correct to talk of Augustine constructing the image, rather than of his discerning or discovering it. I do not deny that he was discerning a reality that is there to be discerned. But these three mental activities are, after all, not the only activities of the mind or self. He picked them out because they suited his purpose, and he quite deliberately tailored them to his theological 'construction' of the divine Trinity (i.e. his construction of appropriate language for it) in the earlier section.

Book VIII, the centre-piece, has no parallels, unless it be both books I and XV. It very neatly concludes the first stage of the great quest and inaugurates the second. In the next few chapters we shall try to accompany Augustine on this awesome quest, an enterprise of infinitely greater moment than the legendary quest for the Holy Grail.

NOTES

1 The subject is dealt with in detail by two works in French. E. Hendrikx, *La Date de composition du De Trinitate* (Paris, 1955), and A.-M. La Bonnardière, *Recherches de Chronologie Augustinienne* (Paris, 1965). The only book in English I know of which discusses the matter is E. TeSelle, *Augustine the Theologian* (London, 1970), but on this point he relies uncritically on another French work: I. Chevalier, *Saint Augustin et la Pensée Grecque; les Relations Trinitaires* (Fribourg, 1940) which is really not at all reliable.

2 *Ep.* 174 (*PL* 33, 757–758).

3 We need to make a little effort of imagination to put ourselves back in a world which had no printing presses, typewriters or carbon paper, let alone duplicating and photo-copying machines. Professional authors like Augustine did not *write* their literary works; they dictated them, probably to three or four stenographers at a time, to ensure several copies. All that Augustine probably ever wrote with his own hand would have been notes and jottings, probably written with a stylus on a wax tablet. There were no publishers as we have them today, but in any town of reasonable size there would have been booksellers who would employ a staff of copyists, who would also write to dicta-tion. The people who got hold of one of Augustine's copies of his unfinished *De Trinitate*, would, I suppose, have had further copies made of it in Hippo, and it

probably did not achieve a very wide circulation. By sending his completed work to Aurelius in Carthage, a vastly more important metropolis, Augustine ensured that it would be more widely published, being copied by the much grander booksellers of that city.

4 *PL* 32, 635–636.

5 The Donatists were a schismatic sect who had arisen in the African Church immediately after the end of the great persecution launched by the emperor Diocletian, some eighty or so years before Augustine became bishop of Hippo. They denied the validity of any sacraments, above all of baptism, conferred by unworthy ministers, and they maintained that all Catholic clergy were unworthy ministers, because they derived their orders from bishops who had handed over (*tradiderunt*) the sacred books to the imperial authorities in the time of persecution, and so were *traditores* (traitors). By Augustine's time the Donatists had become a strongly nationalist sect, very popular in the Punic-speaking countryside, and they had their own equivalent of our contemporary IRA or ETA in roving bands of terrorists known as circumcellions.

6 *Ep.* 143, 4 to Marcellinus (*PL* 33, 586–587).

7 *Ep.* 169, 1 to Evodius (*ibid.* 743). He is telling his friend and fellow bishop what literary work he is busy on. He has finished the first five books of the *City of God*, and is carrying on with that. He has also dictated his explanations of Pss 67, 71 and 77 (68, 72, 78 in our usual reckoning). The rest of the psalms, which he had not yet dealt with, 'are vehemently demanded and awaited from me. I do not want to be distracted or delayed from dealing with them . . . ; so much so that at the moment I do not wish to attend even to the books on the Trinity which I have been keeping in my hands for so long, and have not yet completed. They are extremely difficult, and I do not think that many people will be able to understand them. So works that will, I hope, be useful to more people call more urgently for attention'.

8 The pagan critics had become more vocal after the sack of Rome by the Goths in 410. About the same time Pelagius had voiced his criticism of Augustine for writing in his *Confessions* X, xxix, 40, 'You command continence; grant what you command and command what you will', *da quod jubes et jube quod vis*, which Pelagius interpreted as a negation of free will. So the long controversy began, getting more and more acrimonious, Augustine defending the complete gratuitousness of salvation. Augustine's letters clearly took up very much of his time, letters being serious literary compositions. His sermons, though he regarded preaching as one of his principal duties, were mostly preached extempore, as the spirit of the moment moved him, and did not exact from him laborious hours of preparation. But they were, certainly, the fruit of years of reflection and study.

9 *PL* 42, 822; 959; 1057.

10 Cf. Anselm's version of the Augustinian principle, 'faith seeking understanding', *fides quaerens intellectum*, in his *Proslogion*, proem. (*PL* 158, 225).

11 Cf. *Confessions* III, v, 9 (*PL* 32, 686); V, xiv, 24 (*ibid.* 717–718); VI, v, 7 (722–723); VII, xxi, 27 (747–748).

12 I have not been able to trace this actual phrase. But comparable expressions may be found in *Confessions* X, xxvii, 38 (*PL* 32, 795), and *Enarr. in Ps.* 74(75), 9 (*PL* 36, 953). See also below, Chapter 14, note 8.

9
Missions: *De Trinitate*, books II–IV

In book I, as we have seen, Augustine establishes the starting-point of faith by demonstrating from scripture, i.e. almost exclusively from the New Testament, the absolute equality in divinity of the three persons. In effect it is what we have done above in Chapters 2 and 4, so we have no need here to look over his shoulder as he is composing book I.

As we also observed above (Chapter 7, A, pp. 66–68), the one serious scriptural objection to the equality of the Son and Holy Spirit with the Father is that they are said to have been sent by the Father, and this appears to imply their subordination to the one who sent them. We also noted how Augustine dealt with the difficulty. But besides being a 'difficulty' it also introduces the topic of the missions of the Son (and the Holy Spirit) which he deals with at length in books II–IV, and to which we now turn.

A. NO OBVIOUS MISSIONS OF THE SON AND HOLY SPIRIT IN THE OLD TESTAMENT: BOOK II

In book II Augustine deals with all those theophanies in the Old Testament which the economic theologians from Justin to Tertullian and Novatian had treated as manifestations – or missions[1] – of the Son/*Logos*. He does not actually deny that the Son was sent or manifested on these occasions; he simply shows by a meticulous examination of the texts that we never have any unmistakable evidence from the text itself that it was the Son, and not the Father or the Holy Spirit or all three persons together as the one God, who spoke to Adam in the garden, or appeared to Abraham at Mamre as three men, or to Jacob in his dream, or to Moses at the burning bush, or to all Israel at Mt Sinai when the law was given, or to Elijah on Horeb in the still small voice, or to Isaiah in the temple. In other words, we have no evidence from the sacred text of the Old Testament that the Son or the Holy Spirit was sent by the Father before 'the time had fully come' (Gal 4:4). But we do have incontrovertible assertions in the New Testament that the Son was sent to us in the person of Jesus Christ, and the Holy Spirit manifested at the baptism of Jesus in the form of a dove, and in the mighty rushing wind and fiery tongues of Pentecost.

'So what?' you may ask. To appreciate the theological significance of what Augustine has done we should consider a little more closely what the economic theologians were doing when they assumed that all these Old Testament theophanies were manifestations of the Son. They were demonstrating the pre-existence of the Son or *Logos* by in fact retrojecting the incarnation backwards into the Old Testament, back to the creation itself. Because the incarnation made the *Logos*/Son visible in the man Christ Jesus, they thought of him as always potentially visible – indeed some of them thought of him as always *essentially* visible. I think there can be little doubt that these Old Testament manifestations of the Son (as the economic theologians supposed them to be) were at least *imagined* as – so to say – pre-performance appearances of Jesus Christ. Thus this commonplace assumption (for such it had been before Augustine demolished it) blurred the distinction between his humanity and his divinity, blurred the complete truth of his divinity, and blurred the difference between the Old and the New Testaments, that is, between the old and new dispensations or economies. Paradoxically, the economic theologians enfeebled if they did not distort the very concept of the economy itself.

So Augustine's achievement in demonstrating by his theological exegesis that the missions of the Son and the Holy Spirit were proper to the New Testament was important for three reasons:

(1) it lent unequivocal support to the full and equal divinity of the Son/*Logos*;

(2) it finally scotched any notion that any divine person could be essentially visible;

(3) it re-established the difference, the discontinuity indeed, between the old and the new dispensations.

In this last respect, as in so many others, Augustine shows himself to be a true disciple of St Paul. In particular he may be said to be offering an extended commentary on Gal 4:4–7: 'When the time had fully come, God sent forth his Son . . . God sent the Spirit of his Son . . . ' – but not before! What happened before? Paul and Augustine are quite clear: before that sending, and hence that coming of the Son and Holy Spirit, there was the régime of the law, which is compared both to a status of *servitude* and a status of *minority*. (See for the latter comparison especially Gal 3:23ff.; for the former Gal 4:21ff.) And they are saying to us that the ultimate mystery of God, which we call the mystery of the Trinity, the mystery of the Father and the Son and the Holy Spirit, was not and could not have been revealed to mankind under such a régime, to us as slaves and/or as children. It can only be revealed to us as free people and adult people, to us precisely as 'sons in the Son', and as free with the freedom with which Christ has made us free (Gal 5:1) – which we have been made by God's (the Father's) gracious gift of his Son and his Holy Spirit to us in the new dispensation or economy.

It is the recurring temptation of Christians to return to the womb of the Old Testament. The Galatians were succumbing to it, which is why Paul wrote them that vehement epistle. It seems that the economic theologians were to some extent succumbing to it. The Latin Church, our own Latin Catholic tradition, has succumbed to it, since about 800, time and time again: the symptoms or effects being, for example, the assimilation of our New Testament ordained ministry to the Old Testament levitical priesthood; and the persistent authoritarianism and legalism which are such undeniable blemishes on the ecclesial life of Latin Catholicism;[2] and finally the absence of any deep devotion to the Holy Trinity, any deep sense of meaning in 'the name of the Father and of the Son and of the Holy Spirit' which is such an unfortunate weakness of popular Catholicism.

B. THE MISSION OF ANGELS IN THE OLD TESTAMENT: BOOK III

So the mystery of the Trinity is now related to the economy of salvation by being revealed through the missions of the Son and the Holy Spirit as the climax of that economy. For while Paul and Augustine both emphasize the radical newness of the new dispensation and hence its discontinuity with the old, neither of them makes the mistake of rejecting the old as meaningless or valueless. This was the mistake of Marcion and other Gnostics in the second century, the heretics Irenaeus was engaged in refuting.[3]

The old dispensation was a preparation, a pedagogy, and we of the new dispensation still need to be aware of it, indeed in some sense to be taken through it, just as in ordinary life sensible adults do not reject everything they learned at school even when they have grown out of school, and sometimes can with profit live over again their experience of being educated. So our Christianity, though it should have 'grown out of' the law and the old dispensation, still cherishes its memory and its experience. We with our faith in the mystery of the Trinity have grown out of Israel's experience of and faith in Yahweh,[4] the Holy One of Israel. But our 'memory' of that experience and faith, stored up for us in the Old Testament and in our tradition, is something we have to keep alive, and sometimes live over again in order to give body, as it were, to our own 'adult' experience of and faith in the Father, the Son and the Holy Spirit.

So Augustine as a Christian is still very interested in these Old Testament theophanies, even though he does not find in them any evidence of the Trinity. They are still experiences of the true God.

But, as he has been insisting *ad nauseam*, the true God, and therefore not only the Father but also the Son and the Holy Spirit, is absolutely invisible, beyond any possibility of being perceived as he is in himself by any sense experience. What then were those manifestations of the divine which we call theophanies, and how were they brought about? Augustine insists that they were *created* phenomena, modifications of the physical or material creation in fact, since they were observable by the senses,[5] which represented or stood for God. And taking another leaf out of Paul's letter to the Galatians (3:19), Augustine maintains that these created phenomena were produced by angels. Here with Paul he seems to be perpetuating or reviving a rabbinic idea that had been overlooked by the early Christian tradition. The word 'angel', let us remember, both in Greek and in the Hebrew word it usually translates (*mal'ak*), means 'messenger' and messengers are *par excellence* people who *are sent* with messages. So what Augustine is saying is that it was not after all the Son or the Holy Spirit who were sent in the Old Testament but angels. They were the intermediaries, the mediators – together with specially chosen men like Moses, the prophets and the kings – between God and his people. A very different and merely provisional or preparatory economy from the one inaugurated by the coming (because he was sent) of the Son of God himself.

C. THE MISSION OF THE ONE TRUE MEDIATOR, JESUS CHRIST, IN THE NEW DISPENSATION: BOOK IV

At first sight book IV reads more like an exotic little treatise on Christology than part of a work on the Trinity. Augustine presents the incarnation and Christ's work of redemption in his death and resurrection as God's response to man's need. The need is twofold, or perhaps two-levelled: for reconciliation with God, i.e. to be restored to union and harmony with God; and to receive the perfectly apt sacramental, symbolic means to this end.[6] Man needed to be saved, and in a human way. This is achieved in Christ, the one true mediator between God and man (since he is both divine and human; cf. 1 Tim 2:5), who is also – Augustine here anticipates Schillebeeckx[7] – the perfect sacrament of harmony restored.

I have just called book IV an *exotic* treatise on Christology, because Augustine sets all this out in terms of an elaborate number symbolism with which I will not trouble the reader. It might also be thought exotic as being a bit out of place in a work on the Trinity. But in fact it at least links up with the previous book, where we saw that angels, together with Moses and other chosen figures, were mediators of the old covenant. In this role they also presided over 'the régime of symbols' – the ritual law in particular – which that covenant imposed. But this mediation and this régime of symbols was clearly not enough to meet the needs of mankind just referred to. It had only prepared the way, pedagogically, for the perfect mediation achieved by Christ. This latter, set forth in book IV, is next contrasted with the false mediation offered by the demons masquerading as gods. The perfection of Christ's mediation is splendidly displayed by the perfection of his sacrifice, which perfectly symbolizes and achieves mankind's union with God. It is the perfect sacrament of unity. It in turn is contrasted (following Hebrews) with the imperfect, ineffective sacrifices of the old law and with the false, corrupting sacrifices to the demons (pagan gods).

It is worth quoting in full Augustine's presentation of Christ's sacrifice as this perfect sacrament of unity, this perfect act of mediation:

Now there are four things to be considered in every sacrifice: who it is offered to, who it is offered by, what it is that is offered, and who it is offered for. And this one true mediator, in reconciling us to God by his sacrifice of peace, would remain one with him to whom he offered it, and make one in himself those for whom he offered it, and be himself who offered it one and the same as what he offered.[8]

Still, what has all this to do with the Trinity? The answer is, it explains and as it were defines the mission or sending of the Son. As the angels were sent in the old dispensation for their task of imperfect or incomplete mediation – and continue to be sent on subordinate tasks in the new – so the Son is sent to perform his work of perfect mediation between God and man, and to complete God's economy in the new dispensation. After completing his description of Christ's work of mediation and contrasting it with the vain efforts of philosophers (mainly the Neoplatonists) to achieve such a result on their own, Augustine links this whole Christological excursus to his proper theme of the missions by saying at the beginning of his concluding section of book IV, 'There you have what the Son of God has been sent for; indeed there you have what it is for the Son of God to have been sent'.[9]

Missions are for a purpose. Indeed the English word 'mission' often stands for the purpose or task for which people are sent. So we can talk about being sent on a mission – on what mission? – to survey a territory, to distribute famine relief, or whatever it may be. Thus the mission on which God the Son was sent was to save mankind by performing, or indeed being, the perfect sacramental mediation between God and mankind.

But his mission was accompanied by the mission of the Holy Spirit, and both missions had the effect of revealing the eternal processions of these persons from the Father – that is of revealing the mystery of the Trinity. If I may quote at greater length Augustine's key text on the missions:

Just as his being born means for the Son his being from the Father, so his being sent means his being known to be from him. And just as for the Holy Spirit his being the gift of God means his proceeding from the Father, so his being sent means his being known to proceed from him. Nor, by the way, can we say that the Holy Spirit does not proceed from the Son as well; it is not without point that the same Spirit is called the Spirit of the Father and of the Son [Mt 10:20, Gal 4:6]. And I cannot see what else he intended to signify when he breathed and said *Receive the Holy Spirit* [Jn 20:22] . . . it was a convenient symbolic demonstration that the Holy Spirit proceeds from the Son as well as from the Father.[10]

Augustine, and we, will return to the question of the Holy Spirit proceeding from the Son as well as from the Father in Chapter 12. Rather surprisingly he does not here deduce it from texts that talk about the Son sending the Holy Spirit, like Jn 15:26 and 16:7.

It appears, then, that the mystery of the Trinity is revealed to us precisely as the climax of the divine economy or plan of salvation. For it is by the sending of the Son and the Holy Spirit that we are saved – and by the sending of them that their very being as both one with the Father and distinct from him is revealed. I have seen Augustine criticized for elaborating a theology of the Trinity according to which any of the three persons could have become incarnate. Leaving aside that awkward word 'could' (since who are we to prescribe to the divine persons what any of them could do?), I think what is said in this book IV shows clearly enough that Augustine regards the incarnation of the Son rather than of the Father or the Holy Spirit as supremely appropriate, as – shall we say – aesthetically right. He has after all been reflecting at great length on Paul's key statement of the trinitarian mystery in Gal 4:4–7.

But when the time had fully come, God sent forth his Son, born of woman, born under the law, to redeem those who were under the law, so that we might receive adoption as sons. And because you are sons, God has sent the Spirit of his Son into our hearts, crying 'Abba, Father!' So through God you are no longer a slave but a son, and if a son then an heir.

D.   SUMMARY: IMPORTANCE OF THE NOTION OF MISSION

To summarize under a few headings St Augustine's teaching on the missions:

(1)   It is by the sending of the Son and the Holy Spirit that God enters, as it were, fully and personally into the economy of salvation.

(2)   His doing so is the climax of that economy or drama, and therefore neither person was sent in the old dispensation which was a preparation for that grand climax.

(3)   The sendings of the Son and the Holy Spirit reveal their eternal processions from the Father (and the Holy Spirit's from the Son as well), and thus reveal the inner trinitarian mystery of God.

(4)   And so this mystery of God's being is organically linked to the economy of salvation, above all to the mystery of the incarnation and of the saving death and resurrection of Jesus Christ. As St Paul's text, just quoted, shows us, to be saved is to enter in some way into the divine relationships of the three persons.

(5)   We could add, though Augustine has not discussed it, that the missions of the Son and Holy Spirit have their extension or continuation in the mission of the apostles, hence of the Church, hence of all 'missionaries', hence indeed of all Christians.[11] Our mission is to carry on the mission of the Son (redeeming the world by mediating between God and mankind) in the mission of the Holy Spirit.

NOTES

1   Augustine provisionally defines 'mission' in this context as the making visible of the one who is sent: II, v, 10 (*PL* 42, 851). See also the previous sections, II, v, 7–9.

2   It has often been assumed by persons on both sides, and on neither, that Protestants and especially Calvinist and Puritan Protestants with their psalm-singing and sabbath-keeping are more Old Testament in their religion than Catholics, who notoriously 'don't read the Bible'. These are the received and hoary stereotypes. But while it is true that in this line Catholics don't read the Bible, and certainly don't treat the Bible as an immediate authority governing their behaviour in the way that such Protestants have done, with the Ten Commandments enthroned in their sanctuaries where Catholics have Tabernacle and Crucifix – still Catholics have a long, long tradition of treating their Christianity in an Old Testament manner. Our moral theology manuals and text-books confound moral theology with canon law, and discuss cases of conscience with all the *legal* precision of rabbinic scholars. It is indeed a long-standing – and bad – Catholic tradition, encouraged by documents emanating from the highest authorities, faithfully preserved in the manuals and the catechisms, to treat morals as a science founded on law, rather than the other way round. What happens to grace in such a scheme? It is handed over to dogmatic and controversial (polemical) theology, and/or is treated as an extrinsic factor which is supplied on request to help us – keep the law.

3   It is the counter-mistake of the adolescent reaction to infantilism. And of course, the more massively entrenched the infantilism is and has been, the more extreme and disturbing the eventual juvenile reaction. It is what we have been suffering from these last twenty years with our post-Vatican II blues. But what I find more disturbing still than the adolescent reaction that dismisses all old traditions as irrelevant is the backlash of infantilism trying to reassert the old authoritarian positions and prescriptions. If we are to be condemned to a ding-dong battle between juveniles and infantiles, when will we ever be allowed to become adults?

4   The Jehovah Christianity of many of the sects is another variant of the back-to-the-womb movement.

5   Such observable phenomena would also include dreams, visions, voices, which are modifications of the subject's psychic apparatus – memory and imagination, or sub-conscious, *animus* and *anima* etc., according to your preferred psychology.

6   A 'definition' or rather description of man favoured by many contemporary anthropologists (e.g. Mary Douglas) is 'a symbol-making animal'.

7 In his book *Christ the Sacrament of Encounter with God* (ET; London, 1963).
8 IV, xiv, 19 (*PL* 42, 901).
9 IV, xix, 25 (*ibid*. 905).
10 IV, xx, 29 (*ibid*. 908).
11 The key texts are Jn 17:18, and 20:21. In the first Jesus says to the Father, 'As thou didst send me into the world, so I have sent them into the world'; and in the second, after his resurrection he says to the disciples, 'As the Father has sent me, even so I send you'. The sense in which the mission of disciples is both an extension and also a kind of analogue of the mission of the Son is better conveyed by Jn 13:20, 'He who receives anyone whom I send receives me; and he who receives me receives him who sent me'. This echoes Mt 10:40, where Jesus is speaking to the twelve, and the same idea is put negatively in Lk 10:16, 'He who hears you hears me, and he who rejects you rejects me, and he who rejects me rejects him who sent me', where Jesus is addressing the seventy/seventy-two disciples. These texts are commonly interpreted as covering the 'canonical mission' of ordained ministers and missionaries. But Mk 9:37 has a more radical version of the same concept: 'Whoever receives one such child in my name receives me; and whoever receives me, receives not me but him who sent me'. Christ's mission is passed on to and shared with even children, with the least of these his brethren – and hence I think one can say with all Christians, who do not have to wait, therefore, for a canonical mission from due ecclesiastical authority before they start carrying out their mission, the mission of the Son and of the Holy Spirit, of helping to redeem the world by proclaiming and bearing witness to the gospel.

10
Divine Relationships: books V–VII

A. RELATIONSHIPS CONSIDERED BEFORE PROCESSIONS

We have just been led at the end of book IV to the point that the divine missions reveal the divine processions. It is these processions, the Son's eternally being born of the Father (the Father eternally begetting the Son) and the Holy Spirit eternally proceeding from the Father – and from the Son – that constitute the mystery of the Trinity, that cause (if we can use that word about divine realities) there to be three in God whom we name Father, Son and Holy Spirit. So one might expect Augustine, having discussed the missions of the Son and the Holy Spirit, to investigate next the divine processions. They are the heart of the matter, they are the ultimate object of his quest.

But in fact he does not do this. He goes on now to answer the Arian objections to the orthodox doctrine of the equality of the three. These objections, as we saw above in Chapter 6, B (pp. 55–57), are based on the absolute simplicity of God, and hence on the real identity of all names predicated of him, and hence the impossibility of predicating of him names that exclude each other, like 'begotten' and 'unbegotten'.

In these three books, then, Augustine discusses not the divine processions but the divine names, that is to say the words we use when talking about God and the right and wrong ways of using them. As we also saw above in Chapter 7, B (pp. 69–71), he picks out words or names signifying relationships as the only ones by which we can distinguish the three divine persons from each other. So these three books can also be said to be about the divine relationships. But it is more accurate to say that they are about the divine names signifying relationships and a comparison of them with other names signifying (in God) substance.

What is the connection, then, between the divine processions, which are as we have said the heart of the matter, the goal of the quest, and the divine relationships? Just as the missions *reveal* the processions, so I think we can say that the relationships and their names *express* the processions. Perhaps we could amplify Augustine's statement a little by saying that the missions reveal the processions *through* the relationships. For what these names manifest to us is the Son – and hence by reciprocal implication the Father – and the Holy Spirit as *subsistent relationships*. But this needs explanation and defence before we can go on through these relationships to contemplate the eternal processions.

This whole section of Augustine's work, books V-VII, is the one most thoroughly appreciated and developed in the subsequent Latin scholastic tradition. So here I will not confine myself to considering what Augustine had to say about these matters, but will try to present the fruits of the developed tradition in its most mature form, which means in effect as formulated by Thomas Aquinas.[1]

There is no need to repeat what we saw in Chapter 7, B, that it is only by their reciprocal and mutually exclusive relationships that the divine persons are really distinguished from each other. But some further amplifications of the point will be useful.

B. SUBSISTENT RELATIONSHIPS

The relationships do not simply distinguish the persons from each other – they *are* the persons.[2] In the technical language of the schools they are subsistent relationships. For we are, of course, all the time talking about God, whose absolute simplicity is the keystone of the transcendental theology. As we have seen, this means that God is his attributes; he is not only good, he is his goodness, his eternity, his omnipotence etc. Now the Father, of course, is God. Therefore he is not only Father, he is the fatherhood (the relationship) by which he is Father. So too the Son is the sonship by which he is Son. And the Holy Spirit – well, we have already remarked (Chapter 7, B, p. 70) on the peculiar difficulty of finding proper names for the Holy Spirit; but he is whatever you like to call the relationship by which he is Holy Spirit. The scholastics in desperation called it by the same name as the procession by which the Holy Spirit proceeds and which founds the relationship – and they could not find a proper name for that either, so they just called it 'procession'. So in the technical language 'procession' can either mean each of the goings-forth by which both Son and Holy Spirit proceed eternally in God, or it can mean in particular the going-forth of the Holy Spirit, as distinct from that of the Son which is called 'generation', or it can mean the relationship of the Holy Spirit to the other persons set up by this particular going-forth – all according to context. The Holy Spirit in any case is this relationship. In Augustine's preferred language it is the relationship of being Gift, the relationship of 'givenness' if you like.[3]

C. RELATIONSHIPS AND SUBSTANCE

The cardinal principle of the absolute simplicity of God leads us to a further conclusion. If the mutual divine relationships are subsistent, constituting the three as really distinct hypostases, subsistences or persons – really distinct because mutually exclusive – they are also, on the other hand, identical with the divine substance or nature. The rule is that in God all accidental predications turn into substantive ones; God is his accidents, though we do not use that word about God but substitute instead the word 'attributes'. In you or me a relationship is an accident, it adheres or is added to our substantive being or our nature. But this cannot be so in God. We cannot say that the subsistent relationships, i.e. the three persons, are affixed or added to the being or nature of God, for that would immediately make him complex.

By the same token we must avoid saying or thinking that the three persons add up to God. The expression 'God consists of three persons' should be avoided because it gives this impression – that Father plus Son plus Holy Spirit add up to God. But again that immediately introduces multiplicity into God, which is a form of complexity. The truth is, as it says in the Athanasian creed, 'The Father is God, the Son is God, the Holy Spirit is God [i.e. these three subsistent relationships are identical with the divine essence, substance, nature or being] and yet not three Gods but one God' (Chapter 1, C, above, p. 5).

How in that case, we ask in exasperation, are they three really distinct persons? Aquinas puts the objection very clearly: 'It seems that the relations which are in God are not distinct in reality from each other, because all things identical with one and the same thing are identical with one another. But every relation in God is identical in reality with the divine nature. Therefore the divine relations are not distinct from each other in reality'.[4]

His answer is extremely ingenious. He says that in talking about ordinary things (creatures) we can observe two aspects in their relationships. The first is that the relationships of things, like their qualities, sizes etc. are 'accidents' which adhere to or go with their substantive natures. As a man my relationships qualify me as much as my weight and height, my virtues and vices, and are liable to change just as these other accidents are, without my thereby ceasing to be a man. The second aspect of the relationships of things is that unlike their qualities and quantities they refer them (relate them) to other things, not simply to themselves. Applying this now to the divine case, we can say that relationships under the first aspect, like all other accidents (attributes), turn into substantive predications. They are subsistent, and they are identical with the divine nature or substance. But as referring to another, under their second aspect precisely as relationships, they must be really distinct from the other (i.e. the opposite relationship) to which they refer.

They are distinct, really so, only from each other, *not* from the divine being or nature. The Father is distinct from the Son. Neither is distinct from God;[5] and they are each distinct from the Holy Spirit, not as Father and Son, but as 'from whom he proceeds'.

D.   OUR RELATIONSHIPS WITH THE DIVINE PERSONS

It is only as related to one another that the divine persons are really distinct from each other. They are subsistent *mutual* relationships. But as related or referred to creatures they are not really distinct from each other. Again, to quote the Athanasian creed: 'The Father is Lord [i.e. lord and master of creation], the Son is Lord, the Holy Spirit is Lord; yet not three Lords but one Lord' (Chapter 1, C above, p. 5). From the fourth-century transcendental theologians onwards – including of course St Augustine – it has been another cardinal axiom that all divine activity *ad extra*, i.e. with reference to creatures, is common to all three divine persons, and not peculiar to any of them. It is not only the Father who creates, only the Son who redeems, only the Holy Spirit who sanctifies, although it is quite legitimate to 'appropriate' these activities to these particular persons (see above, Chapter 8, C, p. 79, and below, Chapter 11, D, pp. 103-105). But all three persons are commonly, i.e. indistinctly, acting in all these divine operations directed towards creatures.

So far so good. To say otherwise, i.e. really to divide up divine activity with regard to creatures between the three persons, and to say the Father does some things, the Son other things, the Holy Spirit yet other ones, would again be to introduce complexity into God; indeed it would be implicitly to posit three Gods.

But an inference has commonly been drawn from this axiom, drawn tentatively by Hilary and Augustine[6] and all the scholastics – certainly by Thomas Aquinas[7] – that is not only wrong but ultimately destructive of any relevance to us of the whole mystery of the Trinity.[8] This inference is that we, as creatures, made, redeemed and sanctified by God indistinctly (these activities being common to all three persons), cannot and do not have any real relationships with the divine persons as such, i.e. as distinct from each other. And so it becomes a commonplace of the schools that when we say 'Our Father' as taught to do by Jesus Christ, we are not addressing God the Father specifically, but just God or the whole Trinity, because we are calling him our Father as our creator (or even as our redeemer[9]), and it is the whole Trinity, God without distinction of persons, who created and redeemed us.

But if we cannot be really related to God the Father as our Father, it follows that we cannot be really related to God the Son as our brother or to

God the Holy Spirit as recipients of him as God's gift to us. In all these cases –
on this showing – our relationship is just to God. What then is the bearing of
the mystery of the Father, Son and Holy Spirit on our lives? None, it seems.
The transcendent mystery has been set completely adrift from the economic
realities of creation and salvation that form the context of our lives as
creatures and as Christians. That is why I say that this commonplace of the
schools and the textbooks and the catechisms is and has been not only wrong
but also destructive of a lively faith in the mystery of the Trinity.

Fortunately it is contradicted by scripture, by the liturgical practice of the
Church, East and West, Latin and Greek, Catholic and Orthodox, by the
theologians themselves who make use of it,[10] and by the central economic
dogma of Christian revelation and faith, that of the incarnation.

To prove my case let me take, not just any creature or any human being,
but the topmost of creatures and the supreme human being, the man Christ
Jesus. Now that he was 'hypostatically united to the Word of God', or
assumed into personal union with God the Son, to form one hypostasis or
one person with him, was indeed the work of all three persons of God the
Trinity. This is certain, as Augustine states in his profession of faith (Chapter
1, D, p. 6 above – last sentence but one of the quotation). But it is even more
certain that the man Christ Jesus is related to the divine person of the Son (by
the relationship of union) in a way in which he is not related to the other two
persons. It was the Son only, not the Father or the Holy Spirit, who became
man, as Augustine says very firmly in the same text. There is no common
relationship to all three persons here in this respect, in spite of the common
operation *ad extra* of all three persons in bringing the incarnation about. It
follows that the man Jesus of Nazareth is related to the Father and again to
the Holy Spirit in specific proper ways – as well as being related to all three
persons indistinctly as their creature. To say otherwise would certainly be
heretical.

If him, why not us? If he, as man and not only as God the Son, can address
God the Father (and not the whole Trinity) as 'Abba, Father' (Mk 14:36),
why cannot we (Gal 4:6)? To be sure, we are not the offspring, the sons and
daughters of God the Father in the same way as Jesus is; we are so by
adoption (Gal 4:5), he is the only-begotten Son by nature (Jn 1:14, 18). But
while our relationships to the Father are not the same specific relationship as
Jesus Christ's, there is no logical or theological reason why they should not
equally be relations to him, God the Father, the first person of the Trinity, as
such.

For we call him Father, not in fact because he has created us or even
redeemed us, but because (by the saving action of all three persons) we have
been incorporated into and spiritually identified with his incarnate Son. That
surely is the implication of Paul's great text, Gal 4:4–7. That must be the

effect of the Father sending the Son and the Holy Spirit into the world, each distinctly revealed by distinct created effects, when the fullness of time had come.[11]

NOTES

1   Thomas Aquinas, born about 1225 and dying in 1274, was the greatest of the scholastics in the great century of scholasticism. He became a Master of Arts (after joining the Order of Preachers, the new order of Friars which together with its sister Order of Friars Minor was invading the universities of Europe in the thirteenth century) and spent his life teaching philosophy and theology at Paris and at the papal court. He wrote innumerable commentaries both on the books of scripture and on the works of Aristotle, and above all he wrote a *Summa Theologiae*, a theology textbook, which probably remains unsurpassed as a work of systematic theology.

However, it did not become the ordinary textbook of theology in Catholic academies for centuries, if indeed it ever has done. The textbook which Thomas himself studied and taught from, and which remained the theology textbook of the universities until the seventeenth century at least, was the *Sentences* compiled by Peter Lombard in the twelfth century, *c*. 1140.

Scholasticism simply means the style and method of the schools, i.e. of the universities or institutes of higher learning which began to flourish in Europe from the end of the eleventh century onwards, the two oldest being Paris and Oxford. It thus signifies a technical, academic manner of philosophizing and theologizing which is very different from the more literary and homiletic or rhetorical style of the patristic age. The difference is not unlike that between the dry, professorial notes of Aristotle on the whole range of academic subjects taught in his time, and the literary dialogues of Plato.

2   See Aquinas, *STh* Ia, 40, 2 ad 1 – and indeed the whole of question 40 (ET, vol. 7).

3   One might ask why in this case we cannot talk about the three divine relationships instead of the three divine persons. It would save us introducing this somewhat problematic word 'person' – or if we are Greeks, 'hypostasis'. The answer is that we cannot do so because there are in fact *four* relationships in God. There are the two relationships, fatherhood and sonship, relating the Father and the Son to each other; there are also the two relationships relating the Holy Spirit to the other two. There is the relationship of the Holy Spirit to them, which we have just seen is scholastically named 'procession', and it is indeed the subsistent relationship constituting the person of the Holy Spirit. But the opposite relationship to this cannot be either fatherhood or sonship, because they only relate to each other. Just as the relationship of sonship is founded on the procession of the Son from the Father, which we call generation or being born, and the relationship of fatherhood is founded on the act which gives rise to that generation, which we call begetting; and just as the relationship of the Holy Spirit to the other two which we call, for want of a better term, procession is founded on the procession of the Holy Spirit from the other two; so the relationship they have to the Holy Spirit must be founded on the act which gives rise to his proceeding from them. And this act, and the relationship founded on it, is called by the scholastics 'common spiration' or 'breathing forth' – common because it is common to the persons of the Father and the Son.

But this relationship is only opposite to that of procession, not to either fatherhood or sonship. So it does not constitute a fourth person. It is subsistent in the Father and the Son, really distinguishing them, not from each other, but from the Holy Spirit. They are really distinguished from each other only as subsistent fatherhood and subsistent sonship. See *STh* Ia, 28, 4 and 30, 2 (ET, vol. 6).

This diagram and key may help:

DIAGRAM OF THE MOST HOLY TRINITY

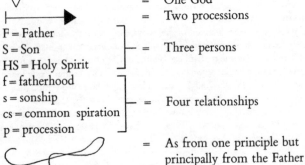

4 *STh* Ia, 28, 3 obj. 1 (ET, vol. 6).

5 See *ibid*. 28, 3 ad 1; the answer to that particular objection. Compare also 28, 2 (ET, vol. 6) and 39, 1 (ET, vol. 7).

6 Hilary: *De Trinitate* III, 11 (*PL* 10, 82). But Hilary is here doing no more than distinguishing very properly between Christ's true or natural sonship and our adoptive sonship. He does not so much as suggest that adoptive sonship can only relate us to God without distinction, and not specifically to God the Father. Augustine: *De Trinitate* V, xi, 12 (*PL* 42, 919). Augustine does suggest that we call God the Trinity 'our Father' since he regenerates us by his grace. But he nowhere implies that we cannot call God the Father, as such, our Father too. This harder – and mistaken – inference may have been read into both patristic authorities by Peter Lombard in his *Sentences* I, 26, 5 (*PL* 192, 593).

7 *STh* Ia, 33, 3, obj. 1 (ET, vol. 7); also IIIa, 23, 2, sed con. and ad 2 and 3 (ET, vol. 50).
8 One should not lightly charge a whole long tradition with being erroneous. But sometimes one has to do it, especially where some clichés of the schools are concerned, that are simply repeated from textbook to catechism without any reflection on their implications. A number of them go back to Peter Lombard's *Sentences*. Some were corrected by St Thomas, e.g. the erroneous cliché that the trinitarian image in man consists of the three powers of the soul, memory, understanding and will: Ia, 93, 7 ad 3 (ET, vol. 13). But for all the prestige of St Thomas, this mistake of Peter Lombard continues to be propagated in, for instance, q. 30 of *A Catechism of Christian Doctrine*, published by the Catholic Truth Society, revised ed. (London, 1971). Erroneous traditions are very tenacious.

As for this particular cliché, which St Thomas does not seem to have corrected – but see note 10 below – my judgement of it is shared by the translator of vol. 7 of the *Summa*, T. C. O'Brien. See App. 1 of that volume, para. 7, pp. 245–251.
9 See above, Chapter 3, A, p. 22.
10 By scripture – see, for example Gal 4:4–7. The mediaeval theologians did not realize what more modern exegesis puts beyond doubt, that the New Testament writers for the most part 'appropriated' the name 'God' to the Father, and the name 'Lord' to Jesus Christ (i.e. to the Son – see e.g. 1 Cor 8:6).

By liturgical practice – notably the custom of praying in the divine offices and the mass to the Father (usually addressed simply as 'God'), through the Son in the unity of the Holy Spirit.

By the theologians themselves – the whole tenor of Augustine's *De Trinitate*, especially the last seven books, is against the cliché. As for Thomas Aquinas, O'Brien, *loc. cit.* in note 8, refers to his commentaries on Matthew, John, Romans, 1 Corinthians and Galatians.
11 A rather technical qualification perhaps needs to be made to what has been said in this section. But it would still need to be made even if one followed Peter Lombard's mistaken axiom. It is that while creatures can have real relations to God, and as I maintain to each of the divine persons distinctly – and do have such relations – the corresponding relations in God are not real but only notional or 'relations of reason'. That is to say, they do not connote any change or modification whatsoever in God. They are attributed to God by our way of thinking and talking only. If I point out to you a man standing 'to the right of that post', it does not mean that the post *really* has a right and a left side. These relations are merely attributed to it by our minds for our convenience.

11

'Person' and 'Hypostasis': Appropriation of Essential Names to the Persons: books V–VII

A. THE PROBLEM OF 'PERSON' AND 'HYPOSTASIS'

Here let us just recapitulate what we saw in Chapter 7, B, pp. 68–71 above. Augustine answers the Arian objections by showing that besides substantive (essential) predications (which absorb, as it were, all accidental predications when we are speaking of God) there are also relative predications, like 'Father' and 'Son', which enable, indeed require, us to say that there are real distinctions between the persons without compromising the total simplicity and hence unity of God. God is one in respect of all substantive predications, yet three in virtue of certain relative predications which, following the scriptural revelation, we make of him.

But three what? – or three who? Nobody recorded or writing in the New Testament appears to have asked and therefore answered this question. But in the course of time, chiefly in argument with the modalist Sabellians, it was answered negatively by saying 'Not just three names or three modes', and positively by saying, if you were Latin-speaking, 'Three persons', and if you were Greek by saying for preference 'Three hypostases'. The Greek equivalent of 'person', *prosōpon* (both meaning primarily theatrical masks), sounded in Greek ears too like a 'theatrical rôle', and hence perhaps liable to encourage Modalism again.

That is the tradition of ecclesiastical usage as it reaches Augustine. The problem it presents him with is that neither of these words is a name signifying a relationship. Just as well, perhaps, that they do not signify a particular relationship, because we say there are three of them, and it is of the necessity of the case that the relationships which constitute the persons are each different from the others, each unique.

But since in fact both 'hypostasis' and 'person' signify substance, it is hard to see how we can say there are three in God, since we are certainly forbidden by the tradition to say there are three substances (*ousiai* in Greek), just as we are forbidden by scripture to say there are three Gods or three Lords. That is the problem.

B. THE SCHOLASTIC SOLUTION OF AQUINAS[1]

We saw Augustine's solution to the problem in Chapter 7, B above, and we shall return to it in the next section. Meanwhile it is worth looking at St Thomas' solution which implicitly rejects St Augustine's – Augustine's at least as it had become petrified in the conventional Augustinian tradition.

Thomas begins with the accepted definition of 'person' given by Boethius as 'an individual substance of a rational nature'.[2] Boethius (and therefore Thomas) is of course well aware of the original meaning of the word as a theatrical mask, from which he traces its transferences to the character or *dramatis persona* so represented, and thence to 'persons having a certain dignity', or as we would say, 'personages', those to whom we accord VIP treatment. Boethius, I suspect, was considerably influenced in framing his definition by the use of the word in Christian theology in both the trinitarian and the Christological contexts. He was writing, we should not forget, some hundred years after Augustine.

'Person' as so defined signifies the concrete particular individual of a rational nature, because it is applicable (in the ancient theatre, one supposes) only to human beings and individuals above them in the scale of being, like demi-gods, spirits, gods and goddesses; in the Christian scheme of things, to angels (and demons) and the divine persons.

And it is applicable to the divine persons, and properly so in Thomas' view, because it designates the subsistent individual who is distinct from other individuals of the same nature. The Greek 'hypostasis' likewise signifies the concretely subsistent individual, but is not limited to those 'of a rational nature'.

Now in God, as we have seen, what are distinctly subsistent are the mutually opposed and corresponding relationships. So the words 'person' and 'hypostasis' can properly be used in talking of God to refer to these relationships, even though in themselves they do not signify any kind of relationship. Thomas adds that since 'person' means that which is most perfect in the whole of nature, namely what subsists in rational (or intelligent) nature, it is peculiarly apt for use in talking about God.[3]

C. AUGUSTINE'S SOLUTION RECONSIDERED

But Aquinas adds a most important proviso, one we should be used to by now, but which we are congenitally prone – with our *human* processes of thought – to overlook. He continues, 'But the word cannot be used in the same way of God as of creatures, but in a superlative way, as is the case with other names which we apply to creatures and then attribute to God'.

What this superlative or more excellent way actually means, to come down with a bump from the heights, is that these words actually tell us nothing whatever about God. To call the Father, Son and Holy Spirit three persons tells us nothing at all in addition to what we already know from calling them Father, Son and Holy Spirit, apart from being our way of saying that they are really distinct from each other; that each is not the other two or either of them.

And this is really the point Augustine is making when he concludes that these words are no more than just labels, without any intrinsic significance when we apply them to God, so that we might just as well, in answer to the question 'Three what?', reply 'Three Xs', or more elegantly 'Three someones'.

I take it that this is why Fr Panikkar congratulates the African bishops at Vatican II on their languages having no equivalents of 'nature' and 'person'.[4] They are, initially at least, free of the mystification imported from foreign languages and traditions; and what is even more important is that they should understand that there is absolutely no need for them to import these foreign concepts in order to enter more deeply into the mystery. Each culture/language has to wrestle in its own way, according to its own grammatical structures and its own semantic tradition, with the problem of how to talk about these ineffable mysteries.

Take Sesotho, the only African language I have any knowledge of at all – and that very scanty. Its word for 'person' in the ordinary sense, as applied to people, is *motho*, pl. *batho*. But it means, very definitely, human beings, distinguished by a number of grammatical rules (e.g. the class of nouns to which it belongs) from non-human beings like animals, or spirits – or gods. You could no more suitably talk about the three divine *batho* than you could talk in English about the three divine people. So the first translators of catechisms – but do 'persons' have to occur in catechisms? – transliterated 'person' into *moperesona*, pl. *baperesona*. But what good does that do? To the ordinary Mosotho ear you might indeed just as well say three Xs or three hiccoughs, except that in their open simplicity they will assume that *baperesona* must mean something very important, very mysterious, which they cannot possibly understand. It is about as disconnected from any experience they could conceivably have as anything can be – unless and until they start learning Latin or theology or something esoteric like that.

It is scarcely for me to suggest what genuine Sesotho word they should use. But I think the translators would have been better advised to try and think of some equivalent to 'hypostasis', which just means 'subsistent individual', and is not confined to those 'of rational nature'. So a general word meaning 'things', or an equivalent for the common African English way of using 'somebody', as in the expressions 'a certain somebody' or 'they are very nice somebodies'.[5]

For a further point arises, which I think is scarcely touched on by St Thomas. Being persons is not something that the divine persons have in common, as it is something which human persons have in common. Whatever the divine persons have in common is the divine nature or substance or being, and is therefore not distinct, not personal to them. Each of them is 'a person', i.e. distinct from the others, in a unique and incommunicable way – by their proper and unique relationships. The Son is a person by sonship – which he is (he is his sonship); and the Father is so by the fatherhood which he, in his turn, is. The Son cannot share his sonship with the Father, nor can he share in the Father's fatherhood. So, as I believe St Teresa of Avila once remarked, not only is the unity of the three divine persons, in their total identity with the divine being or nature, infinitely more 'one' than the unity of a single human person (who is only too easily fragmented, physically and/or psychologically), but also they are infinitely more distinct from each other than any three or more human persons, who are always liable to lose their precarious individuality in some common neurosis or collective consciousness, or mass hysteria.

While I appreciate the point St Thomas makes and grant that it can help us in our appreciation of our Latin–English terminology, I still incline to the opinion that St Augustine's view has the greater pedagogical and catechetical value.

D.   THE APPROPRIATION OF NAMES TO THE PERSONS

Augustine uses the text of 1 Cor 1:24, 'Christ the power of God and the wisdom of God', to test the validity of his proposed theological axiom that the divine persons can be really distinguished from each other only by relationship names. He asks if we have to treat 'wisdom' and 'power' here as such relationship names (rather blurring, for the time being, the meaning of this expression), so that they are somehow proper to the Son (Christ) and not applicable to the Father or the Holy Spirit. In that case, presumably, it would mean that the Father is wise and powerful with the wisdom and power which the Son is.

But if that is so with 'power' and 'wisdom', why not with any other divine attribute that we have been assuming to be predicated of God absolutely and not relatively? Should we not then have to say that the Father is eternal with the eternity which the Son is, and so on, until we come to the point of saying he *is* with the being or 'is-ness' which the Son is – and even that he is God with the godhead which the Son is? Thus Augustine achieves the *reductio ad absurdum* of the hypothesis that such names as 'wisdom' should on the authority of scripture be treated as relationship names, proper to the Son. At times Augustine is something of an intellectual contortionist, and loves tying himself up inextricably – as it seems – in knots, for the pure pleasure of then extricating himself from the tangle. This is Houdini showmanship, which is – more seriously – often a valuable theological exercise. It is proper that theologians should be rigorous, more so than perhaps they often are, in testing their axioms, their hypotheses and above all their generalizations.

He eventually concludes that we can call the Son wisdom in the same way as we can call him God; which is to say that he is wisdom from wisdom just as he is God from God and light from light. Augustine then goes on to ask why the scriptures in fact nearly always refer to the Son when they personify wisdom, as is shown by the way they talk of wisdom as either begotten or created (cf. Prov 8:22, Sir 24:3, 8 etc.). As begotten or 'coming forth from the mouth of the Most High' it would be equated with the Son/*Logos*; as 'created' (Prov 8:22 according to the LXX, also Sir 24:8) it would be referred to the Word *made flesh*.

In other words, Augustine discusses the propriety of scripture's 'appropriating' the name 'wisdom' to the Son. In Chapter 4, E (p. 36 above) we already remarked on the wisdom background to John's use of the name *Logos* or Word for the Son. Augustine too makes the obvious connection between them and says that by the name 'Word' – which he regards as a true relationship name, peculiar to the Son – we mean 'born wisdom'. Once you accept the name 'Word' as suitable and proper for the second person – its propriety will emerge much more clearly when we come in Chapter 13 to discuss the image of God in man – then the appropriateness of also giving him the name wisdom is not very hard to see. It belongs to the same intelligence group of concepts.

But Augustine tries to make a further point, though not very clearly, as he would perhaps admit himself since he makes it mainly by asking tentative questions. 'Is it perhaps', he asks, 'to commend to us for our imitation the wisdom by imitation of which we are formed, that wisdom in those books [scripture] never speaks or has anything said about her but what presents her as born of God or made by him, although the Father too is wisdom itself?'[6] What he is suggesting is that the Son is our model: he is the perfect image to whom we as created and very remote images must try to conform, in order to reach God. Again, as we saw Augustine telling us in Chapter 9, C (pp. 87–88 above), the Son is the perfect and proper *mediator* between God (the Father, the Trinity) and man,[7] and this mediation essentially involves making the two parties between whom the mediator mediates *known* to each other – a work of intelligence/wisdom which must be received wisely by the two parties. In this case, of course, God being one of the parties is already wise, and indeed is wisdom, and knows the other party (us) perfectly. But it is the function of the Son precisely as Word – born wisdom – to reveal the Father to us, and it is our challenge and vocation to receive that revelation by imitating or responding to the revealing Wisdom. Once more, in admittedly a rather confused way, Augustine is suggesting why it is fittingly the Son and not either of the other two persons who was incarnate and became man.

Augustine limits himself to discussing 'wisdom' as an instance of appropriation. Aquinas generalizes the matter, discusses a few other instances, and says that it is a useful theological practice as it provides us with analogies which make it easier for us to grasp the distinctions between the persons. I am not too sure of the strength of his logic here: not a step I would care to put all my weight on. We have after all established that the three cannot be really distinguished from each other in terms of essential or non-relative names. So how such names can clarify distinctions made by relative names it is hard to see.

But perhaps the point is that we are not here dealing with a matter of strict logic. And so there are no strict or rigid rules for this kind of appropriation. It is always a question of what seems appropriate in any given context. Scripture and the tradition of patristic exegesis have indeed established an overwhelming bias in favour of appropriating wisdom to the Son. But there are one or two texts (Wis 7:22, 25; Jn 14:17, 26; 15:26), and indeed the very name of Paraclete or Advocate or Counsellor for the Holy Spirit, that would allow us to appropriate the name 'wisdom' to the third person of the Trinity.

And what about 'power'? In 1 Cor 1:24 Paul calls Christ 'the power of God'. But this name is certainly not usually appropriated to the Son. The Greek for it is *dunamis* and dynamism is something one might think more suitably appropriated to the Holy Spirit. That is certainly the sense imparted by the Pentecostal and other symbols used to refer to him – fire, mighty rushing wind, fountain of living water, finger of God casting out demons. St Thomas, without developing the point beyond a quaint and very unconvincing argument, thinks mistakenly that Augustine thinks it should be appropriated to the Father.[8] The truth is, as I said, that it is not a question of rigid logical rules. It is rather a matter for the disciplined poetic imagination. Any divine attribute can, according to the requirements of context and the control of such poetic discipline, be appropriated to any of the three persons.

E. THE APPROPRIATION OF 'GOD' AND 'LORD' IN THE NEW TESTAMENT

A point that the Fathers and scholastic theologians seem to have overlooked is that the New Testament, almost as a matter of course, appropriates the name 'God' to the Father and 'Lord' to the Son. Perhaps 'appropriates' is not quite the right word, since neither of these names signifies an attribute. St Thomas does consider the question whether they can stand for (*supponere*) the persons singly and decides that they can, as in the Nicene creed, for example, in the phrase 'God from God'.[9] But he leaves it at that and never seems to remark that in the New Testament 'God' nearly always stands for the Father (and most infrequently for the Son or Holy Spirit), and 'Lord' for Christ, the Son (almost always for the Son incarnate, Jesus Christ).

The value of noting this fact is that if we bear it in mind we are enabled to read the New Testament in a more explicitly trinitarian way, which is in my opinion a more authentic way. It also saves us from that faulty commonplace, which we tried to demolish in Chapter 10, D (pp. 95–97 above), that when we say 'Our Father' we are praying to God indistinctly, not to the Father personally. If 'God' usually stands for the Father, it is not likely that 'Father' is often going to stand for God. It is possible, it may even be the best way of reading such an Old Testament text as Isa 63:16, 'For thou art our Father, though Abraham does not know us and Israel does not acknowledge us; thou, O Lord, art our Father, our Redeemer from of old is thy name'. But it can surely never be necessary so to read 'Father' in the New Testament, in which through the revelation of the mystery we are invited into personal relationships with the three divine persons, Father, Son and Holy Spirit.

NOTES

1 *STh* Ia, 29, especially arts 3 and 4. Cf. also q. 40 (ET, vols 6 and 7).

2 *Ibid.* 29, 1 and 3 (ET, vol. 6). Boethius was an interesting man, a learned Catholic layman, a senator and aristocrat who lived from about 470 to 538, when the Roman empire had finally disintegrated in western Europe and Italy was ruled by the Ostrogoths. He was for many years a chief minister of the Ostrogothic king Theodoric, until eventually he was suspected of treason, thrown into prison, where he composed his most famous work, partly in verse, *The Consolation of Philosophy*, and finally put to death. As a cultivated man in a world that lay in ruins, he set himself in his writing to preserve what he could of the classical tradition of education. He was also a theologian, and the work St Thomas is here quoting was *De Duabus Naturis*, on the two natures of Christ (*PL* 64, 1343–44).

3 *STh* Ia, 29, 3 (ET, vol. 6).

4 Chapter 6, p. 63 above, note 17.

5 What I can scarcely do in the text perhaps I may attempt in a footnote. Counting in Sesotho after 10 is a very clumsy proceeding, so that for 26 you have to say 'two tens

and six units/digits'. Now the word for 'units' is *metso*. I wonder if you could not talk about the three *metso* in God. The word for 'who?' is *mang*, pl. *bomang*; perhaps you could talk about the three *bomang*. Anything but *baperesona*!

6   VII, iii, 4 (*PL* 42, 937).

7   By 'man' here is meant human beings in general, female as well as male – and this raises the problem of sexist language. I myself do not think that this problem can be solved, with reference to this syllable 'man', simply by decreeing that henceforth it will only be used for the male of the human species, and not for the species as such, or for its members irrespective of their sex. That seems to me to be not so much eliminating sexist language as doing violence to the English language, which over the course of centuries has given this syllable 'man' these two meanings: (a) the human being, irrespective of sex, equivalent to Latin *homo*, Greek *anthrōpos*, German *Mensch*, Dutch *mens*, Sesotho *motho*; (b) the male adult human being, equivalent to *vir*, *anēr*, *Mann*, *man* and *monna*.

But I agree that the campaign against sexist language very usefully compels us, especially if we are men, to be more careful in our use of the word 'man' in sense (a). Here and elsewhere in this book I will try to use it in this sense only when its reference is general (i.e. to all human beings and to each and any human being), and when no other word is readily available without objectionable clumsiness. I will not use it in this sense in the plural (where 'people' usually serves), or with the article.

8   *STh* Ia, 39, 7. The actual source for this appropriation is Hugh of St Victor, *De Sacramentis* I, 2, 8 (*PL* 176, 209). The appropriation rule proposed is that some attributes are appropriated to persons by way of similarity, like wisdom to the Word/Son, because it is an intellectual property; and others by way of dissimilarity or unlikeness (as when very tall men are nicknamed Shorty), and this is how power is appropriated to the Father, since human fathers are usually weak, from old age.

St Thomas' treatment of appropriation covers articles 7 and 8 of question 39 (ET, vol. 7).

9   *Ibid.* 39, 4.

12

The Procession of the
Holy Spirit

A. INTRODUCTORY STATEMENT OF THE CASE

As we have not yet examined the divine processions in detail, this may seem an odd place to discuss in particular the procession of the Holy Spirit. But as we have already seen, the processions of the divine persons are revealed by their missions, their being sent, and expressed by their mutual relationships. And so it is as a conclusion from his consideration of the divine missions and the relationships of the persons that Augustine establishes to his satisfaction the necessity of saying that the Holy Spirit proceeds from the Father *and from the Son*.

Now this, in the course of the following centuries, became the received orthodoxy in the Latin West. The extra word *Filioque* ('and from the Son') found its way into the Latin version of the Nicene creed first of all, probably, in Spain in the seventh century and finally, after long resistance on the part of the Popes, it was accepted at Rome in the beginning of the eleventh, in the year 1014.

It was this that really vexed the Greek East – the unilateral addition by one section of the Catholic Church of a phrase to a creed that had been finally determined by ecumenical Councils (Nicaea in 325 and Constantinople in 381) representing the universal Church. But the Greeks also found that they objected to the doctrine in itself – and they still do. So let us first look at Augustine's position on the matter; next trace its history briefly in the West; then consider first the dogmatic and secondly the canonical objections of the Orthodox.

B. AUGUSTINE'S DOCTRINE

In Chapter 9, C (p. 89 above) we saw Augustine affirming that the Holy Spirit proceeds from the Son as well as from the Father. He had just stated his understanding of the missions of the Son and Holy Spirit in time as revealing their eternal processions. So he implies – but curiously enough fails actually to state – that because the Holy Spirit is said to have been sent by the Son as well as by the Father (e.g. in Jn 15:26, 16:7), we can infer that he proceeds eternally from the Son as well. What he quotes are texts that call the Holy Spirit the Spirit of the Son (Gal 4:6) as well as the Spirit of the Father (Mt 10:20), and also Jn 20:22 where the risen Lord breathed on the disciples and said 'Receive the Holy Spirit'.

He returns to the matter a little more fully in book V, in which as we have seen he is preoccupied with names of relationship. His constant starting-point is that the Holy Spirit is both the Spirit of the Father and of the Son. He amplifies this into saying he is the gift of both the Father and the Son; both Father and Son give him. And this leads him to what is perhaps his favourite idea, that of the Holy Spirit as being 'a certain inexpressible communion/ fellowship/sharing/partnership/comradeship of the Father and the Son'. And he says this is perhaps why he is called 'Holy Spirit' (which as we have seen is not in itself a relationship name). 'For he is called properly what they are called in common, since the Father too is Spirit and the Son too is Spirit, the Father too is holy and the Son too is holy. In order therefore to signify the communion of them both by a name that suits them both, the gift of them both is called Holy Spirit.'[1]

For the Holy Spirit to be given is, in Augustine's understanding, for him to proceed (see the quotation in Chapter 9, C again, p. 89, from book IV) even before there is any creature for him to be given to. You could say he is the eternal, uncreated generosity of God. But he is given by both Father and Son; therefore he proceeds from them both. Both Father and Son are the source or origin (*principium*) of the Holy Spirit, not two origins but one. 'For just as Father and Son are one God, and in relation to creatures one creator and one Lord, so in relation to the Holy Spirit they are one origin; but of course in relation to creatures Father and Son and Holy Spirit are one origin, just as they are one creator and one Lord.'[2]

In book VI he enlarges a little on the Holy Spirit's being the communion, or 'something common' (*aliquid commune*) of Father and Son. He wonders whether we can call him 'the unity of both, or the holiness or the love of both, or their unity because their love, or their love because their holiness'.[3]

At this stage of the work Augustine says no more about the matter. But he returns to it in book XV in a few places, when he is summing up the whole course of his quest and critically reflecting on it. Three affirmations deserve to be quoted extensively. In the first he writes:

It is not for nothing that in this Triad only the Son is called the Word of God, and only the Holy Spirit is called the Gift of God, and only God the Father is said to be the one of whom the Word is born, and from whom the Holy Spirit originally (*principaliter*) proceeds. I added 'originally' because the Holy Spirit is found also to proceed from the Son. But this too was given the Son by the Father – not given to him when he already existed and did not yet have it; but whatever the Father gave his only-begotten Word, he gave by begetting him. He so begot him, then, that their common gift would proceed from him too, and the Holy Spirit would proceed from them both.[4]

The crucial word 'originally' here is the adverb from *principium* which I earlier translated 'source or origin'. It certainly somewhat qualifies what Augustine said in book V, namely that both Father and Son are the origin of the Holy Spirit – not two origins but one. Here we observe that while this is so, the Father is still 'originally (or principally) origin' and the Son is, so to say, 'derivatively origin' from which the Holy Spirit proceeds – or 'origin from origin'.

Later on he writes, on the analogy of the text 'As the Father has life in himself, so he has granted the Son also to have life in himself' (Jn 5:26):

We should understand that just as the Father has it in himself that the Holy Spirit should proceed from him, so he gave to the Son that the Holy Spirit should proceed from him too, and in both cases timelessly; and thus that to say the Holy Spirit proceeds from the Father means that his also proceeding from the Son is something which the Son has from the Father. If the Son has from the Father everything that he has, he clearly has from the Father that the Holy Spirit should proceed from him.[5]

Later in the same section he repeats 'But the Son is born of the Father and the Holy Spirit proceeds from the Father *principaliter*'. What he means by this, as is clear from the passage just quoted, is that the Father is the origin of the Holy Spirit and so is the Son, but the Son is 'origin from origin', whereas the Father is purely and simply origin.

Lastly, let me quote Augustine quoting himself in a sermon preached on the gospel of John (*Tr. in Joh. Evang.* 99, 8–9: *PL* 35, 1889-90):

It still remains of course extremely difficult to distinguish generation from procession in that co-eternal and equal and incorporeal and inexpressibly unchangeable trinity. So I hope it will suffice those who cannot stretch their minds any further over the matter to read what I said about it in a sermon preached to the Christian people, which I later had written down. Among other things I had been teaching from the evidence of the holy scriptures that the Holy Spirit proceeds from them both. I then went on to say:

So if the Holy Spirit proceeds from both the Father and the Son, why did the Son say *He proceeds from the Father* (Jn 15:26)? Why indeed, do you suppose, unless it was the way he was accustomed to refer even what was his very own to him from whom he had his very self? For example, that other thing he said, *My teaching is not mine but his who sent me* (Jn 7:16). If in this case we can accept that it is his teaching, which he says however is not his but the Father's, how much more should we accept in our case that the Holy Spirit proceeds also from him, seeing that he said *He proceeds from the Father* without also saying 'He does not proceed from me'? He from whom the Son has it that he is God – for he is God from God – is of course also the one from whom he has it that the Holy Spirit proceeds from him as well; and thus the Holy Spirit too has it from the Father that he should also proceed from the Son as he proceeds from the Father. Here we begin to see some sort of reason, as far as people like us can understand it, why the Holy Spirit is not said to be born but rather to proceed. For if he too were called Son, he would be called the Son of them both, which is the height of absurdity. The only two that anyone is the son of are father and mother. It is unthinkable we should imagine any such thing between God the Father and God the Son; for in any case a son of human beings does not proceed from his father and mother simultaneously, but when he proceeds from his father into his mother he does not then proceed from his mother, and when he proceeds from his mother into the light of day he does not then proceed from his father. But the Holy Spirit does not proceed from the Father into the Son and then proceed from the Son to sanctify the creature. He proceeds simultaneously from them both, even though the Father gave the Son that the Spirit should proceed from him as he does from himself. Nor can we say that the Holy Spirit is not life, while the Father is life and the Son is life. And thus just as the Father, while having life in himself, also gave the Son to have life in himself, so he gave him that life should proceed from him as it proceeds from himself.[6]

To summarize Augustine's teaching on the matter:

(1) He teaches that the Holy Spirit proceeds from the Son as well as from the Father, because he is convinced that this is, shall we say, exegetically necessary. He gets the doctrine from the New Testament – not in so many words, indeed, because it is not there in so many words, just as the consubstantiality and equality of the divine persons are not there in so many words – but by a process of genuine and rigorous exegesis. It is revealed by the Holy Spirit being sent by the Son as well as by the Father, by his being called the Spirit of the Son as well as of the Father, by his being given by the Son as well as by the Father.

(2) The Holy Spirit, as proceeding from both the Father and the Son, is 'a certain inexpressible communion or fellowship or comradeship or love between the Father and the Son'.

(3) He proceeds from them as from one origin or principle – i.e., if you like, they share his proceeding from them; and yet this does not (so to say) obliterate the distinction between them as persons, since he proceeds from the Father *principally*. That is to say, the Father is 'the origin of origins'; the Son is 'origin from origin', receiving from the Father (by being begotten of him) that he should be with the Father the origin of the Holy Spirit; and what is more, the Holy Spirit receives from the Father that he should proceed from the Son as well as from the Father.

(4) Thus the Father's 'monarchy' or 'principality', his being the *primus inter pares* of the divine persons, is in no way compromised by the doctrine, and the proper order – an order of origin – is preserved between the Father and the Son, as joint principle from which the Holy Spirit proceeds.

(5) It is to be noted (a) that nowhere does Augustine argue from relationship to procession, though this is a valid argument in my view which the scholastics will develop; (b) that his teaching is not, as it frequently is in other matters, polemically directed against anyone. It is spontaneously produced from his reading of the New Testament and the whole drift of his inquiry. The matter only became a polemical issue centuries after his death.

C. THE *FILIOQUE* IN THE SUBSEQUENT LATIN TRADITION[7]

The doctrine that the Holy Spirit proceeds both from the Father and the Son began to be proclaimed as official Church teaching in the Church of Spain, from the third to the sixteenth Councils of Toledo, i.e. from A.D. 589 to 693. At the third the Visigothic ruler of Spain, King Reccared, renounced the Arianism which the Goths had professed for two centuries and became a Catholic. So the confession of the so-called double procession (which was contained in his profession of faith) was clearly seen by the Spanish Church as a counter to the Arian heresy, which apparently regarded the Holy Spirit as a creature of the Son just as the Son according to this view is a creature of the Father. A heresy of the opposite sort was also prevalent in Spain at this time, Priscillianism, and against this sect (which seems to have been modalist in tendency) the real distinctness of the Holy Spirit had to be affirmed.

However, though these Councils of Toledo continued to repeat the doctrine in their professions of faith, they do not seem to have added the word to the Nicene-Constantinopolitan creed – or not at least by any official act. But their doctrine on the point was also shared by the Churches of France and England, and by the late eighth century and the time of Charlemagne the *Filioque* was firmly ensconced in the creed of these Churches, which had the custom, not shared either at Rome or in the East, of reciting it every Sunday at mass. Not having any very learned scholars in their ranks, they assumed the word had always been an integral part of the creed of Nicaea.

We are now poised on the threshold of the polemical era. But it began, not with polemics between East and West or Latins and Greeks – that is far too sweeping and simplistic a generalization. More accurately, there was a confrontation, in the main political, between the Franks and the Byzantines who deeply resented the pretensions of the Frankish kings to the imperial title (Charlemagne had himself crowned emperor by the Pope in Rome on Christmas Day, 800). The Franks were not sympathetic to the Byzantine Church's campaign against the Iconoclasts and in favour of the veneration of images.[8] Charlemagne summoned a Council of the Frankish Church at Frankfurt in 794 which insisted on the *Filioque*, and accused the Greeks of dropping it from the creed.

In none of this were the Franks supported by the Church of Rome. In 809, after another provincial Council at Aachen which insisted on the *Filioque*, Charlemagne asked the Pope, Leo III, to confirm the decision. The Pope confirmed the doctrine, but refused to add *Filioque* to the creed. Being rather better informed than the Frankish bishops, he knew it had been added by the Western Churches, not dropped by the Greeks. To make his position perfectly clear he had the creed inscribed on silver shields in Greek and in

Latin, in the traditional text without the *Filioque*, and hung up on either side of the high altar in St Peter's.

It was not until 1014 that the Roman Church gave in to the pressure of the emperor Henry II and introduced the creed into the mass – the creed of the Frankish Church which contained the *Filioque*. One is left wondering what had happened, or what then happened, to the silver shields of Leo III. Very probably they had been looted by Saracens or Vikings or other such coarse persons, which would just show the unwisdom of churchmen making a display of wealth, even with the best intentions. It must in fact be remembered that the Roman Church had been going through well over a century of dismal degradation, which it was only beginning to be dragged out of by the German emperors of the Bavarian dynasty. When the definitive break came between Rome and Constantinople forty years later in 1054, the difference over the *Filioque* was made one of the *casus belli* – by the Roman legate, the singularly undiplomatic Cardinal Humbert.

D. THE SCHOLASTIC STATEMENT OF THE DOCTRINE

St Thomas deals with the point in *STh* Ia, 36 (ET, vol. 7), a question of four articles which is about the name 'Holy Spirit'. In other words he is dealing with the procession of the Holy Spirit under the heading of 'Relationship', the names of the persons being relationship names, and not under the heading of 'Procession' (Ia, 27: ET, vol. 6), just as we are doing here, following the example of St Augustine.

He first repeats Augustine's doctrine of the Holy Spirit being the communion or 'sharing' of the other two persons – hence his 'common' name. But Thomas adds that the name 'Spirit' can suitably be seen as a relationship name in its own right (and not just by theological convention) if we take the word in its basic sense of 'breath', the term of the action of breathing forth (Latin *spirare*), just as 'Word' is the term of the action of uttering.

Then he goes on to make the point that if the Holy Spirit is distinguished from the Son, it can only be in terms of a relationship of opposition. He remarks that the Father has two relationships (which means, in God, that he *is* two relationships), one to the Son, fatherhood, another to the Holy Spirit, 'breathing forth' (*spiratio*), i.e. the relationship resulting from the act of breathing forth. Yet these two relationships do not constitute the Father as two persons, because they are not opposed to each other. One is opposed to *sonship*, the other to what we call *procession*, meaning here the relationship resulting from the act of proceeding. And these are not opposed to each other either. So by themselves they will not serve to distinguish the Son from the Holy Spirit. If we leave it at that, these will just be two names for one person

– the Priscillianist error corrected by the Councils of Toledo.

If therefore the Spirit's relationship of procession is to relate him, by a relationship of opposition, to the Son as well as to the Father, then it can only be by his proceeding from the Son as well as from the Father, and the Son will then share with the Father (*communio* again) the breathing forth of the Holy Spirit. He also adds another argument from the *nature* of the divine processions. But we are not ready for it yet since we have not yet examined the nature of these processions. For that, Augustine will make use of the divine image in man, and we shall follow him in that scrutiny in the next chapter.

St Thomas goes on to ask whether we can also say that the Holy Spirit proceeds from the Father through the Son, and decides that we can, with suitable qualifications. It is a way of stating, he says, what we have seen Augustine say, that the Son receives from the Father the power of being joint origin or 'breather-forth' of the Holy Spirit. It is also – a point of more practical significance – a kind of gesture of good will to the Greeks who allow the phrase 'through the Son', which is used by several of the Greek Fathers. Whether they will readily take it in the same sense is another matter.

Finally Thomas states that Father and Son are one principle or origin of the Holy Spirit, again following in Augustine's footsteps. They have to be, because as breathing forth the Holy Spirit they are not distinguished from each other by any relationship of opposition. But here (as I understand it) lies perhaps the major difficulty of the Greeks. If Father and Son are not distinguished from each other as origin of the Holy Spirit, it means that they are here being considered as one in the divine nature, essence, substance or *ousia*. And this means in effect that we are saying the Holy Spirit proceeds from the divine substance or *ousia*, not from the other two persons precisely as distinct persons or hypostases – and that once again upsets the whole applecart of the distinctness of the persons and their inter-personal relationships. We are at an *impasse*. For the Latin objection to the Greek position (denial of the *Filioque*) is that it results in fusing the persons of the Son and the Holy Spirit; the Greek objection to the Latin position (affirming the *Filioque* and adding 'as from one origin') is that it results in fusing the persons of the Father and the Son – de-hypostatizing or de-personalizing them.

How far Augustine was alive to this problem it is impossible to say. Perhaps it was niggling away at the back of his mind, and that is why in book XV, as we saw in section B above, he said distinctly that the Holy Spirit proceeds from the Father *principaliter*, principally or originally. Aquinas repeats this, but also offers a more subtle and satisfying solution. He says that the power (*virtus*) of breathing forth the Holy Spirit is one in the Father and the Son, and is indeed a power of the divine nature. But, he argues, this is no different from the case of the power of generating by which the Father begets the Son; this too is a power of the divine nature. For persons, he says – here reverting to the human analogy – indeed generate other persons, but by a power of their common nature. Otherwise, if individual persons generated in virtue of a property of their personal individuality, 'Socrates would generate Socrates', which is absurd.

But all the same, just as it is the person Socrates who generates another human being by a power of his own human nature, so it is the person of the Father, as the acting subject or hypostasis, who generates the person of the Son, and it is the persons of the Father and the Son, as the two acting subjects or hypostases, who breathe forth the Holy Spirit. So in fact Thomas qualifies the statement that Father and Son are one origin or principle of the Holy Spirit: as regards their power of breathing forth (*virtus spirativa*) they are one; but 'if we consider the subjects (*supposita*) of the breathing forth, here the Holy Spirit proceeds from Father and Son as several; for he proceeds from them as the Love uniting the two' (Ia, 36, 4 ad 1).

E. ORTHODOX OBJECTIONS TO THE *FILIOQUE*: THEOLOGICAL

In this section, as in C above, I am relying almost entirely on Yves Congar (*I Believe in the Holy Spirit*, III, pp. 72–78 especially). But before I relay to the reader his summary of the contemporary Orthodox position, I wish to warn against certain fashionable current generalizations – a habit of stereotyping Latin and Greek, Catholic and Orthodox theologies. The stereotype that concerns us here is one favoured by many scholars of great learning and distinction. Even Fr Congar, though he warns against taking it as a truth of universal validity, seems to me to make a little too much use of it. In my opinion it ought simply to be thrown into the theological dustbin.

It goes like this: in reflecting on the mystery of the Trinity the Latin or Catholic approach is to start from the unity of God, the one divine substance, and to proceed from that as a primary assumption to explain the trinity of three distinct persons. The Greek or Orthodox approach is to move in the opposite direction: to start from the three distinct hypostases or persons as the basic datum of the New Testament revelation, and from there to explain their unity in the one divine substance. So the tendency is for the Latins to be afraid above all of tritheism (saying there are three Gods), and in their less ecumenical moods to accuse the Greeks of this heresy, while what the Greeks dread is modalism (reducing the three hypostases to three modes or names or aspects of God), of which they have not at times been too scrupulous to accuse the Latins.

Now this may be more or less true of the *present* style of doing theology among Catholics and Orthodox respectively, although given the state of flux in contemporary Catholic theology, and the probable diversity of theological schools among the Greeks, I suspect there are so many exceptions that the rule disappears in vapour; and in any case I wonder if it helps ecumenical dialogue between the two sides to start with such stereotypes of oneself and particularly of the other party.

But where the stereotype is positively harmful to fruitful discussion is where it is read back into the past, as it nearly always is by the learned scholars just alluded to.[9] Such discussions are bound to involve quoting the authorities of the respective traditions, above all the Fathers. And to read them as automatically conforming to the stereotype is not only to do violence to history, but also to misread them from the start. It is rather like reading Tacitus on the Germans in the 'light' (or rather darkness) of anti-German prejudices and stereotypes about 'Huns' widely held in Britain after the two World Wars.

Augustine and Ambrose wrote in Latin, Athanasius and Basil and John Chrysostom in Greek. But to cast over them the shadow of this modern stereotype is simply to overlook the fact which was of paramount importance in the fourth and fifth centuries – that Athanasius stood in the Alexandrian or Egyptian tradition, Ambrose in the North Italian, Augustine in the African, Basil in the Cappadocian and John Chrysostom in the Syrian. It was these *local* traditions that counted then, not the later crude divide between Greek and Latin, East and West. They influenced each other, of course, but not just the Greek-speaking Churches on one side and the Latin on the other. Thus in the fourth century, after Nicaea, Athanasius of Alexandria found his staunchest support in Rome and Gaul, and his severest opposition from some of the Eastern, Greek Churches. It was the Syrians and Cappadocians who were for a long time most suspicious of the term *homoousion* (consubstantial) because it seemed to them to compromise the reality of the three hypostases.

So this stereotype does not in the least help, in my view, to explain Augustine's development of the doctrine of the procession of the Holy Spirit from the Son as well as from the Father, nor the Greek opposition to it – which was not in fact voiced until the time of the Patriarch Photius about 850, over four hundred years later.

To represent the modern Orthodox position Congar cites three theologians, all Russians as a matter of fact: Vladimir Lossky, Sergey Bulgakov, and Paul Evdokimov. Of these Lossky is the most critically opposed to the Latin doctrine and Bulgakov the one who is most sympathetic to it.

One objection is that the Latin doctrine represents a rationalization of the mystery – an attempt to push rational speculation on divine matters much further than it can legitimately go. While it has certainly been a vice of much ultra-scholastic Latin theology to pursue rational speculation almost as an end in itself, with scarcely any reference to the biblical revelation and the patristic tradition, I do not think this objection can fairly be made to the reflections of Augustine or even Thomas Aquinas, who were both steeped in the tradition of the Church as it flows from the scriptures, and well aware of the limits of reason in exploring divine mysteries. In any case, the Latin doctrine of the procession of the Holy Spirit from the Father and from the Son is not offered as a rational *explanation* of the mystery, but as part of the statement of the mystery, being no more essentially rationalistic than the Greek statement of the Holy Spirit's procession from the Father alone.

A second objection, of more substance, which we have glanced at already, is that the procession of the Holy Spirit from the other two persons as from one origin, by one common breathing forth (*communis spiratio*), merges them in the divine essence or substance, and thus has the third person proceeding not in fact from the other two persons but from the one divine substance – in which of course the Holy Spirit shares. We saw in the last section how St Thomas meets the difficulty and how Augustine and he both have the Holy Spirit proceeding *principaliter* from the Father.

Perhaps the fundamental Orthodox case, as far as I can grasp it, is that it is a mistake to think of the persons as constituted by their relationships of origin. Their distinctness as hypostases is prior to their relationships. Somehow, both the distinctness and the unity of the three hypostases are derived from the first person, the Father, who is the 'monarch' (meaning literally in this case 'the sole beginning') and the only cause of divinity, which he communicates wholly to the Son and the Holy Spirit.

Furthermore, the inter-personal relationships of the three are much fuller than the four relationships of origin we have seen analysed in the scholastic Latin tradition. There is an eternal inter-communication of wisdom and love and glory between the three which the Greeks term *perichōrēsis* and which is translated by the Latins as 'circumincession'. The Greek word in its secular use means a revolving or a revolution – the revolution of a wheel. It conjures up the rather lovely picture of an eternal divine round dance, and indeed a pun in this sense is possible in Greek, where the word for 'dance round' or 'dance in a ring' is *perichoreuō*, with a short *o* in the middle. While Western theology has not explicitly made much of this concept, Augustine in fact touches on it when he is working out the structure of the trinitarian image in man;[10] and there is certainly space for it, as a subject of mystical contemplation, in the Latin framework. It is in terms of this *perichōrēsis* that many modern Orthodox theologians will explain the statements of several Greek Fathers that the Holy Spirit proceeds from the Father through the Son. We have seen St Thomas discussing this expression.

The Council of Florence (1438), which achieved an abortive union between the Greek and Latin Churches that was repudiated by the Greeks within a few years, in fact said that the expression 'through the Son' was acceptable provided it was interpreted as meaning the same as the Latin *Filioque*. That was hardly ecumenical – no one was very good at ecumenism in those days! But I personally do not see why the Orthodox should not allow us to treat 'through the Son' as equivalent to *Filioque* in the way Aquinas suggested – provided we Catholics allow them to explain *Filioque* as equivalent to 'through the Son' in the sense they understand that expression. This is in fact what Sergey Bulgakov suggests.

F.   ORTHODOX OBJECTIONS TO THE *FILIOQUE*: CANONICAL

At its simplest the objection is that the Latins had no right unilaterally to add to a creed put out by an ecumenical Council (the second, Constantinople, 381) in the name of the whole Catholic Church, especially as the next Council (Ephesus, 431) expressly forbade the making of any further creeds or 'symbols', as they were called in Greek and ecclesiastical Latin.

If insisted on in a simplistic kind of way, this objection has always struck me as a piece of unrealistic legalism, like the laws of the Medes and Persians (Est 1:19, Dan 6:8, 12). Times, after all, change. The Church's formulation of doctrine developed strongly up to 381 and 431, and it is impossible that such development should be halted there. In fact, as we have seen, the *Filioque* was not 'added' to the creed in an act of deliberate decision. To recapitulate briefly, the *doctrine* of it, following Augustine, was formulated in several councils of the Spanish Church at Toledo, and then, since the French and English Churches in particular developed the liturgical custom of chanting the Nicene creed at mass, the word crept in among them spontaneously, in such a way that in all innocence they thought it had always been there, and when a quarrel arose with the Greeks over something else, the Franks accused the Greeks of dropping the word from the creed. To which baseless charge the Greeks naturally enough responded by the counter-accusation of unlawful addition. We have seen how the Roman Church resisted the addition in the early ninth century, only to give in to it in a moment of weakness two hundred years later in 1014.

But it is worth investigating the complexities of the matter a little further. The creed we are discussing is usually called the Nicene creed, affirmed at the Council of Nicaea in 325. But that creed, after affirming the faith in one God the Father, and one Lord Jesus Christ and his consubstantiality with the Father, concludes with the bald statement 'and in the Holy Spirit' – full stop.

It was, as we have seen, the Council of Constantinople in 381 which elaborated the formula of faith in the Holy Spirit to include, among other things, the phrase 'who proceeds from the Father'. *But* the Council of

Constantinople was not in fact convened, like that of Nicaea, as an ecumenical Council. No Western bishops were invited to it. It was convened as a Council of the East. To be sure, it came eventually to be recognized in the West as well as in the East as an ecumenical Council, and hence its creed came to be accepted as universally binding on all Christians. But this certainly had not happened by the time of the Council of Chalcedon (the fourth ecumenical Council in our present reckoning) in 451. For that Council in its 28th canon reaffirmed a decision of Constantinople in 381 which gave the Church of Constantinople, as the new Rome, precedence over that of Alexandria and second place after the Church of 'old Rome'. But the bishop of old Rome in 451, the redoubtable Leo the Great, refused to ratify this canon, since he knew nothing about the precedent of Constantinople in 381 and saw canon 28 of Chalcedon as an infringement of the rights of Alexandria which had been solemnly affirmed by the only ecumenical Council he recognized – that of Nicaea.

It is true that in the course of the next few centuries the Roman Church came to acknowledge the right of Constantinople to the second place, and by the same process of 'creeping canonicity' to accept Constantinople 381 as the second ecumenical Council. This offers an interesting parallel to the way it came to accept the *Filioque*. The point I am making is that 'creeping canonicity' – in this case the 'creeping canonization' of Constantinople 381 as the second ecumenical Council – cannot be made the grounds of severe canonical censures about breaking ecclesiastical law.

The point of substance in this canonical objection of the Orthodox seems to me to be reduced to this: a clause – the *Filioque* – added to the creed by one section of the *oikumenē*, the universal Church, namely by the Latin Churches, without the sanction of another ecumenical Council cannot be regarded as binding on the universal Church. Therefore the Orthodox cannot be obliged by the Catholics to add the *Filioque* to their text of the creed. But I do not think the Catholics (apart from some ignorant Franks more than a thousand years ago, and the more culpably ignorant Cardinal Humbert in 1054) have ever required them to do so. They certainly make no such demand now.

On the other hand, some Orthodox theologians at least *are* putting pressure on Western Churches to drop the *Filioque* on the grounds that it has been added uncanonically. That I indeed object to as legalism – as legalism tinged with a flavour of ecclesiastical imperialism. It does not strike me as very ecumenical in spirit. If it were dropped, it would inevitably give the impression to the ordinary faithful that the *doctrine* was being admitted to be erroneous. Some Orthodox theologians, like Lossky, think it is. But no Catholic theologian thinks it is, nor in my view could any begin arguing that it is without repudiating a whole, and *good*, strand of our tradition. Such repudiations, surely, are not called for in genuine ecumenical dialogue. There are many points of ecclesiastical practice, especially the practical interpretation of the doctrine of Roman or papal primacy, that I as a *Catholic* would like to have the Holy See gracefully surrender in the interests of Christian unity and reconciliation. But the *Filioque* is certainly not one of them.

I would ask the Orthodox, then, to have the magnanimity to allow us to keep the *Filioque*, while we in the same spirit accept their not including it, and indeed their hesitation about the doctrine it expresses. We must certainly not accuse them of heresy for not accepting the doctrine, but neither should they accuse us of heresy for holding it.

NOTES

1 V, xi, 12 (*PL* 42, 919).

2 V, xiv, 15 (*ibid.* 921).

3 VI, v, 7 (*ibid.* 928).

4 XV, xvii, 29 (*ibid.* 1081).

5 XV, xxvi, 47 (*ibid.* 1094).

6 XV, xxvii, 48 (*ibid.* 1095–96).

7 For this section I am indebted to Yves Congar OP, *I Believe in the Holy Spirit* (London/New York, 1983), III, pp. 49–53. He quotes his own authorities and sources in his footnotes. The only ones I will pick out here are H. B. Swete, *On the History of the Doctrine of the Procession of the Holy Spirit* (Cambridge, 1876), and three references Congar gives to Migne's *Patrologia Latina* for Rome's refusal to include the *Filioque* in 809, and its acceptance of it in 1014: *Acta Collationis Romanae, descripta a Smaragdo Abbate Sancti Micahelis* (*PL* 102, 971–976) describes Leo III's conversation with Charlemagne's envoys and his refusal to add the *Filioque*. The *Historia de Vitis Pontificum* by Anastasius Bibliothecarius, no. 410 (*PL* 128, 1237–38) relates how Leo had the creed inscribed on two silver shields (not scrolls as in the English edition of Congar's book), but does not mention the omission of the word *Filioque*; this is to be inferred from the previous reference. The *Libellus de quibusdam rebus ad Missae Officium Pertinentibus* of a certain Berno, ch. 2 (*PL* 142, 1060–61 – in Congar wrongly given as 1061–62) describes how the emperor Henry insisted on the creed being sung at mass. Again it makes no reference to the inclusion of *Filioque*, but this too is a certain historical inference.

8 Iconoclasm was a puritan movement that started among the Christians of Asia Minor early in the eighth century. Prompted possibly by the example of the Moslems, with whom they were engaged in ceaseless warfare on the Syrian frontier, they declared war on the use of images, or icons, in Christian worship. Their cause was taken up by the dynasty of Isaurian emperors in that century, whose origins were in that part of the Byzantine Empire. Iconoclasm – which means 'Image-breaking' – was condemned by the second Council of Nicaea in 787, but the battle against it was not finally won until the ninth century. It seems that at this period the cult of the images of Christ, our Lady and the saints had not developed so far in the Latin Churches of the West. Their piety was sustained much more by the veneration of relics.

9 By G. L. Prestige, for example, in *God in Patristic Thought*.

10 e.g. IX, v, 8(*PL* 42, 965), where Augustine is discussing his preliminary image-trinity
of mind, its self-knowledge and its self-love, and points out that each of these three
entities is not only in itself but also in the other two: 'How they are all in all of them
we have already shown above; it is when the mind loves all itself and knows all itself
and knows all its love and loves all its knowledge, when these three are complete with
reference to themselves. In a wonderful way therefore these three are inseparable from
each other, and yet each one is substance and all together they are one substance or
being, while they are also posited with reference to one another'. The mutual co-
inherence of the trio in the image can also be applied to the divine three.

Again, in X, xi, 18 (*PL* 42, 983–984), when he has refined his image to the three
mental acts of self-memory, self-understanding and self-willing, he spells out at great
length the mutual co-inherence of these three, in a manner that can easily be transferred
to the divine persons.

13
The Image of God: Illustrating the Divine Processions: books VIII–X

A. SETTING THE CONTEXT

We have seen that the method Augustine has been following up to the end of book VII has been to begin with faith and go on to understanding. First he establishes the faith (i.e. faith in the Father, Son and Holy Spirit, three in one God) in books I–IV, basing himself on the authority of scripture; and then he goes on in books V–VII to defend this faith by rational argument against the Arians.

But he is not at all satisfied that this process so far has led us to an *understanding* of the mystery. It has certainly enabled us to state the mystery with more precision – a precision greatly refined by the scholastics – and so to clarify our use of words, like relationship names for example, in talking about the Trinity. But all this, though necessary and to some minds fascinating (dangerously fascinating in the opinion of people like the Orthodox theologian Vladimir Lossky), still does not get us any deeper into the heart of the mystery. It does not enable us to *see*; and that is what Augustine is all the time seeking, well aware of course that he will never achieve the goal in this life.

So in the prologue to book VIII he declares his intention of discussing the matter (i.e. the mystery of the Trinity) all over again, but 'in a more inward manner', a typically Augustinian phrase.[1] He wants to get beneath the words and names we have been playing with so far to the realities they refer to or signify. He is going to have to revise, or indeed reverse, his method.

In the middle of the book, therefore (which is the middle of the whole work – there is a definite artistry in the somewhat baroque manner in which he introduces and intertwines his key notions), he raises the problem of faith. It is no longer enough to say, 'Believe first, proceed to understanding second'. For not only have we come to realize that we have not proceeded to understanding in any profound sense; we have come up against the crucial problem of the very possibility of belief, belief, that is to say, in God, and especially in God as three, Father, Son and Holy Spirit.

An axiom Augustine repeats again and again is that you cannot love what you do not know. He has just been talking about loving God and asking himself how we can love God when by common consent we do not know him or see him. A tentative answer is that although we do not in the strict sense know God, we still have that kind of declension of knowledge which we call faith or belief, and perhaps it is enough to believe in God in order to be able to love him. But then, Augustine points out, even believing things implies *some* anterior knowledge about what is believed. If I exhort you to believe the statement *'Na ke khosi qhobosheaneng* you will very naturally ask me what it means (unless you already know a little Sesotho). And in fact, however willing you may be to believe it because you trust me, you will be quite unable to do so – or to disbelieve it either – until you know what it means. When I tell you that it means, more or less, 'I'm the king of the castle', you will no doubt decide that you cannot either believe or disbelieve it anyway, except in a context of fiction – or make-believe.

Now the trouble with being asked to believe in God, and above all to believe that God is three persons, one God, is that we do not know what it means, and there is no one around, not even God, who can tell us what it means in any human language that human beings could ever speak. God in himself (or in themselves) is (are, was, were, will be, has/have been, shall have been etc.) absolutely incommensurate with any possible human experience in space and time. Augustine says at some length what Thomas Aquinas puts in a nutshell: *Deus non est in genere*, God is not in any class or category.[2] But when we believe anything someone tells us, e.g. that Tokyo is the capital of Japan, pop. 8,000,000, we *know* what we believe because we know the categories or classes of things, the *genera* and *species* in the language of Augustine and Thomas, which the statement refers to. But, once more, there are no such classes or categories in terms of which we may believe whatever anyone, even God, may tell us about God.

Where Aquinas solves the problem, basically, by saying that we can know God, or rather know of God – extremely imperfectly, of course – in the way that we know of a cause through its effects, by what you could call an *objective* procedure, Augustine solves it more *subjectively* by saying we can know him – again very imperfectly – through our inner awareness of certain standards or values by which we make our judgements about things. He gives the example of justice. Why do I love the apostle Paul? he asks. Because I believe he was a just man. But how do I know what that means, or what justice is, seeing that I am not just myself? Even more, how can I love justice, in Paul or in itself, when I am not just myself? It is because my mind is in touch, inwardly and above itself, with the eternally true 'idea of justice'. The line of thought is wholly Platonic, but with a specifically Christian twist to it. For this and similar 'ideas' or truths, moral or mathematical, are for Augustine not real subsistent forms as they seem to have been for Plato, but 'ideas in the mind of God', or refractions of that one simple, infinite, eternal value/truth which God is. So again, as with Aquinas, we can be said to know God as a cause known through its effects; but this time the effects are ideas subjectively perceived rather than the material world objectively observed, and the causality is exemplar rather than efficient.

Augustine chooses justice to illustrate his argument because it concretizes or specifies together the two cardinal ideas of the true and the good. Our minds are capable of discerning, and valuing *truth*, and they constantly make judgements about the *goodness* of things. But God is the ultimate truth and the ultimate good; to be more precise, what we mean by the word 'God' is, *inter alia*, the ultimate truth and the ultimate good. So again, we have some access to God, as to the exemplar through the exemplified, through its refracted *images*.

B.   CONSTRUCTING THE IMAGE IN THE HUMAN MIND

For, of course, all the time Augustine has had in mind the use which he is going to make of the image in his exploration of the divine mystery. He has already remarked that we have absolutely no knowledge of any general categories or classes which might enable us to believe in the Trinity – which is not, he rather drily remarks, a question of the number 3, which we can experience any time we like by flashing three fingers.

Nor do we find any hint of trinity in these eternal ideas of the true and the good to which he has drawn our attention. But wait a minute; truth is the object of knowledge and the good is the object of love. And concentrating on love at the end of book VIII – for we have scriptural authority for saying 'God is love' (1 Jn 4:8, 16) – he points out that in love we do have a trio, of lover, belovèd and love itself. This is his starting point for the construction of the psychological, or more accurately the mental, trinity in books IX and X.

'Construction' is an accurate word for his enterprise. The word 'model' is fashionable nowadays when people are talking about scientific or philosophical method. And the image of God in man is precisely the model (models are after all images of a kind, and images models) through which or in which Augustine intends to achieve what understanding he may of the mystery of the Trinity. And models are modelled or constructed. The operation of modelling or construction in this case is one of selection, not of pure invention. Augustine is authorized by scripture to believe that man is made in

God's image. God is Trinity, Father, Son and Holy Spirit; so we can reasonably expect to find some reflection of the trinitarian exemplar in the constitution of man.

But man has a constitution of enormous complexity and variety. So within the multifarious elements that go to make man man, me me and you you, Augustine quite openly selects those which suit his purpose. As we have seen, he chooses to start with the love trio just mentioned. But he immediately reduces it to a duo. Where it is a case of loving oneself, lover and belovèd are identical. Since we want a model of what Rahner calls the immanent and we have been calling the transcendent Trinity[3] – i.e. of God the three persons in himself/themselves, as distinct from God in his/their economic manifestations and activities, we will naturally look for it in man-in-himself, or the self-in-itself, and in its relations to others. That is why he takes the case of loving oneself.

Almost immediately he makes yet another selection and decides that instead of getting lost in the whole vast complexity of human love, even of human self-love, with its medley of passion and feeling and emotional and physical attraction and sex, he is going to consider only 'the mind (mens) loving itself'. Notice, incidentally, he chooses mind and not soul as the location for his model of the Trinity. And do not jump to the conclusion that he is thereby revealing his indifference to or contempt of the body. Not at all. He will bring our bodily life, i.e. sensation and imagination, into his exploration in book XI, and discuss our mental concern for and relations with the material world, clearly through our bodies, in book XII. But to rid our minds of preconceptions about a dualist (body–soul) versus a unitary (living organism) concept of man, which are in fact strictly irrelevant to what Augustine is doing in this section of the De Trinitate, let me translate his word mens, which is properly rendered 'mind', by 'self'.

So we have, to return to his model, first stage, the self loving itself. Three have been reduced to two: the self, loving and loved, and its love. But we immediately expand it to three again on the strength of our truism that you cannot love what you do not know. So if the self loves itself, this implies that it first knows itself. And here we have the first rough sketch of the image of the Trinity in man – self, knowledge and love (mens, notitia, amor).

Having begun with love (amor), Augustine now concentrates on knowledge (notitia). He is going to fashion it, of course, into a representation of the Logos/Word, and so he gives the name verbum mentis, 'mental word', to the concept or notion in which our actual knowledge of a thing finds expression. He goes on to describe this mental word as 'loved knowledge', amata notitia. But surely we can know things which we hate? Yes; but our knowledge of them is 'that they are hateful', and why so. In other words the verbum mentis, the mental word, is not just a concept in the sense of a kind of mental picture of the thing known and loved or hated, but it is a *true judgement* about the thing known. This is the *amata notitia*. Knowledge is perfected in a judgement.

This mental word can properly be seen as the offspring (*proles*) of the mind, which is thus its parent (*parens*). This is, of course, a very widespread analogy, though I do not know if it is common to all cultures and languages. But at least in the European tradition we talk about *concepts*, and *conceiving* ideas, and of writers or artists being *prolific*, and *in travail* with some great work. It is true this is the language of female rather than male generation, and it is at least to be noted that Augustine in talking of the image never speaks of father and son and begetting, but always of parent and offspring and bringing forth.[4] He justifies the analogy on the grounds that the mental word in which we know something is a true likeness or image of the thing known. So, particularly when we are talking about knowledge of self, the self's knowledge of self is expressed in a mental word of self (a judgement 'that I am I') which is a complete and equal likeness of the self that brings it forth. And consequent upon this 'word' of self-knowledge there spontaneously follows the love of self and of knowledge of self, a pleasure or delight in 'my being myself and knowing myself as myself'. And these three are equal and mutually comprehensive and co-inherent.[5]

But this is only a preliminary draft of the image. It is still asymmetrical to the divine exemplar of Father, Son and Holy Spirit, three persons, one God. For all those three are relationship names, as distinct from 'God' which is a substance name. But in this draft of the image, the trio of mind/self, knowledge and love, only 'love' and 'knowledge' signify relationships – between knower and known, lover and belovèd – while 'mind/self' (*mens*) signifies substance, a thing-in-itself. This trio thus represents, not Father, Son and Holy Spirit but God, Son and Holy Spirit.

At the end of book X Augustine resolves this trio into his complete model, the three mental acts, in one mind, of remembering self, understanding self and willing self, which we abbreviate for convenience to memory, understanding and will; but we must *always* bear in mind that we are talking of three mental acts, not three faculties or powers of the soul.

The process by which he gets to this final resolution is by probing more deeply the matter of self knowing self. As we shall see in the next chapter, Augustine unfolds his model of the image in a distinctly moralizing manner. The image of God is more what we ought to be and are under an obligation to become (by moral acts), than simply what we are. And so he asks himself why we are given the command 'Know thyself',[6] when it would seem that the self (mind) cannot not know itself. If mind can know anything, surely it must know itself simply by being itself, by being as it were transparently or luminously present to itself.

But as the result of sin – the fall – the human mind or self is first distracted from self-knowledge by excessive curiosity and also anxious concern for material things, which distract it not only from knowledge of self but even more from knowledge of God. Think of the thorns in the parable of the sower, Mk 4:7, 18–19. Next as a consequence it is self-deceived about itself because it begins to confuse itself with the images of these things, which as Augustine puts it rather graphically, it has glued to itself in its memory.

So, he concludes, the command 'Know thyself' really means 'Think about yourself' (cogitare) so as to discern self from not-self. Any options you may have about what the self (mind) is, according to various philosophies, materialist, idealist, dualist, monist – and also, we should add today, according to various schools of psychology – put them aside and let the mind/self stick to what it knows with incontrovertible certainty about itself. It may be of the opinion that it consists of one of the elements or is the by-product of organic chemistry, or is a spiritual substance; but it knows that it is, that it lives, and that it understands or is conscious. Now these three, to be, to live, to be conscious – or at least the first two – are substance acts, not relationship ones. So Augustine hunts around briefly for some other things, of which of course there are several, that the mind/self knows about itself, and from them selects his final trio: that it remembers, understands and wills.

Again, to make the image 'immanent' or self-contained (like its divine exemplar) we concentrate on the reflexive acts of remembering self, understanding self and willing self. The question immediately arises, what can be meant by remembering oneself. Incidentally, I think that here one can observe the connection between 'mind' (mens) of the first draft trinity and memory (memoria) of this second trio in the completed model, by noticing the way we can use the verb 'to mind', first in Scots English as meaning 'to remember', as in 'I mind the day I first met you', and secondly in the reflexive 'to mind oneself', as meaning 'to take care by being aware or paying attention to oneself'. So Augustine says, quoting Virgil as his linguistic authority,[7] that you can remember yourself by the same token that you can forget yourself – which is something we are constantly doing.

Self-memory in fact means for him the mind's sheer presence to itself; the verbal opposite of absence of mind or absentmindedness. But the fact is that the mind is always present to itself as long as it is mind. So in a sense it is always remembering itself. It is not, however, always thinking about itself. So until it is doing so, its self-memory is quiescent, or in the Aristotelian language of the scholastics which Augustine would have profited from knowing, it is only potentially remembering itself.

As soon, though, as it thinks about itself (cogitare) its self-memory becomes actual, and in the act of thought (cogitatio) it begets or brings forth a mental word of self-understanding. And from this act of self-memory producing the mental word of self-understanding there spontaneously proceeds the act of self-appreciation or love or enjoyment which Augustine calls rather colourlessly self-willing. Why in his second trio he substituted 'will' for 'love' I do not really understand. It must have something to do with the nuances of the words in Latin.

But now the problem is: is there any *real* difference between remembering self and understanding self? Are they not just two names for, two aspects of, the same mental act of self-knowledge? Perhaps this difficulty of distinguishing really, and not merely nominally, between these two elements of the image reflects a difficulty, that is met more than once in the history of Christian doctrine, of distinguishing really in the divine exemplar between the Father and the Son. We saw in the last chapter how perhaps the most substantial Orthodox objection to the Catholic/Western doctrine of the procession of the Holy Spirit from the Father and the Son is that it confounds the distinction between these two persons.

Augustine deals with the problem – of the difference in the image between self-memory and self-understanding – by the use of lesser or more external trinities in the field of human perception. We are looking at the image in the mind because we are unable to look directly at God the Trinity – one of the key background texts to the whole enterprise is 1 Cor 13:12, 'For now we see in a mirror dimly [i.e. we see a vague image], but then [it will be] face to face'. And now, because we cannot make the discernment we require even when we look at the mental image (since it is very hard for mind to focus on mind), we turn to certain declensions from pure mental activity in what Augustine calls the outer man – rather distorting Pauline language by using it in a Platonic frame of reference. What he means is the sense level of consciousness or perception.[8]

He discerns lesser trinities, first in the sphere of visual perception (the sense of sight standing in for all the senses), and then in the sphere of sense memory and imagination – memory here in its ordinary sense of recalling past experience. Thus in the matter of seeing things we have the trio of the object seen, its image on the retina or in the sense of sight, and the will joining the two together, keeping me looking at what I want to look at. The difference between the sense object and its image in the sense of sight (the two members of the trio which correspond to self-memory and self-understanding in the mental image) is obvious. But the analogy is extremely imperfect since the trio are so disparate in nature, with no unity of substance at all.

But when we move further inward – such a typically Augustinian movement – to the sphere of recollective perception, the analogy becomes more telling. I have experienced and learnt all sorts of things during my life, but I am not actually thinking about them most of the time, and it is only possible, roughly speaking, to think of one thing at a time – at least effectively. Of all the things I have learnt or known and have not completely forgotten, the images are stored in my memory. But when I am not thinking about them, these images are not forming my actual consciousness (what Augustine calls the *acies animi*, the sharp point, the focus perhaps of the mind). When I call one of them to mind and start thinking, say, about the Houses of Parliament, then the image of the Houses of Parliament forms my actual consciousness. And while it is doing so, I cannot perceive any real difference between what is forming my actual consciousness and what is stored in my memory. Yet there must be a real distinction, because one of these vanishes when I stop thinking about the Houses of Parliament in order to think about fish and chips for supper, and the other remains. When I am concentrating my attention on fish and chips, it does not mean that the Houses of Parliament are totally erased from my memory. Not at all. The remembered image remains, always ready to produce again the image that forms my actual consciousness (as a kind of offspring) when I decide, by an act of will 'joining the two together', to turn my attention once more to the Houses of Parliament.

Now you could of course give accounts and explanations of these elementary psychic acts, using quite a different sort of language which would make them totally irrelevant to Augustine's case. But we must remember he is not really trying to prove anything; certainly not to prove any psychological theory of his. He is engaged on an elaborate exercise of illustration, of discernment – you might even say of crystal-gazing: to see in the crystal of the divine image in man some refracted reflection of the divine exemplar, and to examine lesser crystal globes in order to tease out some puzzling obscurity in the master image. And in his own terms I think he succeeds; succeeds in building up a useful series of analogies, imperfect, limping, lame as analogies always are. But to be lame and still limp along is by no means the same as being paralytic and getting nowhere.

C. WHAT WE LEARN FROM THE IMAGE ABOUT THE DIVINE PROCESSIONS

Let us pause for a moment and recollect what it is we are trying to understand. It is the faith we state in the Nicene creed: 'I believe in one God the Father almighty . . . and in one Lord Jesus Christ, his only-begotten Son, born of the Father before all ages, . . . true God from true God, begotten not made . . . ; and in the Holy Spirit . . . who proceeds from the Father and the Son, who with the Father and the Son is equally adored and glorified . . .'. We are trying to understand the eternal birth or generation of the Son from the Father and the eternal procession of the Holy Spirit from the Father and the Son.

To start with the first procession: the language of faith, taken straight from the New Testament, is consistently and persistently about the Father begetting the Son and the Son being begotten by or born of the Father. What makes it hard to understand is its grossness. By that I do not mean its inescapable sexual basis. That need not shock us any more than we saw it shocking Augustine in the last chapter (p. 111 above). It is that such language is surely inapplicable to God in any literal sense because of its material and temporal implications. That is what rules out sex in God. God the Father cannot be the Father of God the Son in the same way as Jack the father is the father of Jim the son, because the divine persons are not material biological organisms living in time.

So why does scripture apply such language to God at all? St Thomas somewhere remarks that the grosser the figure or metaphor we use to talk about God with the better, because then we are in no danger of taking it literally or univocally.[9] Not that the names 'Father' and 'Son' for the first two persons of the Trinity are mere metaphors. But 'literal meaning' is not the only contrary to 'metaphorical meaning'. God is *properly* called Father and Son, not improperly or metaphorically as he is called Rock or Warrior. But he is so called analogically, and the primary point of these names is to insist on the distinguishing personal relationships of Father and Son.

So how does the Son's being born of the Father differ from Jim's being born of Jack? Augustine tells us, taking his original cue from Jn 1:1–18, that it is something like a thought springing from a memory, more precisely like a thought or flash (mental *word*) of self-understanding springing from an act of self-memory. And here the very difficulty of distinguishing between remembering self and understanding self is enlightening. As soon as self remembers itself, it understands itself. It is impossible (logically so) to remember self without understanding self. Granted *a priori* that they are really distinct acts, the act of understanding self springs simultaneously from the act of remembering self. And so we can begin to see what it means to say that the Son is *eternally* begotten of the Father, or born of the Father before all ages. The Father *cannot* exist before or without the Son, as Jack can and must exist before and without Jim. The reason is that what makes the Father the Father is his begetting the Son, just as what makes an *act* of self-memory an act of self-memory is its issuing in the mental word of an act of self-understanding.

But the analogy shows us something more about the divine exemplar. It shows us self-memory as precisely the first and most profound of the acts of self or mind, so that when the mind is not actually engaged in remembering itself and hence understanding and willing itself, self-memory still remains latent or potential, and the other acts, no longer being there as acts, so to say subside into the source of them both, memory.

Now in God there is no back and forth movement from potential to actual activity and back; he/they is/are pure unchanging actuality. The analogy of the image certainly limps. But what it shows us through its refraction of the simple divine light – and I think that this is a point of the Greek Orthodox theology – is that while the Father cannot be Father before and without the Son (he is eternally Father by eternally begetting the Son), still he is not to be defined (so to say) purely and simply with reference to the Son whose Father he is. Self-memory cannot be actuated without thereby giving birth to self-understanding, and both are terms of relationship. And yet you do not *define* memory, not even self-memory, as that which gives rise to understanding. It means self-presence. The Father, then, is 'God-present-to-himself'. As such he necessarily, spontaneously, simultaneously begets the divine Word of God-understanding-himself: God from God, light from light. But his identity with the divine being is somehow prior (in a non-temporal sense of course) to the Son's and the Holy Spirit's identity with the divine being.

I do not think the mental image is quite so successful in illustrating the procession of the Holy Spirit. He is of course represented by the third member of the image triad, love or willing of self – self, remembered and understood, taking pleasure in its self-memory and self-understanding. Augustine several times asks himself why this *voluntas sui* (willing of self) cannot be regarded as a kind of offspring, as can the mental word expressing self-understanding. It is the echo of the question he repeatedly asks about the Holy Spirit, why since he proceeds from the Father he cannot also be called Son. But the answer he gives – not with any great clarity – does not quite seem to fit his doctrine about the Holy Spirit. It is that while he is sticking to his axiom that what is unknown cannot be loved and therefore love or will is subsequent to knowledge or understanding, still there is a kind of will or love that precedes my understanding of any particular thing, namely my desire to know or find out: *appetitus inveniendi*, which he also calls *amor studentium*, the love which students have of study.[10] So there is a sense, it would seem, in which understanding is the offspring not only of memory but also of will. But it is a different will, i.e. a different act of will, from the one which, once understanding has been achieved, 'joins the two together, parent to offspring', i.e. the mind to its object, or in our special case the act of self-memory to the act of self-understanding. It is this latter act of will that is his model for the Holy Spirit. But nowhere, to the best of my recollection, does he spell out how he sees it as issuing (but not as offspring) from the acts of self-memory and self-understanding.

However, here Thomas Aquinas supplies for him. In the last chapter we saw how he had a further argument to justify the doctrine of the procession of the Holy Spirit from the Father and the Son, an argument from the very nature of this procession. And here is the place to give it.

Following Augustine's model of the mental trinity, Thomas understands the first procession, that of the Son, as one *per modum intellectus ut verbum*, according to the way an act of intelligence or mental word proceeds; and the second procession, that of the Holy Spirit, *per modum voluntatis ut amor*, according to the way an act of will or love proceeds. 'And love', he continues, 'has to have a word to proceed from, since we do not love anything unless we grasp it with a conception of the mind'.[11] Thomas has discussed the processions at the very beginning of his treatise on the Trinity, *STh* Ia, 27 (ET, vol. 6). And he says there that since we are considering God-in-himself (the immanent Trinity) we cannot be dealing with a procession from God to things outside, such as the procession of creatures from God. We are dealing with 'immanent acts' that remain within the agent. We have a model for them in the immanent acts of the human mind – he is of course distilling Augustine's construction of the image – where we have the procession of a mental word in consequence of an act of intellect, and in consequence of an operation of will we have a procession of love whereby what is loved is in the lover.[12] So the Holy Spirit as Love proceeds from the Son as Word/Wisdom as well as from the Father, the ultimate and original divine self-presence, *fons totius deitatis*.

NOTES

1 *PL* 42, 947.

2 *STh* Ia, 3, 5 (ET, vol. 2).

3 In this particular context Rahner's word 'immanent' is the more accurate, in that it means divine activities (the processions) remaining within God, and not passing out to some exterior effects; and the same distinction is made in scholastic language, between different kinds of human activity. Those acts are 'immanent' which remain within the agent, notably acts of knowing and willing; those are 'transient' which produce some external effect, e.g. acts of speaking, writing, or any kind of doing or making.

4 Actually, he usually speaks of 'quasi-offspring' and 'quasi-parent' when he is dealing with the lesser trinities of the 'outer man'. The reason is that the act of sensation, or of conscious attention to something recalled, is produced not only by the object (external or in the memory) but also by the living subject of the act, the sense or the mind as the case may be. This scrupulous qualification of his key terms shows how conscious Augustine was of the imperfection of his analogies.

5 See Chapter 12 above, p. 121, note 10.

6 Not a biblical precept but a Hellenic one. The words *Gnōthi seauton* were inscribed over Apollo's shrine at Delphi. Augustine, though, is receiving it via Cicero who in his *Tusculan Disputations* 1.22, 52 interprets the saying as follows: 'So when it says "Know thyself" it means "Know thy mind" '.

7 *Aeneid* III, 628–629:
No such things did Ulysses endure,
    nor did the man of Ithaca forget himself in that momentous hazard;
quoted by Augustine in book XIV, xi, 14 (*PL* 42, 1047).

8 This at least shows that Augustine is not being excessively spiritualist or body-denying

in his construction of the image. In the first place, he locates the image in the mind, and not in the soul, where the distortion of his doctrine perpetuated by the catechisms places it, because he knows perfectly well that the soul animates (from *anima*, soul) the body, including the sense functions, which are all activities of soul. But the trinities he finds at this level, though helping us to understand the mental image better, are not themselves images of the divine Trinity because the disparity between them and the divine exemplar is too great. They are, however, traces (*vestigia*) of the divine Trinity, impressed on God's creation at all levels.

9   *STh* Ia, 1, 9, ad 3 (ET, vol. 1).

10 A *studens* in Latin means one who is eager or zealous about mastering some subject, not like 'student' in English, which usually only means one who is undergoing education, with whatever degree of willingness or unwillingness.

11 *STh* Ia, 36, 2 (ET, vol. 7).

12 *Ibid.* 27, 3 (ET, vol. 6).

14

The Trinitarian Image of God: A Programme for the Christian Life: books XI–XIV

A. THE IMAGE DISTORTED BY SIN

We have been talking about Augustine constructing rather than merely discovering a trinitarian image of God in the human mind or self. One good reason for this which I have not yet broached, but which is very dominant in his thought, is that it is our Christian calling as God-seekers (remember that the whole *De Trinitate* is a sustained quest for God) to construct this image in ourselves. The only way to find God the Father, Son and Holy Spirit is to become truly like God the Father, Son and Holy Spirit – to realize in ourselves the divine image by constructing ourselves into the divine image.

This is all the more necessary because individually and collectively we have already thoroughly deconstructed the divine image in us by sin. It was as much to sketch the spoiling of the divine image by sin as to throw light on the functioning of the image, that Augustine turned to the lesser trinities of what he called 'the outer man'. For his basic picture of sin is one of disorder, especially of disordered love. He has two spatial dimensions (metaphors of course) within which he observes the workings both of order (salvation, freedom) and of disorder (sin, slavery). The first is a vertical one of above and below, the second – domestic perhaps rather than horizontal – is one of within and without. 'Outer' and 'lower' have the same value and significance, and so do 'inner' and 'higher'.

Now the human self (the mind) was created to be below God and above the material world, to which it is related through its own body. That is the right, because the true, order. One lives a well-ordered, good and free life when the mind or self knows and loves God for his own sake; knows and loves itself and its neighbours in God as his image; and knows and loves the world, through the senses of the body, and through the memory and imagination, with reference to God.

This order is wrecked when the self rejects subordination to God, wishing to 'be like God, knowing good and evil' (Gen 3:5), and so sets itself in the place of God. Then it stops loving God, and loves itself perversely, and the material world greedily. In claiming freedom from God's dominion (vainly, of course), it becomes the slave of its desires and of the material things in which it craves (vainly, of course) satisfaction.

We always have to bear in mind that Augustine's notion of the image is not of a statue or picture, which is what the word first implies for most of us. His notion is of a reflection in a mirror. This is quite clear from the crucial importance of 1 Cor 13:12, 'For now we see in a mirror dimly', especially in book XV where he is drawing all his threads together. So in his view the mind or self is only truly God's image when it is, so to speak, looking back at God out of the mirror. Now sin consists in the reflected image of God, as it were, putting its tongue out at its divine exemplar, from the mirror, and then turning its back on it. The result, clearly, is image distortion.

Or take another figure, which is not used by Augustine but fits his use of the space lines, up and down, in and out: a puppet controlled by strings which are manipulated from above. When the strings are connected to the controlling hand above, the puppet's movements are well-ordered and coherent and significant. Cut the strings, and the puppet collapses, its limbs sprawling outwards in all directions. It is a mess, incoherent and non-significant. Unlike puppets we are autonomous and autokinetic. We cut the strings, but continue to have vital movements of our own. But, like puppets, we are creatures of a higher power and intelligence, and our vital movements are only coherent and significant – orderly – when we allow them to be governed by the divine power, wisdom (skill) and love.

It is by the twist he gives his work in books XII and XIII that Augustine shows he is quite as much interested in what we could call the spiritual history of the human self made in God's image, in its disintegration through sin and its reintegration through the grace of Christ, as in the image as a model through which to understand the divine Trinity. In book XI he has descended and come out from the mental image of memory, understanding and will to examine the lower and outer trinities of the outer man in order to find more accessible 'models of the model'. But when he has done that he does not simply return to the mental trinity. Instead he starts a leisurely return journey inwards and upwards to the 'inner man'.

Now by the inner man he indeed means the mind. But he discerns two levels of mental activity, so that we have what you might call an 'outer inner man' and an 'inner inner man' – just, indeed, as we had an outer outer man (sensation) and an inner outer man (sense memory and imagination), both of which we have in common with animals. By the lower or outer function of the mind he means that part of the reason deputed to deal with external and temporal things, roughly what the Aristotelians call the practical intellect. And by the inner and higher function he means that part of the mind 'which presides in the control tower of counsel' and is roughly the equivalent of the Aristotelian speculative intellect.[1] It is the function of perceiving and contemplating eternal truths and values – and God.

Although already in book XI he has had digressions depicting the disorder of sin, as expressed in the outer and lower trinities of sense perception and imagination, still he is perfectly well aware that both sin and conversion are the responsibility of the self as rational, i.e. of the 'inner man'. And since the archetypal sin is the fall of Adam and Eve in paradise, he ties all our sins to that sin by treating the whole story and cast of characters in Gen 3 as an allegory of the self of Everyman. Each one of us, he suggests, male and female, is Adam and Eve and the serpent bundled into one. Adam represents the inner contemplative function of the mind or inner man, Eve represents the outer practical function of the mind or inner man, the serpent represents the sensuality of the outer man, that which we have in common with animals. It is here we meet temptation, but it is with the inner man, both in its Eve function and in its Adam function, that responsibility for consent to temptation lies.

So let me conclude this section by giving Augustine's own account of the moral disintegration of the image. We must bear in mind all the time this allegorical interpretation of Gen 3 which I have just outlined.

As we climb up inwards then through the parts of the soul ... we begin to come upon something that is not common to us and the beasts, and that is where reason begins and where we can now recognize the inner man. But through that reason which has been delegated to administer temporal affairs he may slide too much into outer things by making unrestrained advances; and in this the active reason may have the consent of her head; that is to say the reason which presides as the masculine portion in the control tower of counsel may fail to curb her. In such a case the inner man grows old among his enemies [Ps 6:7] and the sight of eternal things is withdrawn from the head himself as he eats the forbidden fruit with his consort .... Thus they are both stripped naked of the enlightenment of truth, and the eyes of conscience are opened to see what a shameful and indecent state they have left themselves in. So they sew together as it were the leaves of delightful fruits without the fruits themselves, which is to say they sew together fine words without the fruit of good works, in order while living badly to cover up their baseness by speaking well.

'They' in this passage means all the time the human individual, you or me, allegorized as Adam and Eve. He continues, less allegorically:

What happens is that the soul, loving its own power, slides away from the whole which is common to all into the part which is its own private property. By following God's directions and being perfectly governed by his laws it could enjoy the whole universe of creation; but by the apostasy of pride ... it strives to grab something more than the whole and to govern it by its own laws; and because there is nothing more that the whole, it is thrust back into anxiety over a part, and so by being greedy for more it gets less. That is why greed is called the root of all evils [1 Tim 6:10]. Thus all that it tries to do on its own against the laws that govern the universe it does by its own body, which is the only part it has a part-ownership in. And so it finds delight in bodily shapes and movements, and because it does not have these with it inside, it wraps itself in their images which it has fixed in the memory. In this way it defiles itself foully with a fanciful sort of fornication by referring all its business to one or other of the following ends: curiosity, searching for experience through the senses; swollen conceit . . . ; or carnal pleasure . . . .[2]

B. THE RE-INTEGRATION OF THE IMAGE BY THE GRACE OF CHRIST

When these two functions of the mind or self, the 'feminine' practical function and the 'masculine' contemplative functions,[3] are working properly, Augustine sees the feminine function as exercising *knowledge* (*scientia*) and the masculine function as exercising *wisdom* (*sapientia*). His text is 1 Cor 12:8, 'To one is given through the Spirit the utterance of wisdom, and to another the utterance of knowledge according to the same Spirit', interpreted according to Job 28:28, 'Behold, the fear of the Lord, that is wisdom; and to depart from evil is knowledge' (RSV: 'understanding').

As we saw at the end of the last section, the root sin which causes the image to be distorted, the living puppet to collapse and disintegrate, is pride, accompanied by and expressed in greed. So the remedy must begin with humility and abnegation. It must also begin at the bottom and the external sphere of the material, sensible, sensual world, and work its way inwards and upwards to the citadel of the contemplative mind.

The fallen and disintegrated puppet, the cracked and distorted image, cannot begin the process by itself. That is the work of its maker and redeemer. He does it by sending forth 'his Son, born of woman, born under the law' (Gal 4:4). He does it by sending the Word to become *flesh*, his Son to become man (Jn 1:14). 'Flesh', carnality, is here the important word for Augustine. It was at the sensual, sensible level that Satan tempted mankind to sin, according to Augustine's allegory of Gen 3. So it is at the sensual, sensible level that the Wisdom or Word of God begins to lure mankind back[4] to the divine friendship, through his appearance in the flesh (1 Tim 3:16) and his subsequent life, death and resurrection.

Augustine gives a splendid account in book XIII of how Christ by his death overcomes the devil 'not with power but with justice'.[5] It is an account of redemption parallel to that of Christ's mediation in book IV. What it has to do with our theme is this: it is the Word made *flesh*, and the *crucified* Christ, and Christ risen in the *flesh* who is the prime object of Christian faith. This is a faith that raises none of the problems about 'faith in God the Trinity'

which we saw tackled in book VIII. For there is no difficulty in understanding what is meant by the statements concerning the humanity, death
and resurrection of Jesus Christ. The only difficulty is in actually believing
them. And in Augustine's own personal experience, and no doubt in his
cultural world, this was above all a moral difficulty – the difficulty for the
proud intellect to humble itself by believing in these material, carnal, sordid
realities. It was the proud Platonic intellect he was thinking of, which he
shared with philosophers like Plotinus; for them (and him) its proper natural
habitat was the world of eternal ideas, the spiritual world. As he states in the
Confessions, when describing the effect on his intellectual development of
reading the *Enneads* of Plotinus,

There I read, though not in so many words, that *in the beginning was the Word, and the Word
was with God, and the Word was God; all things were made through him and without him was made
nothing. What was made in him was life, and the life was the light of men, and the light shines in the
darkness and the darkness did not comprehend it* . . . . Again I read there that God the Word *was
born not of the flesh nor of blood nor of the will of man, nor of the will of the flesh, but of God. But
that the Word became flesh and dwelt among us* (Jn 1:1–14) I did not read there.[6]

This then is the first stage of reintegrating the true image – to believe in the
flesh of Christ and in his death. And it is primarily an act of the feminine
function of the mind or self, because it is directed to an external, material and
temporal object. Furthermore, true faith, as St Paul puts it, is faith working
through love (Gal 5:6). Augustine spells it out that faith in the incarnate and
crucified Christ requires us to be conformed to him, and so finds expression in
the cultivation of the moral virtues – prudence, courage, justice, self-control,
which are the cardinal virtues of classical Greek ethics. And all this *practical*
activity of living a good moral life is under the direction of the practical
function of the mind and its proper attribute – or task – of *knowledge*. Most of
our education belongs here too, including most of what we study in
catechism, religion classes and theology courses, which is all intended to
nourish and strengthen and give vitality to our faith.

In all this multifarious mental activity, now part of the programme of
reintegrating the true image, we can discern a trinity, or rather innumerable
trinities, of the mind remembering, understanding and willing the objects of
its faith or its knowledge; even more reflexively, the mind remembering,
understanding and loving its own knowledge and its own faith. But this kind
of mental trinity, Augustine is adamant, does not yet constitute the true
image of God, any more than the trinities of the outer man did. The reason is
that it too is not really self-contained. It depends upon input from the
external world, on things coming into the mind 'adventitiously' (including
such things as faith and knowledge) that were not there before. The ascent
inwards and upwards still has to go on.

And so we come back at last to the mind and its memory, understanding and loving of itself. But now no longer just as a model for the divine Trinity; now we come back to it as a threefold act of the mind purified by faith (Acts 15:9). And so the mind or self cannot possibly stop there. Though this is indeed the image of God, the threefold activity of the masculine function and its attribute of wisdom, responding to the challenge *Know thyself*, it is only so if it is immediately referred to God, that is to say if memory of self, understanding and loving of self are transformed into remembering God, understanding God and loving God.

As he puts it himself,

This trinity of the mind is not really the image of God because the mind remembers and understands and loves itself, but because it is also able to remember and understand and love him by whom it was made. And when it does this it becomes wise. If it does not do it, then even though it remembers and understands and loves itself, it is foolish.[7]

This mental trinity of remembering, understanding and loving God (God the Father, Son and Holy Spirit of course, though he does not spell it out) is now the complete image of God as it was intended at creation and as it is restored by redemption. And it is, in my phrase, self-contained. For God, unlike the objects of knowledge or faith, unlike for example the man Christ Jesus, does not come into the mind from outside. We have now not only climbed up to the top, but we have also penetrated to the inmost shrine or sanctum of the self, where God the other, but not purely and simply the not-self, is 'more inmost than my inmost being' (*intimior intimo meo*).[8]

This then is the complete image. But we do not and cannot realize this complete image completely or perfectly in this life, because we are living in a temporal condition and the image, like its exemplar, is properly eternal. In this life we can only realize this image, become what we are and indeed become what we imitate, intermittently and imperfectly. So he says later on in the same book:

It is clear that the image of God will achieve its full likeness of him only when it attains to the full vision of him . . . . The image which is being renewed in the spirit of the mind in the recognition of God, not outwardly but inwardly from day to day [Eph 4:23, Col 3:10, 2 Cor 4:16], this image will be perfected in the vision that will then be face to face after the judgement, while now it makes progress through a puzzling reflection in a mirror [1 Cor 13:12].[9]

C. THE INVISIBLE MISSIONS AND THE INDWELLING OF THE THREE DIVINE PERSONS

The subject of this chapter so far, the reader may feel, has not been contributing any further to our understanding of the mystery of the Trinity. But it has been dealing, I reply, with Augustine's attempt to relate the mystery to our experience – no longer just to the general economy of salvation, but to the personal economy of each one of us. We all experience in our conscious lives the 'trinities' he has been talking about, even though we do not usually think of our experiences of sensation, imagination, memory, practical and moral reflection and decision – and sinning and repenting and being converted and believing, and acquiring a modicum of self-knowledge and praying and meditating and raising our hearts and minds to God – even if we do not think of all these experiences in the terms which he suggests to us.

Now what he is doing, as I see it, is proposing to us a way in which we can interpret all this experience, most of it very humdrum, some of it perhaps 'spiritual' in a more memorable way (like his own experience of conversion) in the light of our faith in the mystery of God the Father, Son and Holy Spirit. We can see it all as part of our quest for God, of our realizing ourselves as true images of God, of undertaking in our Christian lives the imitation of Christ – not as an end in itself, however, but as the way to the final goal of remembering God, understanding God and loving God in the eternal face-to-face vision when we see Father, Son and Holy Spirit as they are. In fact what Augustine is attempting is not to make the Trinity relevant to our lives, but to make our 'image' lives relevant to the Trinity.

But here I think he rather misses something out, at least in this whole section of his work; and that is the active involvement of the divine persons in the whole work of reintegrating the image, and precisely stimulating in us those trinitarian acts of remembering, understanding and loving God. Certainly Augustine, the great doctor of grace, knows that this is all the work of grace. He has said explicitly that it all begins with the Word becoming flesh to challenge our proud intellect into the humble act of faith. But in this particular context – in all contexts, indeed, but specially so here – grace has trinitarian dimensions. This in fact is the place to talk about the invisible missions of the Son and the Holy Spirit, and the indwelling of the three divine persons in the soul, self or mind.

The text to reflect on here is Jesus' farewell discourse to his disciples, Jn 14 – 16, especially 14:15–24. Here Jesus first tells them he will give them another Comforter, the Spirit of truth, if they love him and keep his commandments, and then goes on to say that he himself will come and show himself to his disciples. And when Jude asks how he will show himself to them and not to the world (so the reference is clearly not to be taken as being to the *parousia* or second coming of Christ), he answers, 'If a man loves me, he will keep my word, and my Father will love him, and we will come to him and make our home with him' (v. 23). It is true he talks about giving, not sending, the Spirit, and about himself coming with the Father, not being sent by him; but there are other texts in which he promises to send the Spirit, e.g. Jn 15:26 where the reference is probably not to Pentecost, an event which hardly figures in John's theology. And in the Old Testament there is Wis 9:10 where the author – 'Solomon' – prays about Wisdom, 'Send her forth from the holy heavens, and from the throne of your glory send her, that she may be with me and toil and that I may learn what is pleasing to thee'.

The language of sending in this context is even more figurative than it was when we were discussing the visible missions. What it amounts to is the divine persons beginning to be present in a human person in a new way, the way we at other times call sanctifying grace. But talking about it as a sending and being sent means that their new way of being present reflects and expresses within the human self or mind their own mutual relationships of origin. Thomas Aquinas explains that in this new way of being present God is said to be in someone 'as one known in the knower and one loved in the lover'.[10]

Now as known in the knower he may be said to be present as Son invisibly sent by the Father, and as belovèd in the lover to be present as Holy Spirit invisibly sent or given by Father and Son. Thomas does not discuss how the Father is present, except to say that we cannot say he is sent. According to John, in the passage we have just glanced at, we can say only that he comes. Thomas does not mention Augustine's third member of the mental trinity – or rather the first member – memory. Perhaps we could say the Father is present, or comes, as one remembered in the rememberer; which means to say that his continuous, most intimate presence is recognized, and that from this newness of the Father's recognized presence the Son's presence issues as sent or being formed again in us (Gal 4:19), and so too does the Holy Spirit's as sent or given.

Thomas' profoundest word, perhaps, on these invisible missions and this indwelling of the divine persons, is to be found in *STh* Ia, 43, 5 ad 2 which I here paraphrase:

> Grace conforms us to God. So having a divine person sent to us by grace means our being conformed to that particular person by an appropriate gift of grace. Thus when the Holy Spirit is sent to us, we are assimilated to the Holy Spirit by the gift of charity, because the Holy Spirit is Love. In the same way the Son is Word; not any sort of Word, however, but a Word breathing forth Love; Augustine calls the Word 'knowledge with love'.[11] So when the Son is invisibly sent to us we are assimilated to him, not by any kind of gift perfecting the intelligence, but by such an informing or shaping of the intelligence that it breaks out in an expression of love. So Augustine very significantly says that the Word of God is then sent to anyone when he is known *and perceived* by them;[12] for perception means a kind of experiential awareness, and this is properly called wisdom.

In the next article Thomas is insistent that having the divine persons sent to dwell in the soul with the Father is not the privilege of an *élite* of saints and mystics. It is the divine triad's gift of themselves to any and everyone in a state of grace, from the newly baptized infant to the old sinner emerging repentant and absolved from the confessional, and to the non-Christian of good will who by feeling after God in simplicity of heart enjoys his 'anonymous grace'. Though you could say that it is the special grace of the more perfect Christian to be aware of this threefold divine presence.

When all is said and done, St Paul is still the person who puts it best, in Gal 4:4–7, which we could paraphrase in this special context as follows: When the fullness of time comes for each one of us to be converted, God, always present in our inmost being (the Father), sends his Son into our minds to share his sonship with us by adoption. And because we are now sons, God sends the Spirit of his Son into our hearts, breaking out into the cry of love, 'Abba, Father!'

NOTES

1 *De Trin.* XII, viii, 13 (*PL* 42, 1005). Augustine insists several times that he does not mean two minds, or two distinct faculties or powers, but two functions of one single mind or faculty of intelligence.

2 *Ibid.* viii, 13 - ix, 14 (*ibid.* 1005-06).

3 We must always remember that these two functions, the feminine and the masculine, are to be found in every human being, male and female, man and woman. They may not quite correspond to the *anima* and *animus* of Jungian psychology, but their discernment at least represents a similar insight. I don't think one can conclude that Augustine thought the feminine function to be stronger in women and the masculine one predominant in men. If that is the case, however, then the sooner we men leave women to run the world, and run the Church (and so have a predominantly female clergy, episcopacy and Roman Curia), and ourselves withdraw to a life of leisurely contemplation, the better. Was this the world vision of Sir Pelham G. Wodehouse, with his creation of the Drones' Club and Bertie Wooster's formidable aunts, not to mention the manifestly contemplative soul of Clarence, ninth earl of Emsworth, and by contrast his equally formidable sisters?

4 See Hosea 2:14.

5 XIII, xiii, 17 (*PL* 42, 1026).

6 *Confessions* VII, ix, 13 (*PL* 32, 740–741). It is interesting that Augustine here reads v. 13, *born not of flesh* etc., in the singular as referring to the Word, and not in the plural – the normally accepted reading – as referring to those who believe in his name. This is the reading of one Old Latin MS, possibly supported by one Syriac MS, and was also read by Irenaeus and Tertullian. It is followed, against the overwhelming weight of the evidence, by the Jerusalem Bible.

But when Augustine discusses the whole prologue of John in the *De Trinitate* at the beginning of book XIII, he follows the plural reading. He does so too in his sermon on the text, *In Joann.* tract. 2.

7 *De Trin.* XIV, xii, 15 (*PL* 42, 1048).

8 See above, Chapter 8, p. 83, note 12. I still have not been able to trace this Augustinian saying. Perhaps he never actually used it anywhere. But I have found another text in this very work which almost says it; VIII, vii, 11 (*PL* 42, 957): 'Those who seek God through these Powers that rule the world . . . are in fact being swept away from him and cast up a long way off, not in terms of distance but of divergence of values. They are trying to go by an outer route and forsaking *their own inwardness, where God is present more inwardly still*'. Cf. also *Confessions* IX, i, 1 (*PL* 32, 763), where Jesus is called *omni secreto interior*, 'deeper within than any hidden depth'.

9 XIV, xviii, 24; xix, 25 (*PL* 42, 1055–56).

10 *STh* Ia, 43, 3 (ET, vol. 7).

11 *De Trin.* IX, x, 15 (*PL* 42, 969). Augustine, as a matter of fact, is talking about the mental word. Thomas transfers what he says about it to the divine Word – with Augustine's entire approval, I am sure.

12 IV, xx, 28 (*PL* 42, 907).

V
Losing sight of the Mystery

15

The Drawbacks of Scholastic Method

A. PRELIMINARY REMARKS

I head this part of the book 'Losing sight of the mystery', not because I think that the Catholic tradition or the faithful at large have forgotten the mystery of the Trinity, or lost sight of it altogether. If that were the case this book neither could nor would have been written. What I do think, as I said in Chapter 1 at the beginning, is that the sense of this mystery of God has faded from the centre of the Catholic (or at least Latin) Christian consciousness, so that it no longer means much to the average Western Christian. It has been sufficiently forgotten to require an effort of recall; lost sight of to the extent that a deliberate taking of new bearings is needed. That is what I have been attempting up to this point.

And when I head this chapter 'The drawbacks of scholastic method', I must ask it to be understood that I take as read the enormous achievements of this method, not least in the field of trinitarian theology. Otherwise I would not have referred so frequently in the last three chapters to the elucidations of Thomas Aquinas. But I am saying that this method's all-pervading influence on the field of Catholic teaching, including the catechetical presentation of doctrine, has led to the effectual removal of the dogma of the blessed Trinity from the grasp of the ordinary Christian believer. If we are to restore to ordinary Christians their rightful heritage, it will be useful for us to see how this has happened.

It has been brought about, in my opinion, by a simple reversal of Augustine's method; by substituting an *a priori* procedure for his *a posteriori* one; in Aquinas' own terms, by substituting the *via doctrinae*, the way of exposition, for the *via inventionis*, the way of discovery. The *a priori* way of exposition is only valuable for those who have already been led along the *a posteriori* way of discovery. That is doubtless how the early scholastics intended it to be used. But since their time the compilers of catechisms have tended to treat it as a substitute for the way of discovery – with regrettable results.

B. THE *SENTENCES* OF PETER LOMBARD

The scholastic movement was well and truly launched at the beginning of the twelfth century by two Peters, Peter Abelard and Peter Lombard. They had their precursors to be sure, notably St Anselm of Canterbury. But he, like Peter Abelard's great contemporary and adversary, St Bernard of Clairvaux, was still firmly in the older literary and rhetorical tradition of the Fathers. The two Peters, by contrast, were professional academics through and through. Since Peter Lombard's compilation, the *Sentences*, was to be the standard textbook of theology in the universities (the Schools) for the next five centuries, it is with him alone that we have to deal.[1]

This work is so called because it is intended as a compendium of the teaching of the Fathers, that is, as a collection of their *sententiae*, their judgements and opinions. In such a work the arrangement of the material is all-important. The *Sentences* are divided into four books, which in turn are divided into chapters called, for reasons unknown to me, 'distinctions'. The first book is headed 'On the Mystery of the Trinity', the second 'On the Creation and Formation of Spiritual and Bodily Things, etc.', the third 'On the Incarnation of the Word', and the fourth has no title, but is about the sacraments and eschatology (*PL* 192, 521–962). I do not know if Peter Lombard himself is responsible for these titles.

Book I, in fact, is about God; but after an introductory distinction about 'things and signs' (taken from Augustine's manual *De Doctrina Christiana*, which could be translated *How to Teach Christianity*), the author goes straight into the subject of the Trinity, which occupies him from dist. 2 to dist. 34. Only dist. 35–48 are concerned with what later textbooks would call the subject *De Deo Uno*, on the One God. This fact rather knocks the bottom out of the cliché already criticized (Chapter 12, E, pp. 115–116 above) that while the Greek tradition starts from the three distinct persons, the Latin tradition starts from the one divine substance.

In dist. 2 the author declares his intention of following Augustine's method of first establishing the mystery by the authority of scripture, and then defending it against those who would demolish it by reason. But in fact he can hardly be said to do so. In dist. 3 he starts straight away with the image of God in the human mind. His reason for this is that the Creator is known through creatures, and so the Trinity, we may suppose, can be known through its image in the human mind. But what he fails to appreciate is that we do not know that the human mind bears the image of the Trinity until we already know something about the Trinity: namely those things which Augustine established in books I–VII of his work – (a) that we believe in the Father, Son and Holy Spirit, really distinct, really equal and really one; (b) that the Father has sent the Son and the Holy Spirit in the saving events set forth in the New Testament, and thereby has revealed that there are eternal divine processions; (c) that we have to work out delicate rules of language, terms of relationship and substance and modes of appropriation, for talking about the mystery. Only then does it make sense first to *construct* (not merely to discern) and then to examine the mental trinity, in order with its analogies to throw light on the divine processions.

In the course of his statement of the mental image Lombard makes the mistake of calling the memory, understanding and will that constitute the trinitarian analogues of the divine persons 'natural properties or powers of the mind' (I, 3, 12; *PL* 192, 531), whereas Augustine was always thinking of them as mental *acts*, remembering etc. self and God. To think of them as powers, in fact, robs the whole concept of the trinitarian image of any theological value. Thomas was to correct this mistake of the Master (*STh* Ia, 93, 7, ad 3), but it survives to this day, nevertheless, in the august pages of the *Catechism of Christian Doctrine*, revised edition 1971, authorized for use by the Archbishops and Bishops of England and Wales. Lombard does not, to be fair to him, make the mistake of identifying mind (*mens*) with soul (*anima*). But his editors do, in one of their subheadings (I, 3, 7; *PL* 192, 530) – and so of course does the English Catechism.

He then goes on to discuss the generation of the Son and questions arising from it (dist. 4–9), and the procession of the Holy Spirit (dist. 10–14). In dist. 15–18 he discusses the missions of the Holy Spirit, both invisible and visible, but nowhere is there any mention of the mission of the Son. Dist. 19–34, more or less, deal with the topics of personal names, relationships and properties.

So the Lombard does not in fact follow Augustine's carefully thought-out and – I am sure – *pastoral* procedure, starting from the economy as in some way or other experienced and going on from there to the transcendent or immanent mystery. It is pretty certain that he did not appreciate Augustine's procedure for what it was. But neither does he substitute any very lucid procedure of his own.

C.   THE *SUMMA THEOLOGIAE* OF THOMAS AQUINAS, IA, 27–43

Thomas Aquinas, on the other hand, certainly does do this in a way that is academically or scholastically satisfactory (given certain presuppositions that are not always realized), but pastorally or catechetically is completely out of place. He was, of course, not intending to write a pastoral or catechetical textbook, so he cannot be faulted for this reason. It is simply a pity that later writers of such textbooks took it for granted that his *scholastic* method was suitable for them to follow.

To recapitulate a little, we can summarize Augustine's overall procedure thus: he begins his quest for God, Father, Son and Holy Spirit, by discussing the divine *missions* of the Son and Holy Spirit in the New Testament event, which he sees as both the climax of the divine economy of salvation and the revelation of the eternal processions in God; he goes on to argue with the Arians about the divine *relationships*, and the proper ways of applying the divine names to God and the three – i.e. the proper way of talking about the Trinity; and then he concludes by investigating the divine *processions*, but indirectly through the reflector, so to say, of the divine image in man. From missions to relationships to processions: this is really the *via inventionis*, the *a posteriori* procedure of discovery, going from the clues to the solution, from the effect to the cause.

Now Thomas reverses the procedure. 'Science' in the strict sense is for him knowledge through causes. So the systematic teaching of a science (and in his language theology is most certainly a science), the *via doctrinae*, requires an *a priori* procedure, going from crime as solved back to the clues, from cause to effect. This of course presupposes that the *a posteriori* solution of problems from clues, the discovery of causes from effects, has already been achieved. And I think we may say that in his systematic exposition of the 'science' of theology Thomas and his colleagues all presupposed this kind of discovery (which meant basically the study of Scripture and the Fathers) in their students as well as in themselves as teachers. So he begins his whole enterprise with the study of God, the first cause (very carefully and explicitly stating that he can only be known as a cause is known from its effects, that is to say imperfectly and mainly negatively, by knowing what he is not rather than what he is). God as first cause is the one God, so Thomas indeed exemplifies what is said to be the whole Latin tradition of beginning with the divine unity of substance and only then proceeding to the trinity of persons.[2]

When he goes on next to the mystery of the Trinity, he again starts with the 'cause' – the *processions* – and ends with the 'effect' in time, the *missions*. The *relationships*, i.e. the divine nomenclature, occupy the lion's share of the treatise in the middle.[3] Although he explains the divine processions on the analogy of the mental acts out of which Augustine constructs the divine image in the human mind, he does it without referring to or discussing that image. This is deferred for consideration to his treatise on the creation of man (Ia, 93).

Even within his own terms of reference, I observe two weaknesses in Thomas' treatment of the whole subject. In this question on man made to the image of God, while he summarizes Augustine's 'construction' accurately enough and corrects Peter Lombard's misunderstanding, he does not seem to recognize Augustine's purpose in constructing the trinitarian image in the human mind, namely as an indirect means of understanding the divine mystery and in particular the mystery of the eternal processions; and so he leaves the whole concept of man made to the image of the divine Trinity rather hanging in the air. I do not question the propriety of including the topic in his treatise on man. But since an image is a means of knowing the exemplar of which it is the image, rather than something to be known in its own right, I think St Thomas ought to have made much more explicit reference to Augustine's construction in his question on the divine processions (27), and here in q. 93 should have made it much more obvious, first how the image of the triune God in us is a programme to be lived, something for us to make come true, and secondly how it is a means of introducing us into the mystery of the Trinity.[4] By failing to do this he contributed to the 'irrelevance' of the trinitarian image doctrine for the average Christian, and thus indirectly to the 'irrelevance' of the doctrine of the Trinity. In this respect Peter Lombard's arrangement of matters, directly connecting the image to the divine mystery, was much sounder – though he did not handle it very well.

Thomas' second weakness is his treatment of the divine missions. Here he fails to observe Augustine's cardinal point that the temporal missions *reveal* the eternal processions and thus – since the temporal missions precisely consist in the incarnation of the Son and the Pentecostal gift of the Holy Spirit – make the mystery of the Trinity (the processions) relevant to the economic mystery of our salvation.[5] As we have seen, his chief interest is in what are called the invisible missions and their contribution to our sanctification.

NOTES

1 Peter Abelard, a Frenchman, was perhaps a generation older than his Lombard namesake. The latter, born of a poor family in Novara, studied first in Bologna and then, like so many scholars of the time, wandered off to France and eventually settled in Paris where he acquired a great reputation as a teacher. After writing the *Sentences* he came to be known as *Magister Sententiarum*, the Master of the Sentences. As Paul was the Apostle for the mediaevals, and Aristotle the Philosopher, so Peter Lombard became simply the Master. At the end of his life, in rather quaint circumstances, he was elected bishop of Paris, but held the see for scarcely a year before he died in 1160.

2 The most reasonable procedure, in my view, not only for a systematic treatment of theology according to the *via doctrinae*, but also for the more historical or literary approach of the *via inventionis*. For we came to a knowledge of the one God through revelation – in the Old Testament – long before the mystery of the divine Three was revealed.

3 The processions, *STh* Ia, 27; relationships etc. 28–42; the missions, 43.

4 Thomas does make a reference to this function of images in one place: Ia, 93, 5, obj. 3. But he does it in such a way that he precludes himself from doing justice to the idea in his answer.

5 He adverts to the connection in one place: Ia, 32, 1, ad 3, the last sentence. But this is hardly a prominent statement of a crucial theological dovetail.

16

Indigestible Fruits of Scholasticism: Textbooks and Catechisms

I have before me four textbooks of this century, three Latin, one English. They are: (a) *Institutiones Theologiae Dogmaticae*, vol. I, by R.P. J. Herrmann (Rome, 1908); (b) *Synopsis Theologiae Dogmaticae*, tom. II, by A. Tanquerey (Paris, 1926); (c) *The Divine Trinity, a Dogmatic Treatise*, by J. Pohle, ed. A. Preuss (St Louis, Mo., 1919); (d) *Institutiones Theologiae Dogmaticae II*, by L. Lercher (Barcelona, 1951).

(a) *Herrmann's* textbook, appearing in that particular year, is prefaced by the decree *Lamentabili* of the Holy Roman and Universal Inquisition and by Pius X's encyclical *Pascendi*, both levelled at the Modernists. This will at least ensure that his textbook contains no innovations whatsoever. After two treatises of what he calls 'General Theology', one 'On the true religion', the other 'On the true Church of Christ', treatises that are presumably apologetic/polemic in character, he proceeds in what he calls 'Special Theology' – and Aquinas would simply call 'Sacred Teaching' – to offer a treatise first 'On God as One' and then 'On the Most Holy Trinity'.

In his introduction to this treatise he begins with a *definition* of the mystery of the Trinity. This strikes me as an absolutely horrendous procedure, since mysteries and above all divine mysteries are by definition indefinable. Still, to give him a pious interpretation, he no doubt means what the scholastics call a nominal definition, i.e. not a definition of the reality but of the terms used to state it. So his definition, not of the mystery but of the term 'Trinity' in this context, runs 'One God in three persons', or 'The unity of three really distinct divine persons and the identity of their undivided nature'; very questionable definitions in my view, since they introduce terms – 'person' and 'nature' (Augustine would have said 'substance') – which are themselves, as we have seen, highly problematic. Furthermore, the definitions include *no* scriptural words except for 'God' – yes, and also 'one'. Note the absence of 'Father', 'Son' and 'Holy Spirit'. Right from the start we are in a conceptual stratosphere of abstraction.

He then goes on, in the best logical order, to ask whether the mystery exists, before considering the question what it is. He has already followed this procedure when discussing 'God as One', as Aquinas did before him. But Herrmann improves on St Thomas by also applying it here. Thomas himself did no such thing, since he did not consider the mystery of the Trinity to be something separate from or added to God. It could be said that Herrmann is really doing no more, though in a totally different style, than Augustine did in *De Trinitate* I, where he established the beginning of faith by demonstrating the equality of the divine three from scripture. But the difference of style does have the effect of separating in people's minds (what was probably separate in the author's own mind) the mystery of the Trinity from the mystery of God.

When discussing what the mystery is, Herrmann follows the order set by Aquinas and deals in turn with the processions, the relationships and the missions. On the processions, he makes no explicit reference to the divine image in man. In discussing the missions he begins with the invisible and goes on to the visible ones, without adverting at all to their effect of making known the eternal processions. Thus he simply perpetuates the weaknesses in St Thomas' treatment which we noted in the last chapter (pp. 150–151).

(b) *Tanquerey*. This author is rather less simplistic than our first one. He begins his treatise on the Trinity[1] with a sketch of the *history* of the dogma – hardly more in fact than a list of names, but at least there is something there for the lecturer to amplify, and he includes here the text of the Athanasian creed. So to some degree I have in this book been following in his footsteps.

He too, like Herrmann, goes on to a definition, but he makes it clearer what he does and does not mean by this. The whole section is headed 'A brief exposition of the mystery of the Trinity'. He then goes on 'to prove the mystery from revelation' (i.e. from scripture and tradition). It is in this section, in fact, that he treats of the processions and the missions, but again without observing,[2] let alone emphasizing, the connection between them. What interests theologians from Thomas Aquinas on is the distinction between invisible and visible missions, with pride of place being given quite explicitly to the former. Our next writer, Pohle, will say, 'Aside from the Mission of the Incarnate Logos, an invisible Mission as such invariably ranks higher than a visible mission, because it aims at the supernatural sanctification of the creature' (*The Divine Trinity*, p. 251). The place of the visible missions in the divine economy as precisely revealing the eternal processions, and through them the whole mystery of the Trinity, has thus been totally lost to view.

Tanquerey then goes on to discuss what he calls 'the philosophico-theological refinement [*expolitio*, 'polishing'] of the mystery', in which *inter alia* he chiefly deals with 'the analogies and philosophico-theological theories by which it is explained'. He gives one brief and not very illuminating subsection (695, pp. 424–425) to the trinitarian image in man, and devotes the rest of this part to explaining all those technical terms we have come across, 'circumincession', 'hypostasis', 'substance', 'relationship', 'property', 'notion' etc.

With Tanquerey we begin to get a sense of the importance of history for theology (a very suspect idea during the anti-Modernist witch-hunt), the history at least of the development of dogma. He is still far short, though, of appreciating how the divine mystery itself, about which the dogma has been elaborated, has so to say been inserted into the story/history of our redemption by the divine missions; and into the personal 'salvation history' of each one of us through the programme of the divine image in us.

(c) *Pohle* takes as his starting-point the notion of personality. Thus he takes as a *datum* what has in the history of the dogma been a rather problematic concept or term of explanation – part of what Tanquerey calls the *expolitio* of the dogma. It seems to me that this is to dissociate the mystery at the very start from its place in the common human experience, and to tie it to a philosophical abstraction – an important one to be sure, but still just an abstraction.

For the rest, Pohle's volume is a firmly constructed and lucidly argued treatise, though it does not overcome the basic scholastic weaknesses we have noticed. One interesting feature, though, is his division of the volume into two parts: he first considers 'the Blessed Trinity as Trinity in Unity, or three-fold personality; and secondly as Unity in Trinity, or Triunity'. Thus he, like Peter Lombard, escapes the stereotype of 'the Latin approach' which we have noticed and criticized above (pp. 115–116, 148). In his case, this is probably deliberate.

(d) *Lercher* gives us perhaps the neatest and most typical textbook treatment. *De Deo Trino* follows as usual *De Deo Uno*. The first chapter is about the Mystery 'in the sources of revelation' – why we believe it. But like all its fellows, it fails to address the question of *how* the mystery was revealed, being satisfied in showing only *that* it has been revealed. The second chapter gives a theological exposition of the mystery: (a) about the divine processions; (b) about the divine relationships; (c) about the divine persons – (i) their constitution, (ii) their properties, (iii) their equality and union, (iv) their operation *ad extra* .... But where are the missions? In a second scholion attached to the last subsection, just before the epilogue. R.I.P., buried in the obscurest of corners.

B.   THE DOCTRINE IN THE CATECHISMS

My sample of pre-Vatican II catechisms is as follows: (a) *Deharbe's Small Catechism*, approved by bishops in India, New Zealand, England, Scotland and U.S.A. (1903); (b) the *Explanatory Catechism of Christian Doctrine*, approved by the South African bishops (1934); (c) the *Baltimore Catechism, no. 3*, with explanations by Rev. E. M. Deck (1933); (d) *A Catechism of Christian Doctrine*, approved by the archbishops and bishops of England and Wales, which though in a revised edition of 1971 is still wholly pre-Vatican II in its approach (see the previous chapter, p. 149); (e) *Catholic Faith*, based on the *Catholic Catechism* of Cardinal Gasparri in an American edition for primary grades (1939).

All except the last begin with a few questions on God. Only the English and the Baltimore[3] catechisms ask – and even worse, answer – the theologically monstrous question 'What is God?', as though God were classifiable as a kind of thing. Let us look at their questions on the Trinity, which they all ask immediately after their questions about God (thus following the routine textbook plan, derived from Aquinas), and which those of them which are formally structured on the Apostles' Creed fit into their questions on the first article, 'I believe in God the Father Almighty, creator of heaven and earth'. These in effect ask questions about God at this point, and omit all reference to his being called here 'God the Father'. Thus the English catechism:

16 What is the first article of the creed? . . .
17 What is God? God is the supreme Spirit . . .
18 Why is God called Almighty? . . .

and so on.

But to come to the questions on the Trinity. I shall for the most part just give the questions and omit the replies, except where they are of direct interest to us.

(a)   Deharbe

SECOND TRUTH
OF GOD IN THREE PERSONS

19 How many Divine Persons are there? There are three Divine Persons, the Father, the Son and the Holy Ghost.
20 Is the Father God?

21 Is the Son God?
22 Is the Holy Ghost also God?
23 Is there only one God? Yes, these three Persons are only one God.
24 Is the Father older or mightier than the Son? No, all three Persons have existed from all eternity, and are equally mighty, equally good, equally perfect.
25 By what single word do we call the one Godhead in three Persons?
26 By what sign do we show that we believe in the Holy Trinity?

(b) South African Catechism

2. THE THREE DIVINE PERSONS

20 How many persons are there in God?
21 What do we call the mystery of the three Persons in one God?
22 What has the Blessed Trinity done for us? God the Father has created us, God the Son has redeemed us, God the Holy Ghost has sanctified us. Hence the Father is called Creator, the Son Redeemer, and the Holy Ghost Sanctifier.

(After each answer there is a brief explanation, the first quoting the text of Mt 28:19, and the last adding an explanation of the sign of the cross.)

(c) Baltimore Catechism no. 3

ON THE UNITY AND TRINITY OF GOD

34 Is there but one God?
35 Why can there be but one God?
36 How many persons are there in God?
37 Is the Father God?
38 What works do we ascribe to the Father?
39 Is the Son God?
40 What works do we ascribe to the Son?
41 Is the Holy Ghost God?
42 What works do we ascribe to the Holy Ghost?
43 What do we mean by the Blessed Trinity?
44 Are the three Divine Persons equal in all things?
45 Are the three Divine Persons one and the same God?
46 Can we fully understand how the three Divine Persons are one and the same God?
47 What is a mystery?
48 Why is the knowledge of the Blessed Trinity important to us?

(d) England and Wales, Catechism of Christian Doctrine

After qq. 17–23 on God:

24 Is there only one God?
25 Are there three Persons in God?

26 Are these three Persons three Gods? These three Persons are not three Gods; the Father, the Son and the Holy Spirit are all one and the same God.

27 What is the mystery of the three Persons in one God called?

28 What do you mean by a mystery? By a mystery I mean a truth which is above reason, but revealed by God.

29 Is there any likeness to the Blessed Trinity in your soul? There is this likeness to the Blessed Trinity in my soul, that as in one God there are three Persons, so in my one soul there are three powers.

30 Which are the three powers of your soul? The three powers of my soul are my memory, my understanding and my will.

(e)   Catholic Faith, based on Gasparri's Catholic Catechism

WHAT GOD WANTS ME TO KNOW
THE BLESSED TRINITY

1 Is there only one God?

2 How many Persons are there in God?

3 What do we call one God in Three Divine Persons?

4 How do you show that you believe in the Blessed Trinity?

5 What do you say when you make the Sign of the Cross?

6 Has God a beginning?

(7–14 Questions about God's attributes.)

15 With what prayer do we praise the Blessed Trinity?

Deharbe does not organize his catechism on the articles of the creed, but brings them in at the end of his doctrinal section, qq. 100–118. After the reciting of the creed we have:

102 Who created you? God the Father created me.

103 Who redeemed you? God the Son redeemed me.

104 Who sanctified you? God the Holy Ghost sanctified me.

105 Who is the Holy Ghost? The Holy Ghost is the third Person of the Blessed Trinity, and He is truly God, like the Father and the Son.

106 Why is the Holy Ghost represented in the form of a dove?

107 Why is He also represented in the form of fiery tongues?

108 How does the Holy Ghost sanctify me?

C.   COMMENTS ON THESE CATECHISMS

These old catechisms are nowadays criticized mostly for what many people regard as their pedagogical ineptitude. We are not here concerned with that debate, but only with their doctrinal method and content.

From this point of view I would myself regard Deharbe's catechism as the least unsatisfactory. The author at any rate avoids talking about three persons in one God; instead he talks of God in three persons, and the one Godhead in three persons. This is semantically much more accurate and less misleading.

The questions 'How many persons are there in God?' and 'Are there three persons in God?' have exactly the same form as, and will thus be understood by children – and most teachers too, I suspect – to be exactly analogous to, the questions 'How many inches are there in a foot?' and 'Are there twelve inches in a foot?' God, like Gaul, is implicitly divided into three parts. Whereas to talk of one God in three persons is like talking about one story in three versions, or one play in three performances, and thus does not suggest division into parts.

But the cardinal fault of all of them is that they do not really present the mystery of the Trinity at all. The key terms for the mystery are the names 'Father', 'Son' and 'Holy Spirit'. In all these catechisms these names are introduced only in the second place. In most of them these names never figure in the questions. The essence of the mystery is assumed throughout to consist in the combination of the terms 'three persons' and 'one God'. That is certainly the essence of the mystification. In fact the number 3 and the words 'person' and 'trinity' provide us not with the essence of the mystery but only with what, used rightly, is a convenient shorthand for indicating the mystery once we have grasped its proper terms.

It is to be noted that none of these catechisms introduce the words 'procession' and 'mission', or their equivalents. Their compilers would doubtless reply that these notions are too difficult and abstruse for children and the simple faithful, and must be left to theologians and seminarians only. The South African *Explanatory Catechism* actually marks the different questions as suitable for different school grades. Of its three questions on the Trinity only the first – How many persons are there in God? – is marked as suitable for Standard I. The second is considered suitable for Standard II, the third – the only one that has any actual substance to it – for Standard III.

This seems to me to be turning the whole matter on its head. In fact 'three persons in one God', even Deharbe's preferable 'one Godhead in three persons', are more abstruse and difficult than 'procession' and 'mission', which have a clear connection with the biblical names 'Father', 'Son' and 'Holy Spirit' and are themselves biblical. There is nothing abstruse about the notion of sending and being sent (mission), or about coming forth from, being born of, begetting or bearing, breathing forth and being breathed forth (all variations of procession). These realities, which are not abstractions, constitute the mystery. 'Three persons', 'three in one', 'trinity' simply label it.

It is also to be noted that those catechisms which attempt to show the importance of the mystery and to connect it to the rest of our Christian faith and (in a sense) to the great story of salvation history,[4] resort to a traditional and perfectly respectable appropriation of divine acts, but treat it as though it were a *proper* distribution of these acts to the three persons. We are left with the impression that the Son and Holy Spirit are not involved in creating us, nor the Father and the Holy Spirit in redeeming us, nor the Father and Son in sanctifying us. So we are back with the chief weakness of the old economic theologians, without enjoying any of their assets.

One last observation. All these catechisms have received not merely the *Nihil obstat* but the positive approbation of various hierarchies, provincial councils, bishops and representatives of the Holy See. They are all therefore documents of what is now called 'the ordinary *magisterium*'. And some of them, as we have noted, teach bad doctrine which is not in accord with the authentic and classic Catholic tradition (English Catechism qq. 17, 29, 30; Baltimore Catechism no. 3, q. 24).[5] All of them teach sound doctrine badly in the sense that they render it either meaningless or irrelevant or both, and that they are intrinsically liable to generate erroneous misunderstandings of it.

From this we must conclude that the bearers of the ordinary *magisterium*, the bishops and the Holy See, are open to criticism; and that they will only exercise their magisterial duty effectively and properly if they are willing to accept criticism. The *magisterium* is not in fact, as many persons in high authority would have us suppose nowadays, to be seen as a source of authoritative pronouncements that are to be accepted by the rest of the faithful without question or argument.

NOTES

1 It is preceded by (1) a brief history of dogmatic theology, (2) a treatise on faith (3) a treatise *De Deo Uno*.

2 Except with reference to the procession of the Holy Spirit from the Son: 658 b, p. 400.

3 Only the no. 3 Catechism. Baltimore Catechism no. 2, which seems to be the authentic text, in a revised edition, lacks this obnoxious question.

4 The English Catechism and the one based on Gasparri do not make even this attempt to give the doctrine relevance or meaning for the catechumens.

5 For English Catechism, q. 17 see p. 155 above, and for qq. 29, 30 see p. 157 above. The Baltimore Catechism no. 3, q. 24, is even worse theology and doctrine than the English Catechism, q. 17: 'What is God? God is *a* spirit, infinitely perfect'. My italics; God is unmistakably being classified as one of a genus – 'spirit'.

VI
Recovering the Mystery

17
After Vatican II

A. JUDGEMENT ON THE TEXTS CITED IN CHAPTER 16

The textbooks and catechisms we examined in Chapter 16 represent the nadir in the Latin Catholic tradition of handing on the faith about the Blessed Trinity. I do not think it is too brutal to say that in the catechisms at least – and the textbooks designed for the theological education of the clergy are hardly any better in this respect – this central mystery of our faith is reduced to a sacred rigmarole: 'There are three Persons in one God', and 'This mystery of three Persons in one God is called the Blessed Trinity'; a rigmarole we are excused from attempting to understand because it is labelled a mystery, and mysteries (though apparently definable, pp. 152–153 above) are beyond our capacity to understand. Thus a powerful movement in the Church, scholasticism, which in itself may perhaps be criticized as excessively intellectualist, achieves through a process of 'tradition fossilization' its *reductio ad absurdum* in an anti-intellectualist cramming of children with – mumbo-jumbo.

'Rigmarole' and 'mumbo-jumbo' are rude words. I do not mean that the statements 'there are three persons in one God' or 'the name of the mystery is the Blessed Trinity' are in themselves meaningless rigmarole and mumbo-jumbo. I mean they become so when they are not given their proper context. And that is precisely the fault of these textbooks and catechisms; their teaching of the mystery of the Trinity has no context whatsoever.

Notice how *all* the catechisms end their Trinity sections with the sign of the cross. This means in effect that they proceed from the unknown to the known; they begin with contextless abstraction (rigmarole) and end with a little piece of actual personal experience. For I suppose it is true that all Catholic children and catechumens learn the sign of the cross and its formula 'In the name of the Father and of the Son and of the Holy Spirit' long before they come to their catechism questions on the Trinity. The sign of the cross with its formula is a basic gesture of Christian liturgy. And liturgy, even if it is the rather bad liturgy of modern times, is perhaps the most universal form of religious experience. Going to church, assisting at mass, going to communion, going to confession, making the sign of the cross, saying your prayers, listening (sometimes) to passages from Scripture and gospel stories about Jesus – these are the basic ways in which all Catholic Christians, whether before or after the Council, whether they live in an individualistic or a more communal social atmosphere, experience God and his revelation in Christ. It is from this kind of concrete experience – and other more superficially secular experiences – that formal instruction in Christian doctrine should start. It is where the dehydrated scholasticism we have been examining and criticizing ended – sometimes as a mere afterthought.

B.   VOICES CRYING IN THE WILDERNESS

Now of course the catechetical and theological processes in the Church before the Council were not as uniformly out of touch with reality as what I have just written may suggest. There was the strong liturgical movement, for example, trying to make the worship of God, which is the common religious experience, in different forms, of all Christians, more vital and more instructive and doctrinal, by encouraging active participation, by throwing light on the symbolism of the liturgy, and so forth. This led first to the reforms of Pius XII, particularly his reform of the Holy Week liturgy, and then to the wholesale reforms that followed Vatican II.

Parallel to this movement was a growing sense of the importance of history for a true understanding of Christian doctrine, an appreciation of the elementary fact that Christianity is a *historical* religion, based on a particular historical figure Jesus Christ, and a particular set of historical events, his life, death and resurrection. We have already noted the first stirrings of this historical appreciation in Tanquerey's textbook.

In the line of theological writing, not a textbook but a book of theological reflection for the educated lay reader, I was delighted to discover in our library[1] a book published in 1926, written by Mgr F. C. Kolbe who must then have been in his late sixties and who was for many years chaplain to the Catholic students at the University of Cape Town. He had been a convert to Catholicism from the Dutch Reformed Church about, I would guess, 1880. The title of his book is *The Four Mysteries of the Faith*.[2] These mysteries are the Blessed Trinity, the Incarnation, the Church and the Eucharist.

The book is not in any sense a work of genius. It certainly has a very old-fashioned ring about it today. But it is *real*, about real religion as apprehended by an intelligent, well-educated and by all accounts holy man, who was not content with oft-repeated rigmarole and did not want his public to be so either. The English Catechism tells us that what we mean by a mystery is 'a truth which is above reason but revealed by God' (q. 28). In the context, after what I have called sacred rigmarole about three persons in one God and the mystery of the Blessed Trinity, this does rather read like an anti-intellectualist way of excusing us all from any further thought on the matter, or effort to understand. That will depend on the teacher, of course. Now Mgr Kolbe gives a similar definition of the word – 'a divinely revealed truth which we could not have apprehended without revelation, and which we cannot comprehend even now that it is revealed' (p. 6); but he goes on in the next paragraph to make it abundantly clear that he is not using the word 'mystery' as an excuse for not thinking. He says, 'If then in the middle of my book somebody were to say to me "Yes, but after all *everything* is a mystery", I should reply, "Quite true, but why change the subject so abruptly? . . . " Let no one then interrupt my reasoning with the sentimentalism of "the crannied wall" '.[3] And in some of the following introductory chapters he goes on to talk at length about knowledge of things through symbols and figures and analogies, which is also a necessary element in the concept of mystery, as we shall see again in a moment.

When he comes finally to 'The First Mystery: the Blessed Trinity' (chapter XI, p. 53), he begins, 'My purpose is not to prove the mystery, but *to show the mode of its revelation*' (my italics). And he begins the second paragraph thus: 'The Second and New Creation is represented to us as the result of a Divine Council in which God the Father sends His Son to rebuild the structure which Adam had ruined, and sends His Spirit to animate the work'. Straight into the missions, the mode of revelation. If you say something is revealed, the first thing to investigate is *how* it is revealed, and your investigation will in fact tell you much more about what is revealed. For these words alone Mgr Kolbe deserves, in my opinion, to be declared the first twentieth-century Doctor of the Church. It is a matter of a robust and realistic religious sense triumphing over the cobwebs of conventional abstraction and mystification which had, I presume, constituted Mgr Kolbe's seminary education. In the whole short chapter (five pages) he does not use the words 'person' or 'trinity' once. If one compares this book with *The Faith Explained* by a later and very proficient popularizer of theology, Leo Trese (1959), its merits stand out even further. Trese gives a competent explanation of the Trinity – but does not refer at all to the missions, the incarnation or Pentecost.

Kolbe refers appreciatively in his Introduction to the great nineteenth-century German theologian, Matthias Joseph Scheeben and his *magnum opus, The Mysteries of Christianity*.[4] But he implies that his own reflections were independent of that work. Scheeben's is indeed a great work, not at all musty with cobwebs. But his concern, at least in discussing the Trinity, is to show that the mystery cannot be proved by reason, though once accepted on faith it can be shown to be harmonious with reason. What this involves him in is a consideration, not of notions of 'person' etc., but of the divine processions as constituting the mystery. His treatment of the missions is confined to the invisible missions, and in my view is unsatisfactory. But at least, before he even comes formally to deal with the mystery of the Trinity, while he is talking about mysteries as such in chapter 1, he shows an awareness of the revelatory function of the missions: 'If Christianity's teaching is worthy of the only begotten Son of God, if the Son of God had to descend from the bosom of his Father to initiate us into this teaching, could we expect anything else than the revelation of the deepest mysteries locked up in God's heart? ... And if God has sent us his own Spirit to teach us all truth, the Spirit of truth who dwells in God and there searches the deep things of God, should this Spirit ... teach us no sublime secrets?' (p. 4).

On p. 11 Scheeben gives as an essential component of the notion of mystery, in the strict theological sense, the point 'that its content is capable of apprehension only by analogous concepts'. This is an absolutely fundamental theological principle that is not well appreciated by the kind of theological textbook we have criticized. It only figures in the English Catechism, implicitly, in answer to the question (70), 'What do you mean by the words "is seated at the right hand of the Father"? ... I do not mean that God the Father has hands, for he is a spirit; but I mean that Christ as God is equal to the Father, and as man is in the highest place in heaven.'

At the beginning of Chapter 5 (p. 45 above) I referred to Karl Rahner's 'Remarks on the Dogmatic Treatise "De Trinitate" ' (*Theological Investigations* 4, p. 77). This was originally published in 1960, just before the Council, so it is appropriate to mention it here, though it can scarcely be regarded, at this stage, as a voice crying in the wilderness, since the desert was already beginning to bloom. What Rahner says there has been a major stimulant to me to write this book. I do not say 'inspiration'; that came, as the reader will not be surprised to learn, from reading St Augustine's *De Trinitate*. But when I later read Rahner's *Remarks*, and his thesis 'that the Trinity of the economy of salvation is the immanent Trinity and *vice versa*' (p. 87), I realized that what he says needs to be done today, had already been done by Augustine.

C.   THE COUNCIL AND AFTER

Vatican II tolled the death-knell – at least until a day of resurrection dawns – of theological textbooks. I do not know of anyone who has had the courage to try and write one in the last twenty years. But a book I should mention here (certainly no textbook) is *The Trinity and the Religious Experience of Man* by Raimundo Panikkar.[5] I quoted it above in note 17 to Chapter 6 (p. 63), in support of Augustine's view that the essence of the mystery hardly lies in the metaphysics of the words 'person', 'hypostasis' or 'substance'. For Panikkar is as keen as I am to relate our faith in the Trinity once more to real experience. But he goes about it in quite a different way. In this book I have been trying to bring to light once more the roots of the doctrine in the Judaeo-Christian experience, and then to climb up from these roots (which we can still touch in our liturgical traditions) in the 'economy of salvation' to the highest branches of the mystery 'immanent' in the 'transcendent' deity. As far as I can follow him, Panikkar starts with the immanent mystery as currently formulated, regrets its stratospheric severance from religious experience – typified by anxiety over words like 'person' – and tries to show its links with such experience in *all* religious traditions, not just the Christian one. He is most interested in the religious traditions of India, but he does not exclude others, since his concern is with the universal religious experience and needs of mankind. 'The Trinity', he writes, 'may be considered as a junction where the authentic spiritual dimensions of all religions meet. The Trinity is God's self-revelation in the fulness of time, the consummation both of all that God has already "said" of himself to man and of all that man has been able to attain and know of God in his thought and mystical experience. In the Trinity a true encounter of religions takes place, which results, not in a vague fusion or mutual dilution, but in an authentic enhancement of all the religious and even cultural elements that are contained in each. . . . Only by a deepening of trinitarian understanding will such an encounter in depth come to pass, the synthesis and mutual fecundation of the different spiritual attitudes which comprise religions, without forcing or doing violence to the fundamental intuitions of the different spiritual paths' (pp. 42–43). In this context, what I have been trying to do in this book, namely to help Christians, especially Latin Catholic Christians, to a better understanding of the mystery in terms of our own religious tradition, may be regarded as a preparation for that truly Catholic or universal dialogue of faiths to which Fr Panikkar would devote his theological reflections.

If Vatican II has 'killed' the textbook, it has given new life to the catechism. It inaugurated – or unleashed – a revolution in catechetical methods. This revolution has proved very controversial, and I have no intention, or competence, to get involved in the disputes about method, about the merits and demerits, for example, of the old question-and-answer form. The only point of method I am concerned with in the post-Vatican-II catechisms is their arrangement of matter and their treatment of the Trinity.

The most famous of them, I suppose, is the so-called Dutch Catechism, whose correct title is *A New Catechism: Catholic Faith for Adults* (ET, Burns & Oates, London/Herder & Herder, New York, 1967; latest revised ed. 1983). Its whole arrangement is basically historical, and it succeeds on the whole in linking history with liturgy, that is with the round of the liturgical year. It follows, that is to say, the *a posteriori via inventionis,* not the systematic *a priori via doctrinae.* It begins with Man in Part I, 'The Mystery of Existence'; it ends with God as the second chapter of Part V, 'The way to the End'. That does not mean that God has not been mentioned in the middle. It does mean that we are proceeding, reasonably, from the known to the unknown, from self to the other. The focus of the book is Jesus Christ, in Part III, 'The Son of Man'. We lead up to him with Part II, 'The Way to Christ', 'A: The Way of the Nations' (cf. Panikkar), and 'B: The Way of Israel' (cf. myself). We go on from, or rather with, Christ in Part IV, 'The Way of Christ', which deals with the Church and its life.

Where does the Trinity fit in here? I cannot find it in the index! Nor do I find 'person' there, or 'procession' or 'mission'. Is this catechism so new that they have left out the central mystery of the faith? Not quite; under 'God' in the index I find the subheading 'the mystery of the Father, the Son and the Spirit, 498–502'. That is a reference to the last pages of Part V. So this catechism *ends* with the Trinity. Very proper. Does it do it well? Clearly not adequately – that is not possible in four pages. But on the right lines. The connection of the mystery with the incarnation is to the fore; the mutual relationships and processions of the persons are stated in untechnical language. The bearing of the mystery on our destiny is made clear. The Holy Spirit is skipped over rather lightly, perhaps. But the point is quite well made that the whole book has really been about the Trinity: 'After a volume in which everything spoke of the Father, the Son and the Holy Spirit, a "treatment" in a few pages would be to set the mystery too far apart' (p. 499).

At the beginning of Part III, then, we have already had a simple commentary on 'The Word was made flesh' and related texts, which in a couple of pages takes us on to Nicaea, Ephesus and Chalcedon: briefly, the mission of the Son revealing the eternal generation of the Son (pp. 77–86). On pp. 195–200 we have comments on the giving of the Spirit and Pentecost. But the emphasis is on the gifts of the Holy Spirit rather than on the person of the Holy Spirit, and his relations with and procession from the Father and the Son.

In a word, the mystery of the Trinity is, so to say, 'repossessed' into the whole scheme of Christian faith. In the process it ceases to be cut and dried. But above all it ceases to be rigmarole. There remains perhaps an element of what Rahner calls 'trinitarian timidity'[6] – and the index has not been at all thoroughly prepared. But an excellent catechism for adults, all the same.

One more catechism I wish to notice is the *Catholic Catechism,* officially adopted for all dioceses in Germany (ET, Herder, Freiburg, 1957; 15th impression 1965). It is in fact pre-conciliar, and is certainly less radical in its method than the *New Catechism.* But for all that, it represents the refreshing new realism in catechetics that carried the day at the Council. It is an explanatory catechism with questions and answers embedded in it, but not too prominently.

The first part, 'Of God and our Redemption', is divided as follows: (1) God our Father in Heaven; (2) Of the World's Creation, the Fall and the Promise of Redemption; (3) Of Jesus Christ our Lord; (4) Our Saviour Became Man, Suffered and was Glorified; (5) Of the Holy Ghost and His Action; (6) Of the Mystery of the Holy Trinity.

The first thing to note in its favour, before we see how in fact it deals with the mystery of the Trinity, is that it leads up to it historically. That is, we start with the economy of salvation, and therefore, at least implicitly, with the missions. The structure is in fact that of the traditional creeds.

The first question on 'God our Father in Heaven' (q. 7, p. 9) is, 'Through whom has God revealed himself to us?'; and the answer is, 'God has revealed himself to us under the old covenant through the patriarchs and prophets, and under the new covenant through Jesus Christ and the apostles'. Thus we have a concrete, 'economic' statement of revelation. After that, the questions are all about God's attributes. The appalling question 'What is God?' is very properly never asked. The last question on God (q. 28, p. 32) demonstrates what is at least an improvement on that bad question in the English Catechism – 'Why do we call God a spirit?'. This is not entirely satisfactory either. I would leave out the whole question, and certainly omit that indefinite article in it. I do not know when people first began to bother about God being spirit. I suppose it was thought to be the plain man's way of putting St Thomas' question on the simplicity of God. One regrettable omission in this section is that in spite of its heading 'On God our Father in Heaven', there is no question or explanation of the name 'Father'.

When we come to 'Jesus Christ our Lord', we find constant references to his Father in the text, and q. 44 (p. 53) asks 'What did Jesus say about obedience to his Father's will?'. There should really be some explanation of why Jesus called God his Father – and our Father. Q. 46 (p. 57), 'Who gives us testimony that Jesus Christ is the Son of God and himself true God?', with its explanatory section, introduces us not only to the divinity of Christ, but to his divinity as Son of the Father, which is a great improvement on previous catechisms. Q. 47, 'Who is Jesus Christ?' and q. 48, 'Why did the Son of God become man?' (p. 60) carry on in the same progression: the economy of the *mission* of the Son and the purpose of it. It would in my view be an improvement if it were explicitly stated that the Son of God became man because God the Father sent the Son to become man. This could be put in the answer to the question 'Why did the Son of God become man?'.

When we come to Pentecost and the Holy Spirit, again there is no mention of his being sent: q. 68 (p. 86), 'What did the Holy Ghost do to the Apostles?'; q. 69 (p. 87), 'Who is the Holy Ghost? The Holy Ghost is the

third person of the Godhead; he is true God like the Father and the Son'.
That is too abrupt and there are currents of mystification and rigmarole here
again. But at least the questions are in the right place and context. We go on
to q. 70 (p. 88), 'What do we acknowledge about the Holy Ghost in the
Creed which we say during mass?'. There follow a few questions about the
grace of the Holy Spirit.

Then comes the very brief section on the Trinity, summing up what God
has revealed about himself in the economy. The explanation is better than in
any earlier catechism I have looked at. It does at least mention the missions –
but not the processions, which are essential to any real understanding of the
mystery. Again, in fact, we see that 'anti-trinitarian timidity'. It is encapsul-
ated in the two questions of this section (p. 96). Q. 77, 'What does our faith
teach us about the Blessed Trinity? There are three persons in God: God the
Father, God the Son, and God the Holy Ghost, and these three persons are
but one God'. Q. 78, 'For what favours do we thank the three persons? God
the Father has made us from nothing; God the Son has redeemed us; God the
Holy Ghost has made us holy'. Notice again the resort to appropriation
when the attempt is made to give 'relevance' to the mystery, but without
mentioning that it is appropriation.

But at least, and at last, the mystery is given a context. That the English
bishops, *six years after the end of the Council*, should have reissued their old
'Penny Catechism' in 1971, when they could have produced any number of
simplifications of this *Catholic Catechism* in good, old-fashioned question-and-
answer form – well, to say the least, it is astonishing. Would it be too harsh
to label it a piece of seriously irresponsible negligence? But such, not all that
infrequently, are the workings of a *magisterium* motivated primarily by fear of
change.

NOTES

1 St Augustine's Seminary, Roma, Lesotho.
2 Longmans, London, 1926. Almost certainly long out of print. Well worth another
   edition, in my opinion.
3 Alfred, Lord Tennyson: *'Flower in the Crannied Wall'*:
   Flower in the crannied wall,
   I pluck you out of the crannies,
   I hold you here, root and all, in my hand,
   Little flower – but *if* I could understand
   What you are, root and all, and all in all,
   I should know what God and man is.
4 ET by C. Vollert (Herder, St Louis/London, 1946).
5 Orbis Books, New York/Darton, Longman & Todd, London, 1973.
6 K. Rahner, 'Remarks . . .', *Theological Investigations* 4, p. 81. Actually he calls it *'anti-
   trinitarian timidity'*. Also useful for bibliographical information on other 'voices
   crying in the wilderness', mostly of German theologians.

18

Suggestions for a Catechism of 'Pro-Trinitarian Boldness'

Having made such severe criticisms of old-style catechisms, I think in fairness I should conclude by offering suggestions of my own for a trinitarian catechism. I submit them in the old question-and-answer form for the benefit of those conservative readers who may think it the best one. Professionals in catechetics will easily be able to transpose its substance, if they so desire, into what they may consider more suitable forms. It is not, of course, presented as an independent text, but as something to be fitted into a catechism roughly on the model of the German *Catholic Catechism*.

Introduction

1   Make the sign of the cross.
2   Why do we bless ourselves with the sign of the cross?

Because it was by the death of our Lord Jesus Christ on the cross and his resurrection from the dead that we are saved.

3   What does being saved mean?

Being saved means being redeemed from the slavery of sin and death and restored to the freedom of the children of God, and being given a share in the eternal life and happiness of the Father, the Son and the Holy Spirit.

4   Is that why we make the sign of the cross in the name of the Father and of the Son and of the Holy Spirit?

Yes, and also because we were (will be) baptized in the name of the Father and of the Son and of the Holy Spirit.

5   How do we know that we have been given a share in the eternal life of the Father, the Son and the Holy Spirit?

Because St Paul writes in his letter to the Galatians 'When the fullness of time had come God sent his Son, born of woman, born under the

law, that we might receive sonship by adoption; and because you are sons
God sent the Spirit of his Son into our hearts, crying Abba, Father! So you
are no longer a slave but a son' (Gal. 4:4–7; not RSV).

6   Who are the Father, the Son and the Holy Spirit?
        The Father, the Son and the Holy Spirit are the one God.

7   How do we know about God the Father, the Son and the Holy
Spirit?
        We know about them by faith.

8   What do you mean by faith?
        By faith I mean believing everything that God has revealed.

9   Where do we learn our faith?
        We learn our faith in the bosom of the holy Catholic Church.

10   Who teaches us through the holy Catholic Church?
        Jesus Christ our Lord, the Son of God, and his Holy Spirit teach us
through the holy Catholic Church.

11   What do we call the brief account of our faith and of what Jesus
Christ and the Holy Spirit teach us in the holy Catholic Church?
        We call this brief account of our faith the Apostles' Creed.

12   Recite the Apostles' Creed.

The Apostles' Creed: first article

13   Through what things does God make himself known to us?
        God makes himself known to us (1) through the world we live in;
(2) through our consciences; (3) above all through his revelation.

14   Through whom has God revealed himself to us?
        God has revealed himself to us, under the old covenant through the
patriarchs and prophets; and under the new covenant through Jesus Christ,
and through his teaching as handed on to us by his apostles and disciples.

15   Why is God called 'the Father'?
        He is called the Father because he is the Father of our Lord Jesus
Christ.

16   Is God then not also our Father, and the Father of all people?
        Yes, he is also the Father of us all, because he has given us a share in
the sonship of Jesus Christ by adopting us as his children.

17   Why is God called Almighty?
        Because he has power over everything he has made, which he rules
by his fatherly providence.

18   What do we mean by God's providence?
        By God's providence we mean that he makes provision for all
creatures according to his wisdom and foresight, and that nothing in the
whole created universe is left outside his loving care and control.

19 Can we know in this life what God is?

No, in this life we cannot really know what God is, even though he has revealed himself to us, but only what he is not.

20 What word do we use for saying that God is not made of anything, and that he does not consist of any parts?

We say that he is absolutely simple.

21 How do we say that he is not something bodily or material?

We say he is immaterial and incorporeal. We can also express this by saying he is spirit.

22 How do we say God is not in time, neither beginning nor ending nor moving?

We say he is eternal.

23 How do we say he is not in space?

We say he is immense or immeasurable.

24 How do we say he is without any limitations?

We say he is infinite.

25 How do we say he does not change?

We say he is changeless or immutable.

26 Can we say God is a particular kind of thing, as everything we know in the world is a particular kind of thing?

No, we cannot say God is a kind of thing, because since he is both simple and infinite he cannot be defined or classified.

27 Does this mean that we cannot say at all what God is like?

No; we can say to some extent what God is like; but the likeness will always be a very distant one.

28 Does God exist, like created things?

Yes, God exists, but he does not come into existence or have existence like created things; rather, he is his own existence. He simply is.

29 Is God good?

Yes, God is good; but his goodness is infinite, unlike that of created things; and moreover he is his own goodness.

30 Is God also faithful and true, wise, just, understanding and loving in the same way?

Yes, God is all these things simply by being his own faithfulness and truth, his own wisdom, justice, knowledge, understanding and loving.

31 Why is God the Father Almighty called creator of heaven and earth?

Because he made the whole universe out of nothing.

32 Did God the Father alone make it?

No; he made it through his Son, in the Holy Spirit.

Then after further questions on creation, which after the model of the German Catechism should be followed by questions on evil, the fall, sin and original sin, and death, we come to the second and subsequent articles of the creed. But we come to them with a crucial question about the history of salvation. (I continue to number my questions in sequence.)

The Apostles' Creed: second article

33   What did God do in order to save mankind from evil, sin and death?

   After a long preparation, through the Law given to his chosen people Israel and through the prophets he sent them, God the Father, when the fullness of time had come, sent his Son into the world to become man and dwell among us.

34   Who is this Son of God?

   The Son of God is Jesus of Nazareth, whom we call Jesus Christ.

35   What does 'the Christ' mean?

   It means the Anointed One, and was a title given to the kings of Israel.

36   Why is Jesus called the Christ?

   Because he was a descendant of King David, and God sent him to be the King of kings and Lord of lords, and to establish the kingdom of God on earth.

37   Has Jesus Christ established the kingdom of God on earth?

   He has sown the seeds of the kingdom of God, but it is still only present in a hidden and imperfect manner.

38   When will he establish it in its fullness and glory?

   When he comes again in glory to judge the living and the dead on the last day.

39   Shall we be there?

   Yes, we shall all be there in the resurrection of the dead, to share fully in the eternal life and happiness of the Father, the Son and the Holy Spirit.

40   Why is Jesus Christ called God the Father's only Son?

   Because he was born of the Father before all ages, God from God, light from light, true God from true God, begotten not made, consubstantial with the Father.

41   But if we too are the Father's children, how can Jesus Christ be his *only* Son?

   Because *he* is God's Son by sharing fully with the Father in being the one divine nature, while *we* are God's children by adoption.

42   What do we call the Son's being eternally begotten of the Father?

   We call it the eternal generation of the Son, by which he proceeds eternally from the Father. It is also called his eternal procession from the Father.

43   How is the Son's eternal generation made known to us?

It is made known to us through his being sent into the world by the Father to become man.

44   What is his being so sent called?

It is called the sending or the mission of the Son, from the Latin word *missio*, which means sending.

45   When was God the Son sent into the world?

He was sent into the world when he was conceived and born of the virgin Mary, while Herod the Great was king of Judaea and Caesar Augustus was emperor of Rome.

46   How many years ago was that?

It was about 1,985 years ago.

47   What do we call the mystery of God the Son becoming man?

We call it the mystery of the incarnation.

48   Why do we call it that?

We call it that because 'incarnation' is from the Latin word *caro* meaning 'flesh', and so incarnation means 'becoming flesh'; and John writes in his gospel, 'And the Word became flesh and dwelt among us' (Jn 1:14).

49   Does becoming flesh mean the same as becoming man?

Yes; it was a Jewish way of speaking, as when the prophet Isaiah says 'All flesh is grass' (Isa 40:6).

50   Who is referred to as 'the Word'?

God the Son is referred to as the Word.

51   What is John's Greek term for 'Word', and what is its meaning?

His Greek term is *Logos*, and besides meaning 'word' in the ordinary English sense, it also means 'idea' or 'thought' or 'reason'.

52   Do we learn anything about the eternal generation of the Son from his being called the Logos or Word of God?

Yes, we learn that the eternal generation of the Son from the Father is very different from our generation in time from our human parents.

53   Does that mean that God the Father and God the Son are not truly related to each other as Father and Son?

No; they are truly related as Father and Son, because the Father transmits to the Son his own divine nature, and the Son receives his divine nature from the Father, just as our parents transmit their human nature to us and we receive the same human nature from them. And just as we usually resemble our parents, so the Son perfectly resembles the Father.

54   How do we express the Son's perfect resemblance of the Father?

We express it by calling him the perfect Image of the Father.

55   How then does calling him the Logos or Word of God show that his generation by the Father is different from ours by our parents?

It shows that the Father *begets* the Son in something like the way we *get* ideas in our minds, and express them in words.

56   Do we then also talk about conceiving ideas and bringing them to birth?

Yes; and we sometimes talk about an idea being someone's 'brain-child'.

57   What is the idea or logos which the Father conceives when he begets the Son?

It is the complete and perfect idea of himself, which he expresses by 'uttering' the Word or Logos, which is thus the perfect and equal Image of the Father.

58   Was there ever a time when the Father did not utter the Word or beget the Son?

No, there never was such a time, nor is nor will be, because God's knowledge of himself, and thus his thinking of himself and getting an idea of himself is eternal, and indeed is identical with his being or existence.

59   Why is Jesus Christ, God's only Son, also called 'our Lord'?

He is called our Lord, both because he is the Messiah or Christ, the son of David, and thus the King of kings and Lord of lords, and also because he fully shares the Father's divine lordship over the whole created universe.

After further questions about the virgin birth and the life, death, resurrection and ascension of Jesus Christ, we come to the eighth article, 'I believe in the Holy Spirit'.

Apostles' Creed: the eighth article

60   Why do we also believe in the Holy Spirit?

Because just as the Father sent the Son to become man, so the Father and the Son sent the Holy Spirit at Pentecost in divided tongues of fire and a mighty rushing wind upon the first disciples of Jesus.

61   What is this sending of the Holy Spirit at Pentecost called?

It is called the visible mission of the Holy Spirit.

62   What does the visible mission of the Holy Spirit make known to us about God?

It makes known to us that the Holy Spirit proceeds eternally from the Father and from the Son.

63   Is the Holy Spirit truly God?

Yes, he is truly God, equal in all things to the Father and the Son.

64   What other visible mission of the Holy Spirit do the gospels tell us of?

They tell us how the Holy Spirit came down from heaven upon Jesus at his baptism in the form of a dove.

65   Do these visible appearances teach us anything about what the Holy

Spirit is like and what he does for us?

Yes; his appearance in the form of a dove reminds us of the dove Noah sent out of the ark. So it shows us that he is the Spirit of peace and of the reconciliation of mankind with God. The divided tongues of fire at Pentecost suggest that he has come to kindle in our hearts the fire of divine love, and that he speaks to the hearts of all peoples, of all tongues, languages and cultures. The mighty rushing wind indicates that he has come to us as the power of the living God.

66   What does the name 'Spirit' mean?

The name 'spirit' comes from the Latin word *spiro* meaning 'I breathe'. So the word 'spirit' originally means 'breath'. Then it comes to mean 'air' or 'wind'; and after that, since you cannot see air or wind, it comes to mean whatever is non-bodily or immaterial.

67   Which of these meanings is most suitable to the Holy Spirit?

The first meaning is most suitable to the Holy Spirit. It suggests that he proceeds from the Father and the Son by being breathed forth by them.

68   Did Jesus ever signify the Holy Spirit by breathing?

Yes; after his resurrection from the dead, when he appeared to the disciples, 'he breathed on them and said to them, Receive the Holy Spirit' (Jn 20:22).

69   What are the other chief names for the Holy Spirit?

He is also called 'Gift', because God gives him to us to be our Spirit. And he is also called 'Love', because being God's gift to us of himself, he expresses God's love for us.

70   Is there any other reason he is called Love?

Yes; he is also called Love because he is the expression of the love of the Father and the Son for each other.

71   Besides the visible missions, is there also an invisible mission of the Holy Spirit?

Yes, he is said to be sent invisibly to us when he is poured into our hearts (Rom 5:5, 8:15, Gal 4:6).

72   What is the effect of God's sending the Holy Spirit invisibly into our hearts?

The effect is that we receive God's sanctifying grace, which means a share in the eternal divine life of the Father, the Son and the Holy Spirit.

73   When the Holy Spirit is sent into our hearts, do the Father and the Son come too?

Yes, they come too, because the Father, Son and Holy Spirit are inseparable from each other.

74   Why are they inseparable from each other?

Because their very being consists of their relationships with each other, and because they are one God.

75   What is the common name we give to the Father, Son and Holy Spirit?

We give them the common name 'person', and we call them the three persons of the Blessed Trinity.

76   Why do we call them persons?

We call them persons to show that they are really distinct from each other, that is that the Father is not the Son nor the Son the Father, nor either of them the Holy Spirit.

77   What do we mean by 'trinity'?

By 'trinity' we simply mean 'three' or 'threesome'.

78   If they are three distinct persons having the same divine nature, does this not mean that they are three Gods?

No; they are not three Gods in the way that three human persons, say Tom, Dick and Harry, having the same human nature are three men or three people, because the divine nature is not divisible or multipliable like created natures into many instances of it, but God simply is the divine nature; which means each of the divine persons is the divine nature.

79   Do the three divine persons then add up to one God?

No, they do not add up to one God, because each one is God just as much as all three are God.

80   Are we created in the image and likeness of God?

Yes, we are, for when God created man he said, 'Let us make man in our own image and likeness' (Gen 1:26).

81   Is the image of God in us an image of the Trinity?

Yes; since God is a trinity of persons, Father, Son and Holy Spirit, his image in us is an image and likeness of the Father, the Son and the Holy Spirit.

82   In what does this image of the Trinity consist?

It consists in our minds, and in the mental acts whereby we remember ourselves, understand ourselves, and will or love or appreciate ourselves.

83   How does this image help us to see more clearly the relationships of the divine persons?

The act of self-memory producing the act of self-understanding, expressed as an idea or word of self, is comparable to the Father begetting the Son; and the act of self-appreciation issuing from the conjunction of self-memory and self-understanding is like the Holy Spirit proceeding from the Father and the Son.

84   Is the image of God in our minds fully realized in the acts of self-memory, self-understanding and self-appreciation?

No; the image is fully realized when we proceed from memory, understanding and appreciation or love of self to memory, understanding and love of God.

85   What is the best way of achieving this memory, understanding and love of God?

The best way of achieving it is trying with the help of the grace of the Holy Spirit to live our lives every day in a closer and closer imitation of Jesus Christ our Lord.

Then we proceed with questions on the holy Catholic Church and the closing articles of the creed, and the rest of the Catechism.

And may the blessing of Almighty God,
     the Father,
     the Son
     and the Holy Spirit,
come down upon us
and remain with us always.

                                                              Amen.

Questions for discussion

CHAPTER 1

1   Note and comment on the main differences between the Apostles' or Nicene Creeds on the one hand, and the Athanasian Creed on the other.
2   Set out and discuss the distinctive features of Augustine's personal statement of his trinitarian faith.

CHAPTER 2

1   To what extent do the New Testament writings cited in this chapter express a common understanding of a trinitarian doctrine of God?

CHAPTERS 3 and 4

1   Does the Old Testament's use of such terms as 'Father' and 'Son', 'God' and 'Lord', 'Son of Man', 'Son of God', 'Wisdom', 'Word' and 'Spirit' provide a suitable framework for the trinitarian revelation of the New Testament? Illustrate your answer with examples.
2   Can you conceive of a trinitarian revelation without the manifestation of God in Jesus Christ? Give reasons for your answer.
3   Compare the ways in which the Old and New Testaments use the term 'Holy Spirit'.

CHAPTER 5

1   Give your reasons for thinking that the 'economic' theologians contributed (or did not contribute) to the understanding of the tradition they received from the New Testament.
2   Compare and contrast the theology of Irenaeus with that of Justin or of Tertullian.

CHAPTER 6

1   Why is the argument over the choice between *homo-ousios* and *homoi-ousios* much more important than a mere quarrel over a single iota (the Greek letter *i*)?
2   Explain the 'natural theology' of the simplicity and immutability of God, shared by Arians and Orthodox in the fourth century, and that of 'economic' theologians such as Tertullian. Argue the case for your preference.

3 Explain the difficulties encountered in the Church of the fourth century in thinking in terms of one divine *ousia* and three divine *hupostaseis*.

CHAPTER 7

1 On what grounds can it be argued that the concept of relationship as developed by Augustine is the only key that will solve the problem of the real distinction between the divine persons without prejudice to the wholly simple divine unity?
2 What is the value and purpose of distinguishing between the divine processions and the divine missions?

CHAPTER 8

1 Having regard to its method and purpose, discuss the appropriateness of the structure of Augustine's *De Trinitate*.

CHAPTER 9

1 Is the mystery of the Trinity revealed only in the sending of the divine persons? Give reasons for your reply.

CHAPTER 10

1 Why is great weight placed upon the difference between the category of relationship and the eight other Aristotelian categories of accident? Can it be justified?

CHAPTER 11

1 Compare St Thomas's treatment of the terms 'person' and 'hypostasis' with that of St Augustine, and indicate your preference.
2 What is meant by the notion of 'appropriation' of names? Why is it necessary to use it in the context of trinitarian theology?

CHAPTER 12

1 On what grounds is there a disagreement between East and West over the term *Filioque*, applied to the procession of the Holy Spirit? Can it be resolved?

CHAPTER 13

1 Estimate the extent to which Augustine's analogy of the human mind, in its remembering, understanding and loving itself, is successful in illuminating the mystery of the divine processions.
2 Discuss the opinion that Augustine constructs, rather than discovers, this 'mental trinity'.

CHAPTER 14

1 Comment on the view that Augustine's image of the Trinity in the human mind represents a distortedly 'spiritual' view of man.
2 Assess the value of his elaboration of this image for the Christian spiritual life.
3 Show to what extent his use of this image links up with the 'economic' doctrines of the fall and the redemption.
4 Discuss the degree to which the doctrine of the invisible mission of the divine persons and their inhabitation in the believer can be understood by reference to his teaching about the structure of the mind.

CHAPTER 15

1 Compare the scholastic approach to the doctrine of the Trinity with that of Augustine, indicating and giving reasons for your preference.
2 Do you agree that catechesis has been adversely affected by post-scholastic theology? Give reasons for your view.

CHAPTER 16

1 Do you find the author's criticisms of pre-Vatican II textbooks and catechisms a fair judgement on the material available? Give the reasons for your opinion.

CHAPTER 17

1 Is the author unduly severe in his condemnation of the re-issue of the pre-conciliar 'Penny Catechism' in 1971? Estimate the pastoral pros and cons of the decision to bring it out.

CHAPTER 18

1 Assess the catechetical value of the questions and answers given in this chapter.

Bibliography

Bible: the Revised Standard Version (RSV) is copyright 1946, 1952, 1957 and 1971 by the Division of Christian Education of the National Council of the Churches of Christ in the United States of America.

Ancient writers available in English translation

Thomas Aquinas, *Summa Theologiae*, qq. 27-43: Blackfriars ed., vols 6, 7 (London/New York, 1964, 1975).

Augustine, *De Trinitate: Nicene and Post-Nicene Fathers*, 1st series, 3 (New York, 1887; latest ed. Grand Rapids, Mich., 1956).

Fathers of the Church 45 (New York, 1963).

Both these translations are useful as cribs, but with practically no notes or introductions their value for students is severely limited. A translation by me, with extensive introduction and notes, is at the time of writing in the hands of Fr Walter J. Burghardt, SJ, editor-in-chief of the *Ancient Christian Writers* series. I trust it will be published before 1990.

Hilary, *De Trinitate: Fathers of the Church* 25 (New York, 1954).

Irenaeus, *Against Heresies: Ante-Nicene Christian Library* 5, 9 (Edinburgh, 1868, 1869); *Ante-Nicene Fathers* 1 (Grand Rapids, Mich., 1976).

Justin, *Dialogue with Trypho: Fathers of the Church* 2 (New York, 1948).

Tertullian, *Against Praxeas:* trans. E. Evans (London, 1949).

Modern works

B. Altaner, *Patrology* (ET; Freiburg, 1960).

W. R. Bowie, *Jesus and the Trinity* (New York, 1960).

J. A. Bracken, *What are they saying about the Trinity?* (New York/Ramsey, N.J./Toronto, 1979).

David Brown, *The Divine Trinity* (London, 1985).

R. E. Brown, *The Community of the Beloved Disciple* (New York/Ramsey, N.J./London, 1979).

Catechisms: *The Baltimore Catechism, no. 3* (New York/Cincinnati, 1933).

A Catechism of Christian Doctrine, revised ed. (London, 1971).

A Catholic Catechism (15th impression, Freiburg, 1965).

The Catholic Faith (Baltimore, 1939).

Deharbe's Small Catechism (Freiburg, 1903).

Explanatory Catechism of Christian Doctrine (Cape Town, 1934).

A New Catechism: Catholic Faith for Adults, revised ed. (London, 1983).

I. Chevalier, *Saint Augustin et la pensée grecque: les relations trinitaires* (Fribourg, 1940).

Y. Congar, *I Believe in the Holy Spirit* (ET; 3 vols, London/New York, 1983).

O. Cullmann, *The Christology of the New Testament* (ET; Philadelphia/London, 1963).

A. Grillmeier, *Christ in Christian Tradition* (ET; London/New York, 1965).

E. Hendrikx, *La Date de composition du De Trinitate* (Paris, 1955).

W. Hill, *The Three-Personed God: the Trinity as a Mystery of Salvation* (Washington, 1982).

R. Jenson, *The Triune Identity: God according to the Gospel* (Philadelphia, 1982).

J. N. D. Kelly, *The Athanasian Creed* (London/New York, 1964).

            Early Christian Creeds, 2nd ed. (London, 1960/New York, 1961).

            Early Christian Doctrines, 2nd ed. (London/New York, 1960).

F. C. Kolbe, *The Four Mysteries of the Faith* (London, 1926).

A.-M. La Bonnardière, *Recherches de chronologie augustinienne* (Paris, 1965).

J. Moltmann, *The Crucified God* (ET; New York, 1974/London, 1976).

            The Trinity and the Kingdom of God (ET; New York/London, 1981).

R. Panikkar, *The Trinity and the Religious Experience of Man* (London, 1973).

J. Pohle, *The Divine Trinity: a Dogmatic Treatise* (St Louis, 1919).

G. L. Prestige, *God in Patristic Thought* (London/Toronto, 1936; repr. London, 1952).

K. Rahner, 'Remarks on the Dogmatic Treatise "De Trinitate"', *Theological Investigations* 4 (ET; London/New York, 1966).

            The Trinity (ET; London/New York, 1970).

C. Richardson, *The Doctrine of the Trinity* (New York, 1958).

M. J. Scheeben, *The Mysteries of Christianity* (ET; St Louis, 1946).

E. Schillebeeckx, *Christ the Sacrament of Encounter with God* (ET; New York/London, 1963).

H. B. Swete, *On the History of the Doctrine of the Procession of the Holy Spirit* (Cambridge, 1876).

G. Tavard, *Vision of the Trinity* (Washington, 1981).

E. TeSelle, *Augustine the Theologian* (London/New York, 1970).

L. Trese, *The Faith Explained* (Chicago/London, 1959).

Modern Latin textbooks

J. Herrmann, *Institutiones Theologiae Dogmaticae* I (Rome, 1908).

L. Lercher, *Institutiones Theologiae Dogmaticae* II (Barcelona, 1951).

A. Tanquerey, *Synopsis Theologiae Dogmaticae* II (Paris, 1926).

Indexes

INDEX OF BIBLICAL REFERENCES

Genesis
1	32, 41
1:3	25
26–28	32
26	178
2 – 4	41
2 – 3	24
2	32
2:7	32
3	47, 136, 137
3:5	135
6:1–4	28
2ff.	21
10	22
18	47
26:24	21

Exodus
1:5	22
3	47
3:7–8	49
13	21
14–15	24, 33
4:22	22
9:14	27
13:21–22	38
15:7	27
23:20	26
27	27
33:14	26
34:6	26

Numbers
21:6	27

Deuteronomy
6:4	16, 19, 33
32:8	22

Judges
6:34	26
11:29	26
14:15	26
15:14	26

1 Samuel
11:6	26

2 Samuel
7:14	23

1 Kings
8:10–11	38

Esther
1:19	118

1 Maccabees
4:46	40
9:27	40
14:41	40

Job
1:6	22, 28
28:28	137
38:7	22
8–11	37

Psalms
2:7	23
6:7	136
8:2	18
4	32
5–6	41
22	41
29:1	22
43:3	27
51:11	26
68	83
72	83
75:9	83
78	83
89:6	22
26–27	23
93:3–4	37
104:3–4	37
30	27
105:3–4	77
110:1	32
117	26
147:18	27
148:5	25

Proverbs
8:22–31	25
22	33, 104

Wisdom
1:6–7	27
2:10–20	41
16	23
18	23
5:5	22, 23
7:22–23	27
22	105

Wisdom (contd)
7:25	105
9:10	27, 141

Sirach
24:3	25 (2), 27, 104
8	104
23	25

Isaiah
4:5	38
6:8	27
7:9	6–7, 78
9:6	23
11:2–3	26
35:3–6	37
40:6	175
53	23, 41
55:11	27
63:9–14	26
16	106
64:8	22

Jeremiah
31:9	22

Ezekiel
1:20	26
8:3	26
11:1	26
5	26
24	26

Daniel
6:8	118
12	118
7:13	32

Hosea
2:14	137, 142
11:1	22

Amos
4:10	27

Joel
2:28–29	27

Malachi
2:10	22
3:1	37

Matthew
1:20	39
10:20	39, 89, 109
40	91
11:2–19	37
9	30
10	30, 37
25	18
27	18, 35
12:28	39
17:5	38
23:34	25
26:53	30
28:19	12–13, 35, 40, 156

Mark
1:9–11	18
11	39
15	30
38	27
3:29	39
4:7	127
18–19	127
41	37
7:28	30, 31
8:27–33	34
29	13, 30
31–33	30
9:2–8	18
31	41
37	91
10:33–34	41
45	41
11:3	31
12:36–37	32
13:32	18, 35
14:36	16, 96

Luke
1:4	36
35	39
3:1	38
23	41
4:43	27
7:18–35	37

26	30
27	37
9:31	37
10:1–24	17–18
13–15	18
16	91
21–24	17
21–22	18
21	18
22	18, 35
11:13	39
49	25
22:27	41
23:38	30
24:21	30
26	36
46–47	36

John
1:1–18	130
1–14	24, 138
1–2	36
14	36, 96, 137, 175
18	96
35–51	24
35ff.	29
41	34
49	34
3:13	14
4:10	70
24	70
5	18
5:18	13
19–47	13, 35
20–23	14
26	110
30	13
6:35	34
38–42	14
7:16	110
39	15, 39
8:58	34
10:30	14, 35, 52
12:41	47–48
13:1	14
20	91
14 – 16	14, 40, 140
14:9	35
15–24	140

				96, 109, 177
16–17	14, 40	8:15	177	19	141
16	40	10:14–17	12	21ff.	85
17	105			5:1	86
23	140	*1 Corinthians*		6	138
26	14, 40, 105	1:24	25, 36, 103,		
28	14		105	*Ephesians*	
15:1	34	8:4–6	16	1:9–10	45
15	17	5	41	2:14	37
26	7, 14, 27, 40,	6	17, 19, 33,	4:23	139
	70 (2), 89,		99		
	105, 109,	10:11	30	*Philippians*	
	110, 140	12 – 14	15–16	2:5–11	32
16:7ff.	40, 89, 109	12:3	15, 31, 33,	6–7	33
13–15	14		36	6	52
13	40	4–6	15, 40	7	38, 66
28	14, 27	8	137		
17:18	91	13:12	77, 128, 135,	*Colossians*	
24	37		139	1:13	33
18:5–6	34	15:45–49	32	15–20	33
20:21	91	45	32	25	46
22	15, 70, 72,			2:9	33
	89, 109, 177	*2 Corinthians*		3:10	139
28	34	4:16	139		
		5:16	35	*1 Timothy*	
Acts				2:5	12, 87
1:4	36	*Galatians*		3:16	137
6	30	3:19	87	6:10	137
21–22	29	23ff.	85		
2:36	31, 36	4:4–7	16, 21, 24,	*1 John*	
14:11–12	36		27, 38, 40,	4:8	124
15:9	139		71, 85, 89	16	124
17:3	36		(2), 96, 99,		
			142, 171–172	*Revelation*	
Romans		4	18, 21, 35,	19:13	24
1:4	34		84, 137		
5:5	70, 177	5	96		
12–19	32	6	38, 70, 89,		

INDEX OF REFERENCES TO AUGUSTINE'S *DE TRINITATE*

General	46, 75, 83	VIII, prol.	122, 132
I, i, 1	6	vii, 11	143
iii, 5	77	IX, i, 1	77
iv, 7	6	v, 8	117, 121
II, v, 7–9, 10	90	x, 15	141, 143
IV, ix, 19	88, 91	X, xi, 18	117, 121
25	88, 91	XII, viii, 13	136, 142
xx, 28	141, 143	viii, 13 – ix, 14	136–137, 142
29	67, 89, 91	XIII, i, 1	142
V – VII	55	xiii, 17	137, 142
V, xi, 12	98, 109, 120	XIV, xi, 14	127, 132
xiv, 15	109, 120	xii, 15	139, 142
VI, v, 7	109, 120	XV, ii, 2	77
x, 11	60	xvii, 29	109–110, 120
VII, iii, 4	107	xxvi, 47	110, 120
iv, 7 – v, 11	63	xxvii, 48	110–111, 120

General Index

Adonai 24, 28
Altaner, B. 63, 64
Ambrose 62, 64, 65, 116
angels 21–22, 26, 47, 87–88
Anomoeans: *see* Eunomius
Anselm 83, 148
appropriation (of terms to divine persons) 16, 17, 79, 103–107, 149, 158–159, 170
Aquinas, Thomas 72, 93, 94, 95, 97, 99, 101–103, 105, 106–107, 113–115, 117, 123, 130, 131–132, 141, 147, 149–151, 152, 153
Arianism, Arians, Arius 32, 41, 46, 54, 55–57, 58, 60, 62–63, 68–69, 77, 78, 112, 122
Aristotle, Aristotelian, Aristotelianism 47, 62, 97, 127, 136
Athanasius 5, 58, 62–63, 116
Augustine 5, 6, 7, 46, 48, 53, 55, 59, 60, 61, 63–64, 65–72, 75–143 *passim*, 147–151, 153
Aurelius 75–76, 83

Basil of Ancyra 58, 60
Basil of Caesarea 58, 61, 116
Boethius 101, 106
Brown, R. E. 19
Bulgakov, S. 116, 118

Caesarius of Arles 5, 6
catechetics 147, 164, 171
catechisms 99, 102, 133, 138, 147, 149, 155–159, 163–164, 167–179
Chalcedon, Council of 33, 41, 57, 62, 119, 168

charisms 15
Charlemagne 112, 120
Chevalier, I. 82
chiastic method 81
Chrysostom, John 116
Cicero 63, 132
Congar, Y. 115, 116, 120
Constantine 56, 63
Constantinople, first Council of 4, 7, 56, 108, 118
consubstantial 4, 5, 52, 56, 57, 62, 116
creeds:
    Apostles' 4, 155, 169, 172
    Athanasian 4–6, 95, 153
    Nicene 4, 56, 65, 106, 108, 112–113, 118, 169, 170
Cullmann, O. 32, 41

Didymus the Blind 61, 64
Dionysius Exiguus 41
Donatists 83
Douglas, M. 90

economic theologians, theology 45–53, 66, 67, 71, 85, 86, 159
economy (of salvation) 45, 48, 50–51, 52, 66, 71, 85, 86–87, 89, 125, 140, 151, 154, 167
Elohim 23–24
Ephesus, Council of 118, 168
Epicurean, Epicureanism 47
Epiphanius of Salamis 62, 64
equality (in the Trinity) 13, 14, 66, 84–85, 126
eschatology 30, 32

Eunomius, Anomoeans 59, 68–69, 78
Evdokimov, P. 116
experience (of God) 3, 6, 11–12, 16–17,
    38–39, 46, 54, 63, 86–87, 123, 138, 140,
    149, 151, 154, 163–164, 167

faith 11, 29, 54, 65–66, 78, 80, 86, 122–123,
    137–138, 139, 140, 167
Filioque 7, 62, 70–71, 89, 95, 108–121
Florence, Council of 117

generation (of the Son) 70, 93, 97, 130, 149,
    168
gift, the Holy Spirit as 70, 177
Gnostics, Gnosticism 34, 48, 86
Gregory Nazianzen 61
Gregory of Nyssa 63
Grillmeier, A. 53

Hendrikx, E. 82
Herrmann, J. 152–153
Hilary of Poitiers 60, 63, 95, 98
homoi-ousios 57–58
homo-ousios 57–58, 116
Hugh of St Victor 107
hypostasis 56–57, 58–60, 61, 63, 68, 79, 94,
    96, 100–107

image (of God) 52, 72, 77, 80, 82, 122–143,
    148–149, 151, 178–179
infantilism 86, 90
Irenaeus 46–47, 48–49, 53, 54, 86

Judaism 21, 29, 31, 32, 35, 47
Justin Martyr 46–48, 53, 54, 84

Kelly, J. N. D. 7, 56, 62
Kolbe, F. C. 164–165
Kurios 24, 30–32

La Bonnardière, A.-M. 82
Leo III 112, 120
Lercher, L. 152, 154

Logos: see Word
Lombard, Peter 97, 98, 99, 148–149, 150,
    151
Lossky, V. 116
love 79, 132, 135
LXX 7, 22, 28, 78

magisterium 159, 170
Manichaeans 53
Marcellus of Ancyra 58, 62
Marcion 86
materialist, materialism 53, 64
mediator, mediation 87–88
Messiah 23, 26, 29–31, 34, 40, 47, 48
missions (of the Son, of the Holy Spirit) 13,
    14, 16, 18, 27, 38, 66–68, 71–72, 82,
    84–91, 141, 149, 151, 153–154, 158,
    165, 166, 168, 169, 175, 176–177
modalism (monarchianism, Sabellianism) 34,
    50, 55, 58, 59, 100, 112, 115
monarchianism: see modalism
monophysites 41
monotheism 12, 16, 19, 29, 31, 34, 50
Montanism 50

Neoplatonism 55, 88
Nestorius, Nestorians 41
Newman, J. H. 47
Nicaea, first Council of 4, 46, 54, 55–57, 62,
    65, 108, 116, 118, 168
    second Council of 120
Novatian 52–53, 54, 55, 66, 84

Origen 46
ousia: see substance

Panikkar, R. 63, 102, 166–167, 168
Pelagius 83
person 58–60, 63, 68, 79, 94, 100–107,
    152–153, 154
Philo 32
Photius 116
Plato, Platonic, Platonism 32, 47, 53, 97,
    124, 128, 138
Pliny the Younger 62
Plotinus 55, 64, 138

Pohle, J. 152, 153, 154
polytheism 21, 35, 69
Prestige, G. L. 51, 116, 120
principium 72, 109–110, 111, 132
Priscillianists, Priscillianism 112, 114
procession (of the Son, of the Holy Spirit) 14, 27, 67, 69–70, 71–72, 77, 80, 88–89, 92–93, 97, 108–121, 122–133, 149, 151, 158, 166

Quintilian 63

Rahner, K. 45–46, 71, 125, 132, 166, 168, 170
relationships, divine 61, 64, 69–70, 71–72, 78–79, 82, 92–99, 101, 109, 113, 149
revelation, divine 11–12, 16–17, 18, 21, 29, 49, 54, 66, 71, 80, 86, 88–89, 165, 166, 168, 169

Sabellianism: *see* modalism
sacrifice 88
Satan 18, 38
Scheeben, M. J. 165–166
Schillebeeckx, E. 87, 90
Servant of the Lord 30, 37, 38
Sesotho 28, 102, 106–107, 123
Shorter, A. 11
sign of the cross 3, 156, 157, 163
simplicity (of God) 55
sin 134–137
Son of Man 32–33, 34, 37
sons of God 21–22
Sophia: see wisdom

Stevenson, J. 62
Stoics 47
subordinationism 52, 66
substance (*ousia*) 56–58, 59, 62, 63, 101, 114
Swete, H. B. 120
symbols 88, 164, 165

Tanquerey, A. 152, 153–154
Teresa of Avila 103
Tertullian 46–47, 50–53, 54, 55, 58, 66, 67, 84
TeSelle, E. 82
Toledo, Councils of 112, 114, 118
tradition (of the Church) 12, 33, 65, 71, 79, 86, 87, 90, 93, 99, 100–101, 102, 116, 117, 119, 126, 153, 159, 163, 167
transcendental theologians 46, 54–62, 95
Trese, L. 165
tritheism 59, 115

Ugaritic 21, 28

Victorinus Afer 60–61, 63, 64
Virgil 127, 132

wisdom (*Sophia*) 24–25, 36, 39, 47, 48, 79, 103–105, 132, 135, 137, 139, 141
Word (*Logos*) 24–25, 36, 47, 48–49, 56, 72, 84–85, 104–105, 113, 125–126, 137, 141, 143, 175–176

YHWH, Yahweh 20, 24, 33–34, 37, 86